A Woman in Your Own Right

Anne Dickson Ph.D has degrees in psychology, mental health and environmental science. She has worked as a freelance psychologist, writer and trainer for many years and is recognised as a leading authority on women's development, assertiveness training and interactive communication. Her best-selling, widely translated *A Woman in Your Own Right* is still used as a core textbook for assertiveness trainers around the world.

A Woman in Your Own Right

Assertiveness and You

ANNE DICKSON

Illustrations by Kate Charlesworth

QUARTET

First published in 1982 by
Quartet Books Limited
A member of the Namara Group
27 Goodge Street, London W1T 2LD

This revised edition published in 2012

Reprinted in 2013

A catalogue record for this book
is available from the British Library

ISBN 978 0 7043 7269 6

Typeset by Antony Gray
Printed and bound in Great Britain by
T J International Ltd, Padstow, Cornwall

MIX
Paper from
responsible sources
FSC
www.fsc.org   FSC® C013056

Contents

To those individuals – wherever they are –
who have the vision and compassion to see and
treat other human beings as their equals. It has always
taken courage to resist the norms of aggression and
misuse of power: today it requires much more.

Acknowledgements

I would like to acknowledge the contribution of the women I have trained over the years, both in the UK and elsewhere, many of whom have kept the free spirit of assertiveness alive in their work. They have helped to instil an authentic confidence in women and enabled them to literally find their own voices.

I would like to thank a few women in particular. Stella Salem's loyalty and contribution to the general administration of Redwood in the earlier years needs to be honoured: she has long tried to persuade me to update this book. Patricia Hodgins has also given me much encouragement and support in this venture. My thanks also go to Casey Taylor for our helpful discussion and Arlene Faris for taking the time to read and comment on the first draft of this new version.

Prologue

When my English publishers first approached me with a proposal to create a thirtieth anniversary edition of this book, my response was one of ambivalence: not because I personally believe that assertiveness training has become less relevant now than it was three decades ago. On the contrary, in the face of contemporary cultural values, adherence to the fundamental principles of equality and honesty seem more important than ever in a world where inequalities are glaring, dishonesty often overlooked and individual rights prioritised over compassion or a sense of responsibility for others. My initial doubts were much more to do with whether anybody would be interested in what are now largely considered out-dated and irrelevant principles.

Nevertheless we agreed to go ahead: my brief was to update the original book by removing what were obviously outdated references: to typewriters, for example, or addressing the problem of asking someone not to smoke in a restaurant. It wasn't long before I realised that I couldn't simply tweak a few details: far too much has changed in terms of the social context in which assertive principles have to be understood.

The commitment to equality, for example – at the very heart of assertive behaviour – has been dealt a devastating blow by the shift in social and political values throughout the last thirty years. Neo-liberal economic policies have meant a radical change in life as we know it as economic values have evolved into social values. Sports, education, medicine, politics, broadcasting, the performing arts and the media have been colonised by market values while entailing a corresponding loss of intrinsic values such as gamesmanship, teaching, healing, governing, informing, entertaining and intellectual achievement. The same economic policies have spread through the world with dramatic political and social repercussions and the *absence* of equality as a consequence (economic, social, access to physical resources, education and healthcare, job opportunities and life-expectancy) has been irrefutably documented.

Although it was always crucial to distinguish between an assertive and aggressive response, it is even more difficult to understand the distinction when we all now live within a society where much higher levels of aggression are countenanced as acceptable and often completely normal. One reason for this is that business has become a metaphor for life in the Western world. We are expected to be more entrepreneurial (streamlined, aggressive and profitable) in everything we do: this goal requires the most up-to-date technology, adequate resources, a high profile, the right image and cost-effectiveness. Winning takes priority which means that the ethos of competition has extended its domain from the sports arena and workplace to infiltrate even our closest relationships. Time and time again, we fail to communicate effectively because we are hampered by seeing the other person solely as potential 'winner' or 'loser': every inter-action becomes a contest in which the success or failure of the outcome is apparently dependent on our respective strategies.

Within this wider shift, women's roles in our culture have also altered: the current generation of young women enjoy more independence from the restraints of stereotypically female roles than their mothers did: self-expression, educational attainment and professional achievement are now far more accessible. In earlier years, the concept of the Compassion Trap, for example, was an important aspect of early training programmes and immediately identifiable to women then as a stumbling block to finding the words to make an effective refusal, i.e. to put their needs before those of others. This concept appears less relevant to younger women today who are more certain of their ground when claiming their individual rights.

How and why is this book different from the original? Although the core content remains the same, the evolution of assertiveness training during these three decades means that presenting the subject matter in 2012 is a new challenge. My own experience of teaching and training in a diverse range of contexts and cultures gives me a particular perspective on the path taken by assertiveness training: how it began, how it developed, why it gained popularity and how it eventually came to lose its essential meaning. The following brief history provides some insight into what being assertive means, and doesn't mean, today.

Assertiveness Training 1982–2012

A Woman in Your Own Right first came into being in 1982 in response to the demand for assertiveness training classes. Four years previously, I had taught the first class in this country and the relevance of the topic to women's lives and their consequent interest in learning the skills was immediately and over-whelmingly evident. Adult Education institutions, initially wary of being associated with any 'feminist' agenda, were persuaded by over-subscribed classes and consistent attendance throughout the full ten weeks to open their doors more enthusiastically. Participants in these classes discovered a new concept of em-powerment: one that embraced the importance of communicating feelings and recognising an essential equality with others.

Within a couple of years, the demand for classes and teachers grew exponentially and as a consequence, I established a national and later an international training association which offered a twelve month, in-depth training in assertiveness and sexuality for women who wanted to run courses within their own personal and work contexts.

I wrote the book both to spread the word and to enable women to benefit from some of the principles even if they didn't have access to a class. I could never have imagined how far the relevance of assertiveness would reach: in subsequent years, the book has been translated into over a dozen other languages and it soon became clear that women of very differing cultures identified with similar problems of communication, low self-esteem, expressing anger and problems with confrontation.

In the late-eighties, assertiveness training became trendy here in the UK and inevitably many people jumped on the band-wagon, establishing themselves as trainers of assertiveness, often with little or no experience. The disadvantage, from my point of view, was that the core significance of assertiveness training became diluted as the more radical elements were filtered out. Only the easier and less challenging aspects were retained and this meant, for example, that management of emotions, especially anger, handling criticism and confrontation and crucially, the importance of equality, were often side-lined or omitted altogether from the majority of training programmes.

A second major influence was the issue of gender. In the early days women were able to identify strongly with the disadvantages of not being able to speak up or set limits because of their awareness at the time of obvious inequalities with men in both personal and professional contexts. Men on the whole showed little interest in learning these skills. An unassertive person was stereotypically passive, weak, shy and unable to give orders: an ineffectual image that most men were able to dismiss as entirely irrelevant to their own needs. Over time, however, as they witnessed changes in their colleagues, partners, sisters and friends, some men could see that there was more to being assertive than they had first imagined. In response to a growing demand, mixed courses became available. The early feminist agenda (assertiveness training had been originally taken up by the women's consciousness-raising movement in the US in the mid-70s) slowly evaporated.

As this shift was occurring, assertiveness was taken up within the corporate sector. The early grass roots image of assertiveness changed into a big business image, taught within companies in the private and public sector, as well as academic and medical institutions, usually for men and women together. It was impossible to avoid compromise, I remember, knowing that a breakthrough in understanding and practice that often occurred for individuals during a training programme fell short of challenging the prevailing ethos of competition, dominance and hierarchy within the organisation as a whole.

The deteriorating financial climate was another factor: specialists like myself were no longer economically viable. Those in charge of training departments economised by offering an in-house training package which typically included stress-reduction, time-management, team-building and confrontation skills: assertiveness simply became part of this package. People did the best they could but the central elements of assertiveness training were ever further weakened and the practice of role-play disappeared completely.

When role-play is either not used at all or used inappropriately, group participants learn the concepts intellectually but without the essential opportunity to practise these skills within a safe setting in order to be able to transfer them to real life. The more recent trend towards personal coaches and mentors has further diminished the use of role-play and placed more emphasis on 'the professional pundit' for guidance and advice.

Absence of effective role-play has serious consequences: the individual is unable to be in charge of their own change but more importantly, the function of role-play is to allow the individual to actually feel anxiety and to move *through* that anxiety at both a psychological and physiological level simultaneously. It is this experience which can be carried forward into real life encounters in a way that simply *talking* about what you would like to say will never achieve. Without this opportunity, the potential for effective and lasting behaviour change is negligible.

The combination of all these influences has led to the current anomaly whereby the concept of assertiveness is familiar to a large part of the population and many women have received assertiveness training in some form, though often with only superficial benefit. The practical consequences are seen in organisations. There are many more women managers than there were thirty years ago but women in the most senior positions still remain a tiny minority. Despite occasional optimism and the good intentions behind various government-funded initiatives, the aim of substantially increasing the number of women in senior positions has not been achieved. Women who are either middle or senior managers rarely operate from a core of high self-esteem and often, privately, feel lonely, unsupported, unconfident and believe they have to work harder than male colleagues because of a need to prove themselves 'equal'.

When people refer to assertiveness training, we assume we are all referring to the same thing but this simply isn't the case. Since this book is a new edition, it presents me with an opportunity to emphasise how the model of assertiveness promoted in these pages is fundamentally at odds with the contemporary stereotype of 'an assertive woman'. Although outright hostility and overt aggression are less socially sanctioned in a work environment these days, a more subtly aggressive mode of behaviour has made an appearance.

Being assertive is now associated with being confident, articulate, prepared, unfazed, invulnerable and effective: in short, always and in every way a *winner*. This goal is generally understood to be achieved by learning verbal strategies, with an appropriate script and delivery, thereby implying one's behaviour is based on mastering particular techniques.

So if you believe that you just need a few techniques under your belt to be assertive because otherwise you'll automatically be a 'loser' or if you think being assertive means being able to be tough and sassy and yet always end up being liked by everybody, think again.

This stereotype is more a deterrent than an inspiration: when being assertive implies never being vulnerable or caught on the hop; never confused, lost for words, mistaken or uncertain, in other words, never *human*, we end up waiting. We rationalise our hesitation to deal with difficult situations by telling ourselves 'When I am confident and calm and clear and articulate, *then* I'll speak up': and so we wait.

Instead of being seen as a normal indication of the difficulty of the task ahead, anxiety is interpreted as a weakness, as a sign of inadequacy. The assumptions that guilt or anxiety must be denied (or conquered) or that one must conform to a stereotype of how one *should* behave are both counterproductive. In fact anxiety can be managed much more effectively and with far longer-lasting effects through proper in-depth learning and practice of assertive skills.

In an age when we are encouraged to dedicate ourselves to the expression of our unique individuality, it must be emphasised that this book goes beyond mere self-empowerment: it concerns both the methods and consequences of self-empowerment. It questions the current norm of getting what you want at the expense of everything and everybody else; it also examines the psychological repercussions of both subtle and obvious aggression on all our interaction with others. If you personally are not comfortable with aggression, then you will learn how to avoid it without backsliding into ineffectual compliance: this is assertiveness in action.

A Woman in Your Own Right 2012

The format of this edition roughly follows the original: the sequence remains very similar but with some additional chapters. Like everything else in this thirty year period, the material itself has not stood still and nor has my teaching. I have developed and extended the concepts, with some aspects taking more prominence than in the original version. In this time, I have also expanded several of the original chapters into individual books: sexuality (*The Mirror Within* 1984); assertiveness in the workplace (*Women at Work* 1999); body image and power (*A Voice for Now* 2000) and the art of confrontation (*Difficult Conversations* 2004). The original chapters on feelings and anger have evolved into *Reconnecting with the Heart* (to be published in 2013).

The basic assertive techniques explained in this book are the same although self-disclosure now moves to the fore with its own separate chapter. This is because I have found through experience that this is the quintessential skill, without which an assertive interaction always founders despite our best intentions.

An additional theme throughout is an inevitable reflection

on generational differences: despite some obvious contrasts, my observation tells me that younger women are no more able to challenge authority, be honest, express how they feel or give a clear and effective refusal to a request, than their parents were. At a deeper level I also question whether self-esteem is genuinely higher among younger women of today: once one looks beneath the popularly assumed 'rights' to both freedom of expression and individual fulfilment, there remain deep and pervasive anxieties about appearance, self-worth and a difficulty in remaining independent of the approval of peers, especially of those of the opposite sex.

In response to the transformation of the workplace environment (for both men and women) since 1982, I have added new material relevant to the current challenges for women employees, especially in terms of the skill of confrontation and handling their own authority within hierarchical structures.

There are two further changes from the original, both stemming from my personal circumstances. First, chronological inevitability has prompted a new chapter, one related to the fact that I am now a middle-aged woman. I wanted to address the difficulties of maintaining one's self-esteem as we get older, especially in an era when the process of ageing itself has become fraught with fear and denial in a society seemingly obsessed exclusively with youth.

Secondly, my world perspective was radically altered when I became a student again after many years of teaching. A combination of research in environmental and social sciences opened my eyes to another realm. Having spent most of my working life as a psychologist engaged with the interior of people's psyches, I was initiated into the immense significance of the external structures – economic, political, legal and social – which shape and control our lives. My academic experience has therefore informed some of what appears in this new edition, particularly in terms of the significance of equality and power.

A final consideration: the main aim of this book was originally to provide the reader with an opportunity to try out assertiveness techniques without the aid of a class. Since it is now virtually impossible to find a class or group with whom one might learn these skills, I have decided to retain this emphasis: most of the following chapters end with a section containing suggestions and exercises which readers could use to explore for themselves, on their own or with a friend.

The references, illustrations and examples in the book are all based on the situations presented by participants in classes and training programmes throughout these years.

Personal reflections

Writing this new edition has obviously given me cause to think back. Out of a multitude of memories, two features stand out: one that saddens me and the other remaining a cause for celebration.

A sense of loss

In the deeply competitive society in which we now live, it seems that women compete and compare themselves with other women more harshly than ever before. When I started teaching, there was more of an emphasis on comparing our status with that of men: lack of equality in opportunities of education and work, rates of pay and access to membership of various institutions or activities were open to challenge. The sense of solidarity generated by sharing experiences, failures and triumphs was a powerful catalyst.

I see little evidence of solidarity now. Instead women have assimilated the widespread cultural erosion of qualities of accommodation and inclusivity, co-operation and community by the promotion of individualism, exclusivity, competition and division. We could claim, perhaps, that aggression is now 'gender equal' but not with much celebration. It saddens me that having achieved more equality and more positions of responsibility and power, there is no evidence of the enhancement of family life, the workplace or the world in general.

In the absence of a shared collective goal of challenging visible and obvious forms of sexism, wariness of each other is heightened. Women are more uncertain about their ideals. There is more defensiveness about personal decisions: those staying at home to look after their families criticise those who go out to work and vice versa. Married women and single women dispute the relative superiority of their status.

Despite claims that feminism is 'old hat' and claims of emotional, financial and physical independence, doubts about the reality of gender equality persist. Cross-country research shows that in a two-person working partnership, women still do the lion's share of the domestic chores, especially at weekends; domestic violence continues apace and it hasn't stopped being unsafe for women to walk alone after dark. The need to be sexually attractive as an indicator of personal validation hasn't changed much either: it is one thing to claim equality but it is quite another to live it.

A cause for celebration and wonder

Teaching assertiveness to such a diversity of people has been an extraordinary adventure. I have always believed in the transformative power of the material and that the best way of teaching is not to own it or try and control it but to be the best possible vehicle to convey the principles and encourage others to try them. For me this has meant a certain degree of reluctance to be labelled 'an expert': being an expert in assertiveness is a bit like being awarded a degree in being human.

This doesn't stop expectations that I will conform to stereotype. Thirty years ago, I would turn up for interviews and be confronted by surprise and some disappointment that I wasn't clad from head to toe in black leather adorned with chains. Today, expectations centre more on invulnerability, glamour and financial success: the typical accoutrements of a woman who is assumed to be 'always and in every way a winner'.

The truth though is that in all the years I have been teaching, I have never lost sight of the *challenge* of being assertive. I know what it is like to feel failure; I know what it is like to feel intimidated and fumble for words to speak up in my defence. I know how it feels to be anxious about looking foolish, to fear rejection, to hear my heart pounding as I open my mouth to confront someone.

This is why I've also never lost sight of the miracle of change. My working life has revolved around such miracles and still does: the delight when another person takes the decision to trust me: to agree to try something different and be vulnerable and risk the unknown. The extraordinary dynamic of co-creative change when neither of us knows exactly what will happen, but something does: some part of the person emerges, some new facet, and this is an experience that I can never tire of. Seeing the satisfaction and pride – even if shaky – of someone who has confronted their fear and moved through it is, for me, as exciting as watching the triumphant faces of recent Olympic winners.

I have always said to those I trained to 'trust the material' because it works. There have been occasions when I have had to relearn this. When I was invited first to work in Japan, for example, I was unsure how assertive principles would go across in a society much more traditionally hierarchical than my own. I need not have worried. Alongside cultural differences, there are human similarities: learning to be assertive still meant communicating with the other person as an equal.

Hiromi wanted to learn how to confront his mother, who according to cultural tradition, he had no right to challenge. He described a manipulative and demanding woman who constantly made known her disapproval of Hiromi's wife. As we worked together, he discovered that somewhere between the roles of being a son and a husband, he could also look at his mother as a fellow human being, aging and increasingly insecure about her own position. He could then talk to her with firmness *plus* compassion. He wrote later that this shift in perception had completely altered his relationship with his mother for the better.

On another occasion I sat at a table in the headquarters of an international bank with a dozen Danish women, all of them very senior figures in their own organisations. I had been invited to work with them for the afternoon and, as we introduced ourselves, I looked around this group of immaculately dressed, poised and supremely confident individuals and found myself wondering '*Why* am I here?' After ten minutes of polite discussion, one brave woman, Vibeke, took the plunge and admitted that she actually found it very hard to deal with a bullying colleague. This was the catalyst for the real sharing to begin as others disclosed their own difficulties: feeling intimidated; being excluded by the male-only social activities; having to use a poker face to disguise emotions and feelings; the irritation at being devalued and feeling isolated. We had more than enough to work with.

My trust in the material and belief in its relevance is stronger than ever. This is very much a book for 2012 which I hope will both rekindle learning and renew the resolve among those who read the first edition, as well as offering new readers a practical and useful introduction to important concepts and specific skills which have proved over and over again to be genuinely life-transforming.

Further Reading

The Mirror Within, Anne Dickson, Quartet, *1984*

A Voice For Now, Anne Dickson, Piatkus, Little, Brown, 2003

Difficult Conversations, Anne Dickson, Piatkus, Little, Brown, 2004

Reconnecting with the Heart, Anne Dickson (to be published 2013)

The Perverse Organisation and its Deadly Sins, Susan Long, Karnac, 2008

The Culture of the New Capitalism, Richard Sennett, Yale University Press, 2006

The Spirit Level: Why Equality is better for Everyone, Richard Wilkinson and Kate Pickett, Penguin, 2010

1

When and Where to be Assertive

What has drawn people to sign up for assertiveness training? What has been the attraction for so many women over this time? Most have wanted to change their lives in some way. A few have attended with a clearly defined goal but most have arrived with a general and ill-defined dissatisfaction with their personal or working lives. Many felt that they lacked control over their lives. There were a few good days in a year when they felt confident and secure, but mostly they worried . . . about what they said or didn't say; about how to handle criticism or be taken more seriously at work; about how to manage the work/home balance more effectively; how to set clearer limits with their children or how to address a persistent problem with someone without damaging the friendship or relationship.

The questions which follow are a way of helping you begin to identify the situations which you would like to handle more successfully. Identifying the circumstances in which you would like to respond differently is an excellent first step towards achieving change in your life.

Situations with strangers

How do you respond if you are sitting in a busy restaurant and a waiter ignores you? Do you sigh and tap your fingers on the table? Or do you ask your (male) companion why he doesn't do something? Or do you march out noisily, spitting a few choice remarks over your shoulder as you go? If the food served to you is not properly cooked or bears little resemblance to what you ordered, how do you respond? Do you complain by whining? Do you rudely denounce the establishment? Or do you swallow your dissatisfaction with your food and achieve a slight sense of revenge by not leaving a tip?

If you've chosen to sit in a 'quiet' zone on the train and the passenger next to you seems to be intent on phoning half his call list very loudly on his mobile, what is your response? Do you simmer and say nothing? Do you glare at him and point out the 'quiet' sign above the window? Do you mutter something almost inaudible under your breath? Or do you ask him politely to stop making calls, reminding him that this is a quiet zone?

How do you respond when you find at the checkout that you made a mistake and that the box of cherries you fancied is twice the price you thought it was? Do you cause a bit of a scene and demand a supervisor to check the price because it wasn't clearly marked? Or do you pretend that you knew anyway because you feel embarrassed at not being able to afford them? How do you react when you have been waiting for ages in a queue or you're in a hurry and a sweet little old lady barges in front of you? Does it make a difference if the person who barges in front of you happens to be a six-foot-four male with a belligerent manner? Do you risk stating your opinion and earning disapproving stares from others? How do you respond when you encounter an intransigent sales manager who suggests the electronic article you are returning has stopped working because of your own incompetence? Do you get into a slanging match and storm out or do you lose heart and leave because you don't like confrontation?

When faced with an unhelpful shop assistant who is more concerned with texting on her mobile than attending to your purchase problems, do you react like a sergeant major or do you ask for help, clearly or apologetically? A good-looking salesman has gone to a lot of trouble to unpack every possible article in search of what you want and still nothing fits your requirements. Do you buy something anyway even though it is not what you want, simply so as not to appear ungrateful, or do you thank him for his assistance but decline to buy anything?

Situations with friends

If you have to negotiate where to meet or what film to see or where to eat, do you make your own preferences clear or are you pushed around or manipulated into a choice which you are really not happy with? A friend wants to go out and drown her sorrows after a bust-up with her boyfriend: you want to be supportive but you really don't fancy a long night's drinking because you need to be clear enough to revise for some exams: do you put aside your own needs or pretend you have an alternative engagement? Do you say 'no' or suggest a compromise? If you feel angry with the way someone has treated you, do you communicate your feelings or do you hide them and then make sure you keep the person waiting an hour the next time you arrange to meet? You lent a friend some money several months ago and there's no sign of him paying it back: do you keep quiet hoping he'll remember or let your resentment accumulate until it begins to sour your friendship? If a friend persistently uses you as a shoulder to cry on and rings up just as you are settling down to watch a favourite television programme, do you turn the sound down but keep one eye on the box and mutter 'uh-uh' occasionally? Do you listen patiently, wishing you could see your programme, or do you say that you are busy and could she ring back? If a friend who is important to you is the subject of malicious gossip in a group of mutual acquaintances, do you turn a deaf ear, do you hit out aggressively and put them in their place or do you express how you feel and ask them to stop? A good friend asks you if the dress she is wearing looks OK: you know your truthful answer is 'no' so are you honest or do you tell a lie because you don't want to hurt her feelings?

Situations at home

In your own home are you a martyr, a slave or a tyrant? How do you behave if everyone leaves the washing up, the cleaning, the tidying up to you? How do you respond when you want to say 'no' to a child's request for money or for friends to come for a sleepover? How do you respond if you want to say 'no' to a demanding relative who wants to pay you a visit at a busy or inconvenient time? How do you react when you feel affectionate and put your arm around your partner but find your partner is too preoccupied and wants some distance? What happens if your partner feels sexy but you are not in the mood? Or if you feel sexy but your partner is reluctant? How do you respond to criticism about your appearance from a lover or parent? Do you feel rejected or come back with an aggressive retort? If you want some privacy at home, how do you go about getting it? Do you feel you can set limits or that you should always be on call for your family? How do you confront an irritating habit in someone you love?

Situations at work

Consider how you respond to legitimate criticism from a superior. Do you fly off the handle? Do you deny it at all costs? Do you reach around for someone else to blame? Do you shift uncomfortably from one foot to the other feeling about three years old? Do you adopt a pained expression and sulk for the rest of the day? Consider also how you respond to unfair criticism from a superior. How do you criticise a subordinate for continual lateness, or sloppy work or dishonesty? Do you agonise and wait for ages, ask someone else to deal with the matter, attack the person with all guns firing at once when they are least expecting it, turn a blind eye or even try to find another job?

How do you respond if your male boss makes an offensive sexual comment? Do you launch into a tirade, pretend you did not hear or do you just play along knowing that you can make an official complaint later? If you feel that your employer's demands exceed your contract unfairly, how do you cope? Do you arrange a discussion and assertively put your case? Do you give in and groan under the extra load or do a bad job out of spite? How do you handle nosy colleagues who persist in interfering in your private affairs? Do you tell them to mind their own business or deflect them with some juicy gossip about someone else? How do you deal with a bossy, domineering colleague? Do you give as good as you get or do you avoid confrontation? Do you complain bitterly in private or plan some secret revenge for being bullied?

If someone does a good piece of work or has put in extra time and effort, how to you respond? Do you let it go unnoticed or do you take the time to give specific credit? What happens if someone praises your work? Do you squirm self-consciously and say it was really nothing to do with you or do you agree with them assertively? If someone admires your appearance or a new outfit, how do you respond? Do you dismiss the compliment defensively or accept it graciously?

Four types of behaviour

Having glanced at some typical situations, the next step is to identify the types of response described in the above examples.

There are essentially four ways to react to any difficult encounter. These are best explained by presenting caricatures of four women who exemplify them: Agnes, Dulcie, Ivy and Selma.

I have used women's names because this book relates specifically to women, although the same descriptions could equally apply to men's behaviour. A word of caution: these four are intended as caricatures with the express purpose of underlining the differences between the four types; in reality no such women exist. Each of us is capable of being aggressive, passive, manipulative and assertive. However, it is useful to separate them into four distinct characters as a way of beginning to untangle the overall confusion about how we behave. They can be used to pinpoint the line of action we take at any given moment.

First comes Agnes, the aggressive stereotype. Although Agnes comes across loudly and forcefully, she often has little real self-esteem. She seeks personal aggrandisement through belittling the thoughts, values and capabilities of others. She cannot afford to consider another person's point of view because she is hell-bent on winning. She is always alert to any competitive element and needs to prove her superiority by putting down others. Faced with threatening circumstances, she responds with an outright attack aiming at the other person's vulnerable points. Her compulsive over-reaction often alienates those around her. She may provoke an aggressive response in return but people usually feel constantly on the defensive in her presence. She resorts frequently to verbal or even physical violence and abuse, leaving in her wake a trail of hurt and humiliated feelings. People may harbour resentment towards her but feel reluctant to express this to her directly for fear of more of the same treatment. This silence means that Agnes is sometimes unaware of how much she intimidates others.

Next comes Dulcie, more of a doormat, who represents the  passive stereotype. She makes an ideal target for Agnes. While Agnes tends to opt in and take on all-comers, Dulcie tends to opt out and hide. She finds it difficult to make decisions and avoids taking responsibility for making choices in her life. Consequently others are often forced into making decisions for her which eventually makes them frustrated and resentful. Dulcie prefers to see herself as a victim of unfairness and injustice, always finding something or someone else to blame. As she clings on to her hard-luck stories and stagnates in her passivity and resignation, she infuriates people around her, particularly those in close contact. They will probably feel guilty at first because they cannot do more to help her, to make her happier or to solve her problems. But after a while, this turns to exasperation at her lack of willpower and her persistently negative outlook on life. She puts herself down continually, refuses to acknowledge any compliments and spends a lot of time starting her sentences with 'If only . . . ' She attributes to others the skills, talents, and good fortune that she was not lucky enough to be blessed with. Faced with any kind of confrontation, Dulcie cries and gives in or opts out completely.

Third in line comes Ivy. Ivy is indirectly aggressive. Whereas Agnes hits out with her weapons leaving obvious scars, Ivy's well-chosen barbs hit the mark but leave no obvious trace. As with her two companions, Ivy's behaviour stems essentially from a low self-esteem; this is why she can never risk a direct approach. She does not trust herself or anyone else. She is skilled at deceiving others; she needs to be in control and to manipulate those around her to avoid rejection and hurt. She may appear to think highly of others but they can often detect an undercurrent of disapproval. People around Ivy are confused and frustrated at never being able to pin her down. Her attack is concealed, unlike that of Agnes, and she will often deny her feelings and wriggle away. Her main weapon is guilt. With a marksman's precision she knows how to activate that little guilt button in those around her and she engineers people into all sorts of positions to get what she wants.

Do any of these behaviour patterns strike you as familiar? And if you recognised yourself or someone else in the descriptions, what was your immediate response? You may perhaps feel a little smug if you recognised the faults and behaviour of someone you know, but the uncomfortable recognition of *yourself* may have made you wince a bit. If you find yourself being judgemental and hypercritical of yourself or others, try adopting a more compassionate and realistic viewpoint because, basically, what all three have in common is a lack of any real self-esteem.

This is usually connected to our experience as children. Perhaps Agnes, for example, had to prove herself superior in order to earn approval and love. She feels no real self-confidence in just being herself so is very mistrustful of others. Maybe Dulcie was criticised so often as a child that she is now afraid to make a move or show her true feelings. The Ivy in us has learned that as a woman, she must use whatever subtle devices she can to get others to do what she wants. Direct, honest, straightforward behaviour has never exactly been encouraged in our society.

We all behave in these ways at certain times so when reviewing aspects of your own behaviour which seem to you Agnes-like, Dulcie-like or Ivy-like, skip all excuses, justification or blame. Simply notice *how* you tend to behave. Try to observe the essential person beneath the behaviour. Notice how the Agnes interacts with the Dulcie in you and how easy it is to swing from aggression to passivity and back again.

This seesaw is a common problem. Understandably, women find themselves frustrated and demeaned by a conventionally passive stance and so hurl themselves into the fray in an attempt to redress the balance of power. Unfortunately, they often tip the scales in the other direction. By domineering and insensitive behaviour, they end up alienating and punishing those who are close to them. Realising that this is not what they want either, and usually overwhelmed with guilt, they try to compensate by taking conciliatory steps in the opposite direction. For many women, this to-ing and fro-ing in a cloud of uncertainty represents a major source of tension and discomfort.

It may come as a relief to know that there is an alternative: the *assertive option*. And, what is more, such skills can be learned, which is what this book has always been, and is still, about. One of the main reasons we make such a mess of things is that we simply do not have the skills. We need precise skills to use at those moments when we choose to discard the familiar for the unfamiliar, the dishonest for the honest, the role for the person. We need to know how to communicate our thoughts, feelings and needs neither aggressively nor passively, but assertively.

And so to Selma, the assertive stereotype. Selma respects herself and the people she is dealing with. She is able to accept her own positive and negative qualities and, in so doing, is able to be more authentic in her acceptance of others. She does not need to put others down in order to feel comfortable in herself. She does not believe that others are responsible for what happens to her. She acknowledges that she is in charge of her actions, her choices and her life. She does not

need to make others feel guilty for not recognising her needs. She can recognise her needs and ask openly and directly even though she risks refusal: if she is refused, she may feel rejected but not totally demolished by the rejection. The key is that Selma's self-esteem is anchored deeply *within* herself: she is not over-dependent on the approval of those around her. From this position of strength, she is able to respond sincerely to others, giving herself credit for what she understands and feels.

Many women will identify mainly with one of these four stereotypes, others with two, and still others with all four depending on the circumstances. It is interesting to see if you can identify a pattern in your own life. In what category would you put your mother or your father? Sometimes an aggressive mother will encourage a passive daughter, or a passive mother an aggressive daughter, or a predominantly indirect mother can end up teaching her own daughter that indirect aggression is the most effective strategy.

To recognise is not to blame. No one is at fault: each of us has learned to cope in the best way we could, given the circumstances at the time. Once we can let ourselves off the hook of feeling bad or guilty about our behaviour, we can begin to see choices and make the changes we would like to see in our lives.

It is also important to emphasise again that each of these characters plays a part in our behaviour. Sometimes we make the mistake of believing someone is an absolute Agnes or Dulcie: this is simplistic and unreflective of reality. Each of us can (and does) behave aggressively, passively and also assertively in different situations: a whole number of factors influence which will predominate at any given time. The point of this book is to show you how to achieve optimum communication more often than not. This entails looking at what gets in the way: how we can avoid some obstacles and face others more effectively and how we can draw on those occasions when we are already assertive to inform our thinking and behaviour when we have to deal with other encounters that we find more challenging.

2

What is an Assertive Woman?

What does it mean to be assertive? This question has been put to me innumerable times. More specifically, what does it mean to be an assertive woman? Thirty years ago many people believed that assertiveness training was only relevant for shy, retiring violets who needed to learn to be more outspoken and less afraid of a good fight: in some ways, though things have changed, a similar confusion exists today.

The popular stereotypes of what it means to be 'an assertive woman' remain pretty much the same: the career woman who discards her softer qualities as she climbs the professional ladder (assertiveness becomes synonymous with being unfeminine and hard-nosed); the domineering wife who nags her husband and children into submission (here assertiveness is confused with being overbearing and a bully); the woman who always gets what she wants by using any means available to her (this time, assertive is taken to mean ruthless and self-centred) or the ardent feminist who loudly confronts a sexist gesture or remark (in this context, assertive implies hostility and aggression towards men especially).

No wonder many women conclude they're quite assertive enough already. The above behaviour descriptions, though, relate not to assertive but to aggressive behaviour. This misrepresentation persists despite the noticeable changes in women's role in our society. Certainly there are more women in positions of authority than before but this only means that the stereotypical behaviour of many 'successful' women, including those who have reached the higher echelons of their career ladders, continues to add to the confusion between assertive and aggressive behaviour. Women may come across as direct, confident, ambitious and articulate but, unfortunately, this can often be a veneer which masks a determined and self-concerned ruthlessness.

Even out of the workplace, the preoccupation with individual rights and entitlements has fuelled a determination not to be passive: the pendulum seems to have bypassed assertiveness and settled on the opposite pole of aggressive communication as a norm. This isn't confined to women but women have been caught up in this general trend with the consequence that it has become harder to know how to speak up or to challenge particular behaviour when the only apparent alternative to keeping quiet is being bitchy. Not everyone feels comfortable with the idea of being unpleasant, uncaring or offensive. If women want to avoid aggressive behaviour, where do they look for a true idea of what it means to communicate assertively?

Remember that the *completely* assertive woman does not exist, except on paper. However confident someone appears to be, you can be sure they have their off-days and have to face problems in some areas of their lives. We all have to. You may look at a high-powered career woman or celebrity whose life appears to contain all the enviable features of success and happiness and conclude the last thing she needs is to be more assertive: but maybe in her private life she suffers from one unsatisfactory sexual encounter after another because of her inability to refuse unwanted advances. A woman who has no qualms about telling off a junior or making a big scene until she gets what she wants may find it impossible at home to avoid being a slave to her family. A woman who is apparently in command and uninhibited in a social context may be easily demolished by criticism or quite unable to take the initiative to reach out to another person and show affection. A woman who is an exemplary organiser and always appears to be in charge may find it impossible to assert her own needs and to ask for help when she needs it herself.

Whatever the external image we choose to present – highly confident or timid, very loud or very meek – we all have times when we feel relaxed and comfortable and very sure of ourselves: we also all have our areas of anxiety and difficulty, when we feel vulnerable and less able to say or do what we really want to say and do.

There is no one assertive model which should be aimed for because it is more important to see how *you* can act more assertively in your own life. Below are examples which illustrate how some women felt encouraged to explore their own chosen area of difficulty and to discover a more effective means of communication.

Soni, very proudly devoted to her new baby, was flustered by her well-meaning but over-enthusiastic mother-in-law. She felt overwhelmed by the endless advice on childcare: the best way to hold, the best time to feed, the right moment to stop breast feeding and so on. Soni would continually swallow her irritation because she didn't want to risk provoking a family row. The assertive solution she found was to express her frustration in a way that allowed her to remain sensitive to the older woman's feelings while asserting her need to make her own decisions about the care of her child.

Hayley, an administrator, had been in her new job for a few weeks. She had been looking forward to a rare chance to have lunch with a close friend who was in town just for the day. Just before noon, her manager handed her some urgent work and asked her, as a favour, to work through the lunch hour. She was unhappy about this but didn't want to keep quiet and say nothing. She decided to see if they could reach a workable compromise, which means being able to negotiate around a conflict of priorities. This is an important aspect of assertive behaviour: she explained to her manager that she had a really special lunchtime engagement which was important to her but asked if he would agree to her staying as late as necessary that evening to finish the work before she went home. Her compromise was accepted.

Living in a large flat with six other students, Paula felt unhappy about the refusal of some of them to keep to a task-sharing rota which they had drawn up together and agreed upon. She had fallen into the habit of grudgingly doing more than her fair share of the household chores. Every now and then she would let out her resentment by way of moaning and sighing but nobody seemed to take the hint. The assertive option for Paula was to take the initiative and not continue to play the martyr. In this case, it meant calling a meeting of all the residents and confronting those concerned with a request for action from the whole group.

Denise, a retired schoolteacher, had been looking forward to a drive down to the coast for the day to enjoy some solitude and peace. The evening before, her bossy elder sister had telephoned and invited herself along for the ride. Denise always felt very intimidated by her sister and usually gave in to her demands. This time she lied and pretended she'd changed her mind. Although this worked, Denise felt uncomfortable and realised she would have preferred to have made an assertive refusal, saying a clear, firm 'no' to her sister, stating clearly her preference for spending the day on her own. This helped her to do so in the future.

Sometimes, women would find that being assertive meant that they no longer went 'over the top' when they were angry but that they could express very strong feelings without losing control.

Jed was a friend of Tricia's partner, Mark, and had asked to stay with the couple at their home for a few days because he and his wife had suddenly split up. That was two months ago and Tricia had become increasingly irritated by Jed's presence, his mess and the general lack of space. She had a blazing row with Mark about it when they were out over the weekend but nothing had been resolved. After practising in the class, she was able to set time aside with Mark away from their flat and she expressed her frustration convincingly but without aggression, making a clear and specific request: that Mark ask Jed to find somewhere else to live within the next two weeks. This time Mark was able to hear her and agree.

Assertive action can also mean choosing to take the initiative and make a request in advance rather than waiting for the inevitable to happen and then sulking about it afterwards.

Caroline was faced with this kind of dilemma. By mid-afternoon on the day of her tenth wedding anniversary, she had heard nothing from her husband, Eddie: no call, no card, no flowers, no mention at all. Her feelings of rejection and disappointment were growing by the minute. She considered settling down to wait for his return home so she would be ready to give him the cold shoulder treatment and make sure he'd feel very guilty for having forgotten. She was pleased to report that for once she felt she had been very assertive: she had phoned Eddie at work and reminded him of the date. He had been a little taken aback and embarrassed at having forgotten but delighted when she asked what he would like to do to celebrate.

Some women find that being assertive means feeling confident engaging with someone whom they normally would find intimidating. When we're faced with someone who for one reason or another has more power or a higher status that we do, it can be difficult to assert our rights as an equal.

Marion found this to be true for her. Her eleven-year-old daughter developed irregular but very bad headaches. Various local hospital tests indicated the need for a series of brain scans and she was advised to see a top neurosurgeon. She was normally a forceful and outspoken woman but was obviously anxious about her daughter. She wanted to know how best to care for her and what the likelihood was that it was a brain tumour. Her anxiety about the status and manner of the consultant made her feel quite helpless: when her questions were dismissed, she found herself unable to persist. What she learned to do was to keep calm and persist with her questions which depended on her maintaining her need for information alongside her anxiety. Although the consultant was the expert and had more specific knowledge than she did, Marion could still assert her right to be treated as an equal human being and could persist until he took her questions seriously and answered them.

These are some of the meanings of being assertive. Sometimes people persist in believing that being assertive means you will get what you want all the time. This is not only unrealistic but also means that every interaction automatically becomes a question of winning or losing. This is competitive and aggressive which may be appropriate in other contexts but it is important to understand how these goals differ from an assertive approach.

Choosing to behave assertively may mean not getting exactly what you want but having to negotiate a compromise instead.

> Sue found herself in the minority of four to one in an important meeting at work. Ideally she wanted them all to turn their mobiles off for the duration of the meeting because past experience had shown that with constant interruptions, it was virtually impossible to get anything decided in the time available. Her colleagues were sympathetic but felt unable to get through the meeting without access to their phones. She reinforced her request and offered to compromise by shortening the meeting by fifteen minutes. Three colleagues agreed: the fourth refused to budge. Sue didn't get exactly what she wanted but with fewer interruptions, they got more done. What was important, though, was that she didn't compromise her self-respect. She felt that her wishes had been heard and considered, not over-ruled. If each person concerned feels acknowledged, this is usually a sign that an interaction has been handled assertively, not aggressively.

The above examples show that we are so used to just two positions – top dog and under-dog, the powerful and powerless – that we easily forget there can be a middle path. The tension and effort needed to win does not allow you to develop a genuine respect for the needs, feelings or rights of others or yourself. The principle of equality is one of the most important hallmarks of assertive communication and behaviour.

3

Equality and Power

To truly understand the concept of equality, we first have to understand the nature of power. Power, as evidenced in the institutional, social, national and global structures of the world, has one familiar form: perpendicular. It is easy to image this kind of power as a ladder because this represents the vertical movement along ascending or descending rungs, each related to how much or how little power any person has in relation to another.

We absorb this shape of power as an internal reference from our earliest years: we learn there are only two options, that movement is restricted to either up or down and that we are always – in relation to others – higher or lower at any given moment in time. The up/down ladder system infiltrates into every area of our lives with the result that knowingly or unknowing, we are constantly in a process of mental assessment of our position – our power – in relation to the power of others. This I call perpendicular power, always assessed in terms of over and under.

Perpendicular power operates in four main categories:

Legitimate power

This describes any power that is conferred through the particular social or civic arrangements of the culture in which we live. So whether you're a queen (over one's subjects), a parent (over a child), a manager (over a department) or a teacher (over a group of students), this aspect of power derives from the professional roles that come with a job or appointment or birth-right. We all experience having less or more legitimate power over others at various times in our lives.

Resources

When we have access to resources of some kind that others don't have, we have power over them. Resources include wealth, key information, land, water, weapons, oil and technology. So if you're a teenager with a car or an executive with a private jet or a nation with huge mineral wealth, these resources give you power over others: without resources, we are powerless.

Expertise

When you have knowledge or skills that someone else needs but doesn't have, you have power over them. You can be a computer expert or a plumber, an interpreter or a baker, an eye surgeon or a dog-handler: when someone else needs your expertise, they automatically have less power than you in this particular context.

Charisma

Finally, a less concrete form of perpendicular power but, nonetheless, it is a significant dimension. Genuine charisma describes the power and influence generated by someone's personal presence: their beauty, charm, moral integrity, holiness, sometimes referred to as force of personality. This can have a profound effect on others. Charisma can also be manufactured – as with the cult of celebrity – so it is then more the product of publicity and hype than grounded in any intrinsic personal qualities. The power of celebrity enables stars of stage, sport and screen to exert a larger than life appeal, influencing us to look like them, dress like them or act like them. We may be even influenced into giving them our money or our votes or, in extreme cases, laying down our lives for them.

What do all these four aspects of power have in common?

First, perpendicular power is measured always along the lines of a *ladder*. This means that you may exert some kind of power over others at the same time as being powerless in other contexts. A variety of ladders co-exist in our society: we may have less money but more expertise; be less skilled but more youthful; less intelligent, but far prettier.

Secondly, this kind of power is only ever *temporary*. It doesn't last forever. Professional and personal roles end and when they do, the power that accompanies that role disappears with it. Resources are finite and exhaustible and subject to unpredictable forces such as market fluctuation and political or climatic changes. Expertise is only relevant when it is needed: social and professional needs change, and with them, some skills become gradually or suddenly redundant while others start in ascendance. Even charisma is affected by time as physical prowess, youth and beauty fade and fashion moves on.

Thirdly, such power is conferred from *outside* us: by the organisation in which we work, by the norms of society or cultural trends. This external source means that it can be given and taken away in equal measure: it is not dependent on any intrinsic worth or personal characteristics. Even charismatic power which may emanate from some inner qualities is totally dependent on the existence of admirers or devotees to remain effective.

In this context, power is not dependent on merit: history shows that charismatic individuals can just as easily be sinners as saints. We gain power over others whether we 'deserve' it or not. It is quite arbitrary. Sometimes we don't choose it or even welcome this power: it just comes with a function or particular responsibilities with which we find ourselves.

Perpendicular power, with which we are most familiar, can be seen as a useful structure, an easy way of measuring which gives us useful information – like using a ruler – to assess relative positions. The reason for examining power at this stage of the book is that consciously or unconsciously, structures of power impact on all our communication because they influence our thoughts and perceptions of others.

The relevance to communication lies in the fact that the perspective of the ladder dominates every aspect of life and especially our relationships. Even without being aware of it most of the time, this particular viewpoint affects our communication in subtle ways. When we consider criticising or challenging someone or expressing our feelings or saying 'no' to them, this structure hovers in the mental background so that, even without thinking about it, we automatically approach a difficult conversation with a strategic assumption of winning or losing, largely dependent on how we assess our respective positions on the ladder. All kinds of imaginary outcomes and attendant anxieties – based on these relative positions – prevent us from speaking up: won't it be pointless to challenge someone in that position? Will I get punished? Isn't she too vulnerable for me to be truthful? Is it my place to say anything? Will I end up looking stupid?

These anxieties can be eased by understanding and developing a different kind of power – personal power – which is not attached to our relative positions in the hierarchy. As you will see in the following chapters, embracing personal power provides the key to all assertive communication.

Personal power

Instead of a ladder, this power is more easily understood symbolically as a continuum, a continuously moving force which accompanies us from birth to death. It is something that abides within us alongside all the trappings of external power which come and go throughout our lives. Personal power can wax and wane but it exists *independently* of movement up or down the many ladders of external power. Even in times of anguish and despair, it survives like an ember that can be breathed back into life when circumstances change.

Personal power does not depend on outside circumstances so is not tied to rank or class, wealth or background, beauty or age. It cannot be measured in conventional ways. The natural compassion radiating from a very inexperienced young nurse or the quiet assurance and wisdom of a man who has led a humble but fulfilled existence bear little relation to the structures of power in society.

Some of the more recognisable hallmarks of personal power

are balance, honesty, emotional awareness, integrity and equality. Balance signifies the commitment to weighing up your own needs, opinions and desires against those of others: the underlying goal of all assertiveness training is to develop personal power to the extent that you can interact with others from a place of much more security and balance than when you are teetering on one rung, trying to regain or retain a precarious foothold.

The quality of honesty applies especially to being truthful to yourself about your needs, your limitations and your feelings: not being truthful – being in denial – always weakens our personal power. Emotional awareness follows on from honesty: developing a more familiar relationship, for example, with anxiety or anger helps us move through these feelings and still say what we want to say instead of being overwhelmed. Integrity – being true to yourself – gives a boost to personal power because it provides the inner strength to risk disapproval and disagreement.

Equality is a crucial facet of personal power which derives from responding to both models of power at once: you open your eyes to see the person you are communicating with as either higher or lower than you in terms of perpendicular power, while *also* acknowledging your equality as human beings. This may strike you as a bit vague and unfamiliar at this point but the concept and its implications will become clearer as you read through these pages. Once you're clear about what it really means, you'll see how it provides the key to effective communication.

4

Putting Theory into Practice

In the last chapter we looked at a few examples of the sort of situations that have cropped up in workshops and training programmes. What follows are some exercises which can be done on your own, as well as guidance as to how you could set up a context for working with one or two other people who are similarly interested in learning to be more assertive.

Exercise 1 Set aside fifteen minutes on your own. Find something to write on and make a list of ten situations in which you would like to be more assertive. They can be taken from any area of your life – like those described in the first chapter – with strangers or your family, with friends, relatives, children, neighbours, colleagues, partner, patients or customers – anyone you come into contact with in the course of your life.

When you have the list in front of you, write down next to each interaction how you behave now – aggressively, passively or manipulatively (if you have so far avoided dealing with the issue, this is one for the passive category). You may find that you need to write down more than one response if you behave both aggressively *and* passively, for example, on different occasions.

If you have another fifteen minutes, continue to Exercise 2. If not, then wait until you have the time. It does not matter if you leave it for a while.

Exercise 2 Look at your list and see if you can range the items in order of difficulty. Look through it and find one which you think is the easiest: one which you can *almost* handle assertively but not quite. Write 'Number 1' next to that on your list. Now find the one which makes you shudder when you think about it: the one that you feel is the most difficult and unlikely ever to happen. This one becomes Number 10. Then take the next easiest one and put Number 2 next to it. Find the next most difficult one and make that Number 9. Continue until you have a range of situations, starting with the easiest one and continuing down to the worst. If you cannot manage to find ten or if you find that most of your list is bunched together around the top and bottom, don't worry: the important thing is to have a range with some easy ones to start with so that you can gradually work your way down the list.

'Working down' the list brings us to the principal method we use in assertiveness training, a method called *role-play*. As I said in the Introduction, this aspect of assertiveness training has virtually disappeared because it takes time and it takes commitment: it also takes a belief that the person who wants to change has the answer somewhere in her and, although she may well need guidance and support in finding this answer, she doesn't need steering, general advice or counselling.

Without role-play, change remains in the realm of thought and conjecture. Talking and thinking about your behaviour is a start but only of limited value. The way to *change* is to try it out for yourself: this is how you learn to feel anxiety and move through it; how you learn that when you express what you feel instead of denying it, the physical sensations actually disperse and you find yourself getting stronger (from within) in what you want to communicate.

Role-play is borrowed from the traditional techniques of behaviour therapy. It helps the person rehearse what she wants to say or do in a given situation. Another person takes the complementary role: for example, someone else might sit in for the queue jumper, the shop assistant, the child, husband, friend, parent, boss and so on, in order that the first person can practise handling the dialogue assertively. Without any learned skill, the person taking the complementary role can identify the essence of the exchange and will often surprise herself and everyone else by spontaneously finding the right words to use, the correct intonation, and many subtle ways of making the role-play scenario very real for the person who is practising.

If you doubt the effectiveness of this method, you have only to try it to see how helpful it can be. Most people initially express great reluctance to try it out and everyone feels self-conscious at the beginning but after taking part in role-play, they are surprised and utterly convinced of its value. It is not the same as 'play-acting': once you are involved in the role, you find that you feel the same feelings that you do in the real-life circumstances: anxiety, indignation, guilt or disappointment. What's more, the person taking the opposite role can be a very helpful source of insight and feedback. There are many tiny details – the tone of your voice, the way you stand or your eye contact, for example – details which you do not notice yourself but all of which contribute to the overall impression. In this way, someone else can observe and tell you when you are coming across more assertively.

Setting up a role-play at home The other person can be anyone you feel safe to work with. It is not always advisable to choose one of your family unless you are sure they will take what you are doing seriously and that they understand what you are trying to achieve. For this reason, some women find it easier to practise with a friend, especially if the friend has some understanding of what assertiveness is about. The important thing is that you trust the other person because for role-play to work, you have to be genuine: you have to be able to acknowledge that you don't have all the answers and that you find some situations difficult before you practise dealing with things more effectively. In other words, you have to stop acting and be yourself: this is why you need someone who is on your side and preferably someone who will trust you in turn.

You will probably feel a little silly and self-conscious when you both begin but after a couple of awkward moments, you will begin to get absorbed. I know that whenever I have tried something out with a close friend, I have always felt a little embarrassment at first but it soon disappears. It is quickly replaced by the excitement of learning with someone's interest and encouragement and the satisfaction is shared by both of you when you finally get it right! Apart from being fun a lot of the time, it is also a very useful and positive additional dimension to friendship.

How do you start? Whether just one of you is practising or both of you intend to take a turn, whoever starts must decide specifically on what they want to achieve. It is no good saying 'I want to deal with my messy son', 'I want to feel more confident talking to my boss' or 'I wish my hairdresser would listen to me'. You have to learn to be specific: 'I want my son to tidy his room once a week'; 'I want to ask my boss for a promotion to the next scale' or 'I want to tell my hairdresser not to cut more than half an inch off my hair'.

You do not have to go to too much trouble over this but it helps to recreate the scene a little. For example, the first role-play might need the person playing the son to be at the computer. In the second example, the 'boss' might sit at a desk (you could use a table). The boss could pretend to be on the phone or watching a screen or doing whatever makes the scene more realistic. In the third, the 'hairdresser' could stand behind the other person who could be on a chair, just as you would be in a salon.

Be open to feedback from the person playing the son/boss/ hairdresser: ask them to tell you what you say or do which is unhelpful and suggest how you could improve. The other person's feedback can be revealing and useful. Don't spend too much time in discussion: the most effective use of time is in the actual role-play. Keep practising again and again until you feel happier with the way you handle the conversation.

If you're temporarily in the shoes of the son/boss/hairdresser, you do *not* have to worry about having dramatic ability. Everyone finds it remarkably easy once they relax into it: we are often better observers of one another's behaviour and gestures than we give ourselves credit for.

Start with the easiest first Practise a situation from the Number 1's or 2's on your list. The reason for doing this is important. It is always tempting to dive into the deep end too soon. The hardest problems are the ones you most want to be rid of, the ones which cause you most heartache and frustration.

But any long-lasting problem usually involves a relationship with someone who is or has been important to you in some way: it may be a person at work, a spouse, a parent or close friend. Any relationship that *matters* to you will have a history attached to it and therefore feelings will run high because they have accumulated over time. It is more difficult to be clear about what you really want and feel when the issue is emotionally loaded.

For example, it is almost impossible to say 'no' assertively to your mother when you have been saying 'yes' for thirty years and swallowing back the resentment every time. Long-standing relationships of any kind are fraught with hidden complications. It is no good pretending all you want to do is simply ask your teenage daughter to come home on time when deep down you are feeling sad that she is growing up and growing away from you. If you start with your Number 9's and 10's, you will find that you'll get too anxious and that it won't work. Then you risk becoming discouraged and convincing yourself that there is no way of dealing with it so you might as well give up.

Start with the situations where you can practise your assertive skills with people who do not mean so much to you: a fellow passenger, a salesman, a neighbour, a new work associate or waitress, for example. You can probably find many opportunities which present themselves during your day when you can try out these skills. Nothing is too trivial: every single interaction that you manage assertively will build up your skill and confidence. You can do as little as you want and take as long as you want. You can look at your list as a personal programme. What for you is very easy, and would not even appear on your list, might represent a Number 10 problem for someone else. And, similarly, something which presents you with a lot of difficulty could be easy for someone else to manage. There is no point in comparison because we all have our own areas of competence.

As you read through the book you may find more and more situations you would like to try for yourself: you may want to practise an important interview that you know you are going to have to face or you may want to find a better way of handling a recurring problem. The worst hurdle is making a start. It is always easier to *think* about doing it and even rehearse in your mind the whole dialogue before or after the event but role-play offers the most effective way I know of actually helping people use the skills for themselves through incorporating new behaviour into their lives, translating thought into action.

I remember Anna reporting back during the follow-up meeting when I asked if anyone had practised what we had worked on using role-play during the previous session. Anna, a quiet woman in her late forties, had found it difficult to speak up in meetings at work. We had role-played an alternative strategy so that she would not have to endure yet another meeting without having said what she wanted to say.

Our practice had first involved Anna realising the folly of waiting for 'the right moment'. This moment never comes, of course, but what happens is that our anxiety increases with each passing 'wrong' moment and the tension makes it physically harder to get the words out. Anna had practised several times resisting her tendency to *wait*: for a lull in the conversation or for her colleagues to stop speaking or for the chairman to notice her and invite her to speak. Instead Anna learned to keep breathing evenly and take the plunge. She practised using a specific phrase 'I'd like to make a suggestion' and each time she strengthened her voice in tone and volume so that the others taking part in the role-play meeting instinctively stopped to listen. She was then given a spontaneous burst of applause but she still had to practise speaking once the attention was focused on her. So we did it again and she learned how to continue with her proposal.

This exercise was to teach Anna how to manage her anxiety instead of being restricted by it. As a consequence she was able to try it out in her real-life meeting. She reported that she had felt the same levels of anxiety and noticed she was waiting once again for the right moment when she recalled the experience of her role-play. So she took a deep breath and spoke up a couple of times until the discussion stopped and the attention turned to her: at this point she made her suggestion. She told us that her heart had been thumping so loudly, she had thought everyone else could hear it but she got the words out anyway. Probably none of Anna's colleagues knew how hard it had been for her but that didn't matter. She had managed to make her suggestion and also to invite a response: this was really helpful in taking the spotlight off herself and encouraging others to show interest. She told us she had felt six-feet tall when she'd left the meeting and her sense of triumph was shared by us all: she had taken a big step in building her confidence. Having done it once, she could do it again.

If you try to tackle the more difficult problems before you are ready, you will only come unstuck and do the reverse. On the other hand, with one, two, then three small successes under your belt, you will achieve two things. You will be able to shrug off a failure here and there without too much self-recrimination and also feel better equipped to tackle more difficult areas from a position of strength. In this way, you will avoid the common barrier which prevents people getting started: the trap of thinking that everything is either too trivial to bother about or too difficult to cope with. A lot of us get stuck in this trap and end up doing nothing. The first and major step is to start applying some assertive techniques which are introduced in the next chapter.

5

Assertive Techniques

If by now you are interested in knowing how assertive skills can work for you, take a closer look at the dynamics of a familiar, everyday situation: imagine that you are tired, you go home and the place is in an absolute mess: how exactly do you ask for help with clearing it all up?

What might Agnes do? She storms into the empty lounge, turns off the unwatched television, yells upstairs to her children who are nowhere to be seen, kicks a toy across the floor, finds her husband in the kitchen, pulls the newspaper out of his hands and shouts: 'Why the hell has nobody done anything about tea?'

Dulcie plonks herself down at the kitchen table, puts her head in her hands and then slowly rises and starts to pick up the breakfast things, trudging around thinking to herself: 'They really are an inconsiderate lot. Look at him sitting there doing nothing.' Then, in silence, she sets about preparing the meal.

Ivy comes in and mutters: 'Look at this mess! I don't know how you can all be so inconsiderate.'

She clears the mess sulkily then slowly and laboriously prepares a meal which is served late. She calls her family to eat and when anyone complains about the lateness, she responds with a chilling stare. The whole meal is conducted in a heavy, awkward silence and everyone feels uncomfortable and guilty.

(Notice that not one of them has asked directly for what she wanted: namely some help.)

How could you deal with this issue assertively? Selma arrives

home and finds the same chaos and mess and her husband sitting in the chair. She confronts him with a statement: 'I'm tired and I'd like you to help me get the supper ready. Could you to do the washing up (or wash the vegetables or lay the table)? ' She asks specifically and directly for the help she wants.

This brings us to three skills which are essential to assertive interactions.

You need to:

- Decide what it is you want or feel and say so specifically and directly.
- Stick to your statement and repeat it, if necessary, over and over again.
- Assertively deflect any responses from the other person which might undermine your assertive request.

Being specific If you have ever listened to someone's long-winded preamble, you may have wondered impatiently when they were ever going to get to the point. This is the key to this technique. It means deciding what the 'point' is and stating it without all the unnecessary padding that we tend to use when we are anxious. Look at the following examples of padding (in italics).

'(*I hope you don't mind me saying this, you'll probably think I've got a bit of a nerve, in fact it is unusual for me, but*) could you check this list for me before I send it through to the boss?'

'(*I'm terribly sorry to trouble you but*) I'd like you to change this for a clean cup.'

'(*Oh, I'd have loved to say "yes" but you know, with things as they are, and, you know, really if you'd told me last week, I mean, you haven't given me much notice, so this time*) my answer is "no".'

'(*Ahem, waiter, I'm really sorry, but I'm afraid that*) I've been waiting over half an hour for my sandwich.'

'(*I wondered what you were doing this afternoon, you know, if you were busy, because I, em, have to go to the shops, and well, if you're doing anything, it doesn't really matter, I suppose, but*) I'd like to borrow your car.'

The padding often weakens your statement and confuses the listener. Practise making a clear statement or request without the preamble.

Being specific sounds an easy instruction to follow but I know from teaching this skill how difficult we find it to say what we want exactly and concisely: somehow we seem to have lost the ability to focus on what we want and instead tend to focus on the other person.

Here is an example of a typical dialogue between myself and a course participant. In this instance, Casey had expressed her wish to learn how to make an effective request of her female assistant to produce a report for a monthly area meeting.

AD: What do you want to ask for?
Casey: Well, she's working for three other people not just me.
AD: What do you want to ask for?
Casey: The thing is, she always puts their work first and leaves mine till last.
AD: What do you want to ask her to do?
Casey: I'd like her to go get the typing done. But I think she has a problem with me.
AD: What do you want her to prepare?
Casey: The report.
AD: When do you want it by?
Casey: (*shrugs her shoulders*) I don't know . . . Tuesday?
AD: Is that what you want?
Casey: That would do.
AD: When would you like it?
Casey: Well, people need a few days to look at it.
AD: So does Tuesday give enough time?
Casey: It really should be last thing Monday.
AD: Do you need to see it before it is sent out on Monday?
Casey: Ideally.

AD: So, does mid-day on Monday give you enough time?
Casey: Yes.
AD: So your request is "I'd like you to type this report and
        email it to me by Monday lunchtime."
Casey: Yes.

Casey was intelligent, competent and also articulate but not at all unusual in finding it hard to be specific. The problem is her habit – shared by many – of using the other person as a reference point which will only elicit a spiral of anxieties about the imagined response: 'she'll be aggressive'; 'he won't listen'; 'she seems to resent me' or 'I don't want to appear bossy'. These kinds of thoughts interfere with our ability to focus solely on what we want.

It is only when you say what it is you *want* that you can say it with conviction. It is no use, for example, trying to convey assertively that you want your partner to phone if he's going to be late when secretly you suspect he's having an affair; it is no good trying assertively to arrange where and when to meet someone when your heart is not in it and you really don't want to be going out at all; you will not sound convincing when you ask someone to help you set the table when your real wish is to have the entire evening off, with someone else fetching a takeaway.

With help and discipline, you can learn to work out in excruciatingly specific detail what it is you're asking for. You may not get what you want but this is the only starting point because by asking for it *directly* and *specifically*, you give yourself the best chance of getting it. If you only hint or complain, after a while you will probably hear yourself saying, 'I've asked him *so* many times' or 'I'm always telling her but . . . ' as if the problem lies with the other person who is somehow too obtuse or unwilling to understand your message. This risks reinforcing your own sense of powerless to change what is happening. Every time women complain in this way I can be sure that the problem lies with the manner in which they themselves are making their requests rather than with the response of the other person.

Check your own behaviour to see whether or not you have made a *clear* request or if you have relied on the common belief that the other person *ought* to know what you want and feel, without you having to spell it out for them. We assume that someone should know us well enough or that if they loved us enough, they would understand our needs without us having to be explicit. But we cannot always depend on other people's telepathic abilities. Nor is it safe to rely on dropping hints, however broad they are: uttering a deep sigh and looking heavenwards may still not accurately convey that you want some help with doing the chores. Besides which, if you are not specific, then others can always sidestep the issue conveniently on the grounds that you did not actually ask for anything!

As women we often confuse clarity and directness with bluntness or rudeness. We learn to hint in a roundabout way, to make others feel guilty if they have not responded to our unexpressed needs. We complain, we reproach others, we resort to sarcasm, we sulk. The last thing we actually *say* is what we want. Whether it is the Agnes, the Dulcie or the Ivy which predominates in our behaviour, the problem of identifying the actual need or request poses the same difficulty.

Sticking to it So now you know what you want to say, beginning with an assertive request or statement. But what happens if, as soon as you start, you receive a barrage of abuse or are met with a refusal or even ignored? This is when you move on to the next stage which is to repeat your statement or request calmly until it is understood and acknowledged by the other person.

The purpose of repetition is to help you maintain a steady position without falling prey to manipulative comment, or irrelevant logic, or argumentative bait, some or all of which may be provoked by your assertive request. Here are some examples:

Example 1

At the deli counter in a small supermarket, Selma returns some French cheese which, when opened at home, was revealed to have rather more mould than was healthy.

Selma: I bought this cheese yesterday. When I got home and opened it, I found it was very mouldy and I'd like a refund, please.

Shopkeeper: Nothing to do with me, I wasn't here yesterday. *(Irrelevant logic)*

Selma: I bought it in this shop and as it is inedible, I'd like a refund.

Shopkeeper: That sort of cheese is meant to be mouldy, Madam. It's the way it's made. *(Argumentative bait)*

Selma: I know what kind of cheese I buy. This is past its healthy state and I'd like a refund.

Shopkeeper: Look, there's a queue of people behind you waiting to be served and I'm on my own here . . . *(Manipulative bait)*

Selma: I can see that there are people behind but this is inedible and I'd like a refund.

Shopkeeper: Well, have you got the receipt?

His manner is resigned and unfriendly but he nevertheless complies with the request for a refund.

Example 2

Selma has an unexpected morning off and intends to spend her time finishing a novel for the next meeting of her reading group. Her next-door neighbour knocks on the door in a fluster.

Neighbour: Selma, love, what are you doing this morning?

Selma: I'm going to spend it catching up on my reading.

Neighbour: Oh good. Since you're not busy, would you look after the children while I go to the hairdresser? The only appointment I could get is at 11 o'clock.

Selma: I'm sorry but I'm not prepared to spend the morning looking after your children.

Neighbour: But Selma, what are friends for? *(Manipulative bait)* You know I don't often get the chance to go . . . and I've got a date on Friday. *(More manipulative bait)*

Selma: Yes, I know and I was OK with taking them when you last asked but I'm still not prepared to look after your children all morning today.

Neighbour: It won't be for long, you could read while they played. They wouldn't bother you at all. *(Irrelevant logic)*

Selma: No, I'm really not prepared to look after them this morning. Why don't you try someone else? Marsha's in, you could try her.

The neighbour finally accepts Selma's refusal

Example 3

Robert, a friend of a distant cousin, landed on Selma's doorstep from Australia. He said he expected to stay a couple of nights but it's now three weeks later. He has spent most of the time watching television, lounging around, trawling the internet and smoking dope.

Selma: Robert, I have something to say to you. I feel really uncomfortable with you smoking dope in my flat and I would like you to move on somewhere else.

Robert: Oh come on Selma, what are you being so heavy about? *(Argumentative bait)*

Selma: You may think I'm being heavy, but I don't even know whether it's illegal or not so I don't want you to smoke in my flat and I'd like you to look for somewhere else.

Robert: How can you chuck me out when I haven't any money? *(Manipulative bait)*

Selma: You can get yourself a job if you try. You have been here for three weeks and I'd like you to look for somewhere else.

Robert: Look, just calm down and cool it. If it makes you happy, I'll promise not to smoke any more when I'm in the house. *(Irrelevant logic)*

Selma: I am calm, Robert, and I really want you to make plans to move. *(Robert eventually gets the message.)*

The difficulty with some arguments is that as soon as you reply to them you become hooked and your position is weakened so this technique works in two ways. First, it helps you to project an image of determination and purpose instead of appearing to be a pushover. Secondly, many women find that after the first two or three repetitions, they actually feel the *truth* of their statement which gives them more determination as a consequence which, of course, reinforces the impression of conviction. The technique is remarkably effective, but it does require constant repetition of the key phrase: hence the importance of starting with one!

Once you are able to repeat your phrase and feel your confidence increase, you then need to 'field' the other person's rejoinders. Simply ignoring what they say or pretending you have not heard as you carry on repeating your request is not enough. You won't create an assertive impression sounding like a mechanical parrot: on the other hand it is difficult to respond to a deflection without getting entangled in someone else's line of argument: it's easy to get side-tracked and then lose heart. An assertive beginning all too often degenerates into an aggressive outburst or sulky submission because of this one specific difficulty. This is where the third skill of deflecting the argument becomes relevant.

In order to achieve a smooth verbal interaction and communicate effectively, you need to indicate that you have heard what the other person said but without getting 'hooked' by what they say. Practising this helps you to overcome your anxiety and defensiveness and to continue undeterred. The following examples show how this might be done.

'It may not be usual for you to get complaints *but this is not what I ordered and I want a replacement.*'

'I know there is a queue of people behind me *but I still want an appointment to see Dr Hall this week.*'

'I can see you are feeling let down *but I really don't want to go out tonight.*'

'I appreciate you being a good friend to me in the past *but I just can't lend you any money right now.*'

'I know that you're tired as well *but I'd still like you to do your share of the work.*'

'I understand you're disappointed *but I still have to say "no".*'

In each example, the speaker maintains her statement. She acknowledges the response of the other person without allowing it to deflect her from her main statement.

It is extraordinary that these techniques appear so simple. Yet anyone who practises them, using role-play, will probably discover how difficult it can be to stick to the point, how easy it is to be side-tracked and how essential it is to decide what you want to say before you begin. An approximation will not do: you need a specific starting point if you want to communicate assertively. Once you become familiar with these basic assertiveness training skills, you will see how often you can apply them anytime you wish to assert yourself more effectively.

Following on

1. If you have made the list of situations as suggested in Chapter 4 you will already have a good idea of where to begin. Look towards the top of your list. Using the skills outlined above you can decide what it is you want to say/ ask and then try it out in role-play. Sticking to your statement will probably be more difficult that you think but keep going until you feel the conviction of what you are saying. Practise fielding the response from the other person without getting side-tracked.

2. You can practise the techniques using the following examples:

    a) You have bought a drill and when you get home you find it doesn't work. Set up the role-play with someone to take the part of the shop assistant who implies you don't know how to use the drill because you're a woman and use the techniques to ask for a replacement.

    b) You want to ask a friend if you can have the book back that you lent them two months ago. The friend has not finished it but you are about to go away and want to take the book with you to read.

    c) You are in a department store and the assistants behind

the counter are chatting, apparently oblivious of your presence. Ask for some attention.

d) You see some appealing apples on display on a stall in the market. You ask for a pound of them but the stall-holder goes to another box of apples which you suspect are not as good as the others. Your task is to ask for some of the apples on display.

e) You want to make an appointment to see a busy super-visor at work. Your task is to use the skills to approach him or her in the office or in the corridor and reach an agreement on a specific time.

f) You are sitting on the bus and someone comes to sit next to you: in fact it feels as if they are sitting on top of you! Practise asking them to move over so you have enough room for yourself.

Use these ideas and adapt them to suit you.

6

Rights and Responsibilities

At this point it is important to consider some basic human rights applicable to all of us, women and men, adults and children. These rights are not new or startling or revolutionary. In fact they may strike some readers as quite ordinary at first but many women have been helped to make a start in changing their behaviour by reviewing these rights. They have also found it useful to remind themselves of these rights at moments when they felt assailed by doubts and conflict over the rights and wrongs of assertive behaviour.

The need for this chapter may seem an anomaly in 2012 when it is generally acknowledged that one of the trends in the last thirty years has been to emphasise the rights of the individual while neglecting any of the responsibilities that accompany those rights. This is further evidence of the swing towards individualism and aggression rather than a balance between one person's feelings, needs and limits and those of another.

I decided to retain this chapter, despite the changing context, because I want to reaffirm the need for this balance. In addition, experience has taught me that, simple though they sound, these rights are relevant at a much deeper level than those of being a customer or a consumer: they are not enshrined in our laws but are instead to be considered more as psychological or emotional rights and this is why it is only after repeated affirmation that we cannot only *believe* them but act on them with conviction. Paradoxically, in this aggressive rights-obsessed culture, many people find it difficult to grasp the following more meaningful rights and, as a result, fail to assert themselves on many occasions.

Eleven rights are set out below, with a brief explanation of each one. Keep them in mind as a reference during the following chapters.

1. *I have the right to state my own needs and set my own priorities as a person independent of any roles that I may assume in my life.*

This is fundamental and particularly so for women, whose roles in life often swamp their own personalities. Being a daughter, wife or mother all entail responsibilities and obligations attached to these as well as professional roles which can obstruct the view of what a woman may want for herself.

I remember Carol's sense of triumph when she made a decision to go on holiday alone. Her husband wanted her to go bird-watching with him and Carol felt obliged because she had previously spent two holidays with her mother. Her mother wanted her back and Carol felt torn because she was the only daughter. The conflict between these two roles had lasted several months while Carol fretted and postponed making a decision. When the emphasis was placed on what *she* wanted to do, she suddenly saw quite clearly that she really wanted to go away on her own. When she made this announcement assertively to both her husband and her mother, to her amazement, they both accepted her decision quite easily.

This right does not imply you no longer have to honour the responsibilities within the roles you assume. It simply helps you to be aware that your own needs exist as well as the needs of those for whom you care.

Julie, a hard-working health visitor, had great difficulty in setting aside personal time and felt that her patients should always have priority. So she always made herself available and fulfilled her role admirably except that her own needs were submerged and went unrecognised. They did not disappear though: her unspoken needs emerged in her perpetual tiredness and tension and when she recognised this, she was able to achieve some kind of balance.

2. *I have the right to be treated with respect as an intelligent, capable and equal human being.*

On a good day, this is an easy right to accept but one of the difficulties is that we often do not treat *ourselves* with respect. We do not give ourselves equal credit for intelligence or ability. Intelligence is a quality that many women have consciously played down in order to retain a suitably feminine image. Others who feel comfortable in asserting their intelligence can lose sight of it when faced with a situation in which they feel disadvantaged by lack of technical expertise. After paying a lot for a service on your car, for instance, you find that your brakes do not work any more effectively than they did before. You confront the garage manager who rattles off all sorts of explanations that you suspect are flannel. It is easy to feel confused in this sort of confrontation and it is important to hold on to the fact that you *know* that your brakes are not working, rather than being pushed against the wall by the force of an argument which has you doubting your own intelligence and common sense.

3. *I have the right to express my feelings.*

One of the most important lessons is to recognise what you are feeling *at the time*. Often we agonise over an event hours, days or even months after it happens before we finally register what it was we felt. It is important to identify and to accept that you feel and permit yourself some verbal expression. (As we will discuss later, in Chapter 11, there is a difference between expressing of what you feel and acting on it). This right has three aspects: recognising and identifying your feelings, accepting rather than denying them and taking responsibility for expressing them appropriately.

4. *I have the right to express my opinions and values.*

This includes the right to stand up for your opinions if you choose. This is not to say that you should be bullied into justifying a particular viewpoint if you do not want to, but it means that you have the right to your own opinions even if they stand in disagreement with those of the majority. It is not a question of right or wrong but of differences in perception.

Sometimes we lose sight of our right to assert our own values. Michelle, for example, loved collecting pieces of old china but she agonised over what to say to a friend who treated these objects around her home with a careless disregard for their fragility and value, even on one occasion damaging one of them. When I asked her why she did not confront him, she replied that she felt she had no right: 'It shouldn't matter to me,' she said. 'I shouldn't mind about *things* that much.' She felt that her friend's more casual attitude should be just as acceptable as her own and didn't want to appear too petty. She therefore denied her own values but inside she continued to carry a grudge. It took a long time for her to acknowledge openly that she *did* feel irritated. Eventually she was able to give herself permission to follow through with those feelings, to consider that her own values were different but equally important to those of her friend. She was then able to take responsibility for herself and ask him assertively to treat her objects with the care that she felt appropriate.

5. *I have the right to say 'yes' or 'no' for myself.*

This sounds simple but is very much connected with the first right about roles and responsibilities. Making a choice for yourself because *you* want or do not want something becomes more difficult when you have other roles to fulfil.

Deidre's partner, Mike, had two daughters by a previous marriage and one of them was getting married. Bowing to the resentment of Mike's ex-wife, his daughter had arranged for Deidre not to sit at the top wedding table but had allocated her a place at a table much further away where she would be surrounded by people she didn't know. This was a real dilemma: she and Mike had been together for five years and they were happy but she did not feel at all comfortable with the proposed arrangement. She talked it through with Mike, who felt divided of course but, in the end, he respected and accepted her choice not to go the wedding because she was clear she really did not want to go where she was obviously not welcome.

6. *I have the right to make mistakes.*

Many of us find it extraordinarily difficult to accept this right. If someone points out a mistake or criticises an action, we often feel a level of embarrassment and confusion out of all proportion to the seriousness of the actual error. Whether it is the experience of being punished as children for mistakes or the whole educational construct – of right and wrong, good marks and bad marks – I am not sure, but many of us believe that making a mistake is unacceptable and that it shows we're stupid.

You can learn to shrug your shoulders and accept you mistakes without disappearing into a pit of self-reproach or defensively denying your error. It is important to see that you can do something wrong – behave foolishly, make an unwise bad move, misread a situation, answer incorrectly – without it indicating some chronic personal inadequacy. This right can permit us to acknowledge the mistaken piece of behaviour without losing touch with that central core of self-belief.

You may believe you already have this right but check what happens to your convictions when someone has criticised a mistake in your work? Or when your 'brainwave' turns out to be not so brilliant? Or somebody points out that your argument is full of holes? Or the new hair colour you thought would be perfect really doesn't suit you?

A lot of us set store by competence and achievement and in a competitive society it is difficult to create options other than 'I'm right' and 'you're wrong' or vice versa. In the Introduction, one of the changes I described since the first edition of this book is the increased acceptability of aggression in many contexts. One facet of this trend is defensiveness about mistakes. This is partly due to what is called the culture of litigation which increases fears about the repercussions of being sued and propels individuals and institutions into a kneejerk denial of responsibility for professional wrongdoing, through fear of incurring financial or criminal penalties. What concerns us here is that, even on a personal level, mistakes have become less acceptable as a means to on-going learning and more often equated with being the 'loser'.

This helps to explain why an assertive acknowledgment of a mistake by any individual and a willingness to assume *responsibility* for it is a very rare spectacle in either a private or public context.

7. *I have the right to change my mind.*

This right can be invaluable during the early stages of learning to make assertive choices, that is, choices which reflect what you really *want* rather than what you feel is expected of you or what you think would please the other person. As you look more carefully at the process of decision-making you will develop an awareness of how you make many decisions for the wrong reasons. A wrong decision brings regret. You then have to try to back out in some way. There is usually a period of practice needed before being clear enough to make the right decision at the start and so, at least while you are learning, it is helpful to remind yourself that you can change your mind rather than proceed with a commitment you are unhappy about. This right incorporates the responsibility to communicate your change of mind clearly and assertively giving the other person due notice rather than avoiding them and going into hiding.

8. *I have the right to say I don't understand.*

Have you ever found yourself in a group of people, with everyone listening in rapt attention to the speaker while you sat confused and uncomfortable because you felt unable to speak up and admit you didn't understand and ask for further explanation? If so, then you will recognise the importance of this right. As with the right to make mistakes, we feel an undue amount of discomfort as adults in acknowledging lack of comprehension and ignorance. We can hardly expect to know everything about everything any more than we can expect to be perfect. But to say 'I don't understand' or 'Could you explain that again?' remains difficult for many of us to say without framing it as an apology for one's own limitations.

It is so simple to ask but we hold back time and time again. With this right in mind you can learn to acknowledge confusion or non-comprehension without putting yourself down for being stupid and also to ask for more information or a clearer explanation without feeling ridiculous. It should be added that when you do so, you'll probably find you are not alone!

9. *I have the right to ask for what I want.*

Again this sounds quite straightforward. No one would argue with you. Until, that is, it conflicts with someone else's wishes or expectations so asking for what you want means displeasing them in some way. Whether the conflict is imaginary or real, the fear of displeasing another person can exert a lot of psychological pressure to ignore this particular right which means that a direct request is something that many women avoid. They feel they risk refusal with a direct approach so subtle hints and suggestions are much safer. It is easier to sigh with tiredness and complain of a backache than to ask someone directly to empty the washing machine or move a heavy table.

Many women will go along with what someone else wants for the sake of peace and quiet. I remember a good example of this. At the table next to mine in a restaurant sat a man, his wife, his mother and their teenage daughter. The proximity of our tables and my insatiable fascination with other people's conversations allowed me to overhear the following dialogue.

Husband:	*(as they all sit perusing the menu)* Now, Mum, what would you like?
Mother:	I think I'll have the Chicken Madras
Husband:	*(in disbelief)* Chicken Madras? Have you ever tasted a Madras? It will be far too hot for you!
Mother:	*(a little hesitantly)* But I *like* it hot.
Husband:	Maybe, but you don't really know what you are talking about. A Madras is the hottest curry you can get.

Mother:	But I *like* it hot.
Wife:	It really is very hot, you know, are you sure?
Grandchild:	It really is hot, Gran.
Grandmother:	Well . . .
Husband:	Look, Mum, if you insist then I will order you a Madras, but don't blame me when you can't eat it. *(Waiter arrives to take the order.)*
Husband:	Well, Mum, you've decided on the Madras curry then have you?
Mother:	Emm, I think I'll have a Chicken Korma. Is that a mild one?

The rest of the family sat back in satisfaction, convinced that she had made the right choice. Maybe the Madras would have been too hot but I'll never know: what mattered to me was the way she gave in. It is sometimes easy to spend your life going along with what others want and what other people expect you to want. Too often we settle for something that is not quite right because we don't feel we have the right to persist.

10. *I have the right to decline responsibility for other people's problems.*

If there's one right that has been most obviously affected by three decades of social change, I suspect it's this one. One can almost discern a generational gap in this regard between women now in their fifties and sixties and those in their thirties and twenties. Younger women today would appear to be less conflicted about the concerns of others than their mothers were and many are also more comfortable with asserting their own personal needs on a par with anyone else's.

This is due in part to the important cultural shift in the intervening years which emphasises individual enterprise over collective effort. Changes in economic values have filtered into social values with the result that it is much easier to distance ourselves from other people's problems because we have come to assume that circumstances of poverty and misfortune are the fault of an individual's failure to make the best of his or her life rather than looking for causes in the wider political and social system. If someone is unhappy, in trouble, penniless, out of work or depressed, their plight is attributed to their own inadequacy for which they are expected to take full responsibility.

There will be some readers who are uncomfortable with these attitudes and regret the lack of care or commitment to others less fortunate than themselves. If this applies to you, you must face the fact that your values are counter-cultural, so to speak, and that if you choose to uphold them, you will find yourself in the minority. This is not a reason for not doing so but it is helpful to know what you're up against!

There is no evidence that indifference to others' problems leads to high self-esteem. Under pressure, women of all ages today still give in to all sorts of demands which force them to accommodate the needs of others, rather than setting limits for themselves. Psychological insecurity is a powerful deterrent to achieving a balance between your own needs with those of others. It can come as a revelation to discover that shutting your eyes or ears to others' demands or problems is not the only way to achieve what you want out of your life: an assertive approach offers an effective alternative by showing a way to combine care and respect for another person without losing sight of your own needs and wishes.

11. *I have the right to deal with others without being dependent on them for approval.*

This final right is one which I think still forms a baseline for all of the others and helps explain the chronic insecurity many women – of all ages – continue to feel in relation to self-esteem. The need for approval is the single most important factor at the root of unassertive behaviour and is buried very deeply in most of us. An early association is instilled between behaving in a way which is approved of and the likelihood of earning a loving response. Although this early learning applies to both boys and girls, girls' conditioning includes the need to be good, smiling, attractive and feminine in order to gain the desired approbation. An attractive appearance is intrinsically connected to attractive behaviour.

The result is that many adult women still fear disapproval because it threatens the very roots of their self-esteem. This fear is what holds so many women back from stating their needs, expressing their feelings, standing up for their rights, refusing to do something they do not want to because they do not want to risk being seen as 'unattractive' and thereby earning another person's anticipated displeasure. 'What will they think of me if I say no/ if I don't apologise/ if I express my resentment/ if I say I don't want to or that I don't like that?' 'What will they think of me?' is the stumbling block on which many assertive intentions founder.

The need to be liked and approved of is so powerful that it extends way beyond intimates and friends, whose opinions we feel *do* matter and are important to us. I believe this is an on-going symptom even today. Many young girls agree to sex with a boy before they are ready or really want to because they don't want to be disliked or rejected. Young women fail to challenge and confront or exert authority at work because they don't want to be thought of as incompetent or unattractive. Middle-aged women struggle to hold on to their own sense of self when surrounded by the demands of elderly relatives, young grandchildren, over-worked adult children or husbands who are retired, depressed or have disappeared on a mission of sexual-rejuvenation. And elderly women? It is possible that in one's nineties the need for approval finally gets kicked out of the window but I don't know yet!

Chronic dependence on outside approval is a phenomenon I have encountered working with women across very different cultures: the dependence on approval can be crippling in its effects and it takes courage to challenge it. After a few experiences of surviving someone's disapproval and the realisation that the world did not come to an end, it becomes easier. You also begin to feel proud at having handled an encounter assertively and boosted your *own* morale independently. You learn that you can actually get by quite well without the approval and acceptance of everybody *all* of the time.

These basic rights look simple at first and include ones that sometimes seem too obvious to be spelt out at all, for example, the right to be treated as an equal human being. But as we know, in this world, the difference between having this right on paper and having this right in real terms is enormous. However, even in these circumstances, it is important not to lose sight of the fact that you have this right: when you are treated as unequal, without respect and consideration or as an object rather than a human being, holding on to the truth of this right will affect how you respond to such treatment and whether your own self-esteem survives.

At stressful times, we easily forget these rights. It is here that assertiveness training can help: learning to respond assertively when you are under fire; learning to hold on to the knowledge of your basic rights when you need them most and learning to operate from a base of inner trust and self-acceptance.

7

Body Language

Assertive communication, as we have seen, involves speaking directly and clearly but it also entails much more than the actual words you use. Your entire body helps you to assert yourself. Your posture, your expression and your gestures will all contribute to the overall impression. Non-verbal messages either reinforce or cancel out what you are trying to convey verbally. Any attempt to manage a situation assertively may founder, even though your words are exactly right, if your tone of voice and posture or facial expression reveal uncertainty or self-doubt or hostility. This chapter is concerned with how to use your body to convey an assertive presence and how to avoid giving non-verbal messages which contradict your verbal statement. Developing an awareness of your feelings at the time of communication will help towards exuding assertiveness with your whole being.

Fortunately, you do not have to adopt a whole new set of gestures or expressions to learn assertive body language: this would only make you appear affected and self-conscious. Body language emerges spontaneously from your feelings at the moment. However, there are body patterns that we can *unlearn*. As women, for example, most of us have learned how to smile appealingly, to gesture coyly, to pout, to wheedle and coax with our entire bodies. These habits get in the way of assertive communication. If you take the time to observe how you use your own body, you will see how you can come across more effectively.

Posture The first thing to consider is your posture because the way you hold yourself says a lot about you. Notice whether you hold yourself upright or slouched; whether your shoulders are hunched up around your ears (we often do this when anxious) or are down in a more relaxed position. If you are standing or sitting, notice whether you are balanced or leaning on one leg or balancing on one buttock. It is impossible to be assertive when standing off-balance. Notice how you walk into a room. Do you shuffle in, hoping not to be noticed; storm in like a thunderbolt or move steadily holding your head up and your back straight? Notice whether your head is upright or cocked to one side.

The relative height between you and the other person is another factor and works two ways. If you want to communicate equally, make sure you are not towering over the other person who may be sitting at a desk for example: try and find a way of speaking from a more equal physical position. Also, if you find yourself on the lower end of the dynamic, it helps to stand and face someone eye to eye to reinforce what you want to say.

Proximity and distance Each of us responds to an invisible line between ourselves and another person: too far back from it, the other person feels inaccessible and you feel ineffectual; too far over that line and you feel too close. An important learning point is that we often have differing optimum distances so that what is too close for you may well be comfortable for another and, conversely, someone else may be most comfortable with a distance which feels to you as if you have lost contact altogether. Learn what an effective distance means for you.

Leanne's problem provides an illustration. She complained that when she wanted to approach her boss, she would knock and enter his office. Her boss sat behind the desk and would often not even look up. She would be told to come back later but when she did so, he would still ignore her or talk at her while watching his screen. When we re-enacted her approach in role-play in the class, Leanne found that changes to the way she entered the room and her proximity to her boss' desk made all the difference. Pausing to breathe outside and get herself into an assertive frame of mind, she entered more calmly. Then she moved just two feet nearer the desk and stood squarely in front of her boss and waited until he looked up at her before she started speaking.

In this way Leanne became more aware that, up until then, she had been unknowingly contradicting the importance of what she wanted to say by speaking while he was ignoring her: by doing this, she was simultaneously sending out the nonverbal message that she wasn't worth listening to. Instead she learned to pause whenever his eyes strayed back to the screen and only started to speak again when he was giving her his full attention. In this way she came across far more assertively and was able to communicate what she wanted.

Eyes When we describe the eyes as the 'windows of the soul' we indicate their obvious power of communication. We feel uneasy about shifty gazes and disconcerted when we cannot see the reactions in someone's eyes, if, for example, they are wearing totally opaque or reflective sunglasses. Unconsciously we look for a reaction most of the time. The eyes tell us whether someone is listening or not; whether they are impressed, fascinated or intimidated by what we are saying. It is infuriating to try and talk to someone who has their back to you or has their attention fixed on something else. Maintaining eye contact is not the same as staring which feels intrusive or intimidating. Your gaze can be relaxed and friendly or it can convey hostility and timidity. If you avert your eyes, you probably convey embarrassment. Somewhere in between is the 'normal' interaction: if you are able to look directly at someone while making an assertive request or statement, you'll find this greatly reinforces your message.

Mouth and jaw Moving down to the lower part of the face we find other subtle signals. A clenched jaw and a tightly-held mouth are examples of give-away signs which communicate tension and aggression: although the words the speaker uses may be clear, anxiety emerges when the jaw tightens or the chin juts forward slightly. As soon as that happens – maybe with a slight thrust forward of the shoulders – the atmosphere changes because the body language comes across as threatening and hostile.

In psychological terminology, a give-away signal is known as 'non-verbal leakage'. This describes the clues that don't quite match together, clues that give away the real feelings of the speaker despite the attempt to control and hide them. One example is the smile that is a little too fixed or too wide or which lasts a little too long. Such a smile makes us uncomfortable because we detect there is something false about it. This does not necessarily imply that the person is deliberately trying to deceive the listener: it often occurs when we feel obliged to hide feelings of hurt or embarrassment or anger or when we feel vulnerable and unsafe. Similarly, we make an effort to suppress our fury or disappointment because we are afraid we might blow up in a temper or burst into tears, neither of which is considered socially acceptable. The consequence of keeping feelings at bay is that we tend to smile without realisng it.

When it comes to expressing anger, most women will make angry statements while unconsciously smiling at the same time. This is certainly not because they are feeling happy or friendly at that precise moment! It is usually because of the nervousness and inhibition they feel about expressing anger: the automatic smile is basically a non-verbal message saying 'Please don't be angry with me' or 'I don't want to appear nasty.'

Many of us have been so conditioned to be 'nice' that this smile is a vestige of that niceness, of the encouragement to be sweet, appealing and placating. A smile can indirectly express anxiety (about a confrontation) or our own resentment or hurt (unspoken). If you are trying to get across to someone that you feel angry or offended when you have a broad smile on your face, it is bound to confuse the other person and detract from the force of your statement. The two elements don't match up and, if this becomes a habit, you may well end up wondering why people don't ever take you seriously.

Voice If you have ever felt irritation at being in the company of someone who continuously speaks in a very loud voice or been frustrated by always having to lean forward and say 'pardon?' to someone who talks in a scarcely audible whisper, you will understand the difference the volume of your voice can make. Between the 'little girl' or 'sing-song' voice and the foghorn, there is a balance. Practise using the higher and lower registers of your voice. Breathing and relaxation help release the constriction of the throat and chest to enable a deeper breath to project your voice more fully.

The difference between an assertive and aggressive outcome to your conversation is marked by subtle changes in the pitch and tone of the voice. Notice whether your voice has a whine or whether it carries an apologetic, sarcastic or hostile tone. Speaking more slowly and audibly instead of mumbling or muttering some garbled statement will ensure clearer comprehension. The inflection of your voice is also important. An edge to your voice can make a refusal or comment sound like a put-down instead of a firm but non-aggressive statement, simply because of a sarcastic tone that will be picked up by the other person.

If you are making an assertive statement, don't let your voice rise up at the end, making your statement sound like a question. This tendency is much more common than it used to be and although it may seem a harmless habit, it does interfere with making a serious or authoritative statement when you need to. Phrasing a statement as a question makes it half-hearted and weakens the sense of conviction behind it.

Gestures Twiddling a piece of hair, scratching your scalp, clasping and unclasping your hands, biting your fingers or the side of your mouth or fiddling with jewellery are all examples of gestures which convey tension and nervousness. Tapping or shuffling feet send out messages of impatience and embarrassment. 'Chopping' movements of hands and arms can convey aggression as can the common gesture of the pointed index finger. This last gesture is unconsciously imitated from authority figures in our childhood and it is extraordinary how it remains outside of our awareness, even when it automatically seems to appear whenever we wish to reinforce our statement and show the other person who is boss! The problem is that, on the receiving end, that finger is bound to trigger a defensive response to what you are saying, whether you intend it or not.

Once you are aware of your gestures, you can learn to keep them under control. The practice of role-playing provides an opportunity to observe and comment. This is both illuminating and helpful. Sometimes only slight readjustments are necessary: refraining from twiddling; standing up straighter; breathing three times calmly before approaching a difficult confrontation; sitting or standing in a well-balanced position; altering the tone of your voice; holding your arms by the side instead of clasping them together anxiously behind your back; relaxing your shoulders instead of hunching them up around your ears. These minor alterations can make an enormous difference to how you feel when you are about to embark on any interaction when your anxiety tends to be at its highest: even during a conversation you can counter rising internal tension with a deep breath to help you regain some composure.

Appearance One final aspect of non-verbal communication is appearance. Drawing your attention to appearance is *not* an instruction to conform to any convention of dress for the purpose of attracting an onlooker. It is much more to do with how you feel about *yourself*: our appearance says a lot about our mood and how we feel about our bodies; the colours we choose to wear, the parts of our bodies we draw attention to or cover up and the style of clothes we wear.

Feeling assertive can have the effect of making you want to express yourself clearly through your appearance. Many participants in classes have begun to make little changes, to do something out of the ordinary, not out of a need to impress but out of a new-found wish to express their own individuality. Finding a personal style, discovering something which expresses *you* does not always require a lot of money or time and can boost your sense of self-esteem.

Every one of these separate aspects of body language contributes to the total impression. The way to start changing the overall effect is to focus on the detail. Most of us are unaware of a facial expression or habitual gesture which is immediately obvious to an observer in a role-play scenario so the best way to learn is by asking someone else to comment. Use their eyes to see where you can make some correction. Improve your body language and you will find that, with only minor adjustments, you will be able to produce a major change in the general effectiveness of your communication and self-presentation.

As I said earlier, there is no *one* kind of body language that is assertive. The key is something called congruence. Congruence describes the effect you achieve when your body language matches what you are saying because what you saying matches what you are feeling. Whether you're feeling nervous or proud, vulnerable or angry, joyful or awkward, if your words match your feelings at any given time, your body will reflect this match and this is when congruence occurs, making your communication extraordinarily effective.

Communication by email

Obviously, the relevance of non-verbal communication is diminished in circumstances which mean you are not face to face with the other person. When I started teaching these skills, we had the options of speaking face to face, speaking over the phone or writing a letter. Now we are presented with more choices and I have often been asked what difference it makes to the effectiveness of assertive communication if we are using emails or texts to convey our messages.

I would still, even today, encourage people to speak face to face if this is possible. The significance of body language lies in those tiny little non-verbal changes which accompany our speech. As described earlier in this chapter, we are usually unaware of them despite the fact that they make up a very large part of the overall impression we are conveying to the other person. Even when speaking over the phone, we are not entirely aware of the other person's facial expressions and therefore we are more sensitive to what we hear in the tone or nuances of the voice.

With emails or texts, we have absolutely nothing to go on at all. And even the words used are often abbreviated to such an extent that all we can pick up is a general message. My own experience of both receiving and sending emails about anything significant is that they are widely open to misinterpretation. It is really hard to know exactly what someone means because you have only the minimum to go on without the whole context in which communication usually takes place. Not hearing a tone of voice means you can imagine resentment, sarcasm or irritation when it is not intended or be left completely puzzled because you don't know what the person was implying between the lines.

Sometimes participants in workshops insist that email is the only available means to confront a busy colleague or issue a refusal to a relative or friend but I tend to challenge this. There is almost always some possibility of arranging five minutes with a colleague or thirty minutes with a friend to speak to them *if* it is important. And this I believe is the key. Electronic communication is fine for dealing with trivia or the day-to-day business of arranging schedules or meetings or where to rendezvous, informing others of missed trains or a change of plans, consulting about shopping decisions or establishing someone's whereabouts.

However if you want to communicate about something that's important, see if you can possibly arrange a face to face meeting where you'll have more chance of being clear in what you are saying as well as gaining a better understanding of how the other person reacts to what you have to say.

Assertive communication is far more likely when you choose not to use an email or text to avoid having to deal with the other person's response.

8

Saying 'No'

When a woman says 'no', she really means 'yes' . . . or so the saying goes. We may feel frustrated at its implications but it remains as prevalent and influential today as thirty years ago: one doesn't have to look too far among the headlines to find allusions to the apparently incontestable ambiguity of a woman's refusal, particularly in a sexual context. One of the unfortunate aspects of this issue is that, for many women, a difficulty in saying 'no' clearly and definitively *does* exist: when we do say 'no', we often do so indirectly or directly, but without much conviction. Learning how to make an assertive refusal – with clarity, persistence and without aggression – is the focus of this chapter.

Consider some of the situations in which it is difficult for you to make a refusal: to a request for money; to a social invitation; to a loan or a lift or to giving some information that you'd rather keep to yourself. Who do you find most difficult to refuse: a stranger, your partner, a child, an elderly person, your boss, your mother? When do you find it difficult? When you are tired, in a rush, in front of a group of people or while speaking on the phone?

Although the specific difficulty will vary from person to person, there are common beliefs which come up time and time again. These are some of them:

- Saying 'no' is callous, uncaring and mean. It's selfish.
- Saying 'no' over little things shows you're churlish, small-minded or petty.
- Saying 'no' directly is rude and aggressive. It's too abrupt and blunt.
- Saying 'no' will cause others to take offence. It will make them feel hurt and rejected.

- Saying 'no' will make you look inadequate. Others will question your competence to do the job.

If any or all of these fears have some meaning for you, you will probably find you have a problem with making direct, clear statements of refusal. Perhaps you find yourself falling into the following traps like Ivy, padding out a refusal with a string of excuses, including dishonest ones, such as 'It doesn't belong to me, otherwise I'd love to lend it to you . . . ' 'The dog's sick, otherwise I'd love to come . . . ' or 'My husband wouldn't be comfortable with it'. Or have you ever tried to avoid saying 'no' directly by making the other person feel guilty: 'I don't know how you could ask that of me when you can see what I've been going through . . . ' Have you ever tried to soften the blow with a winning smile or a patronising manner which you hope will convince everyone you are not just being nasty? Excuses, avoidance and pussyfooting around the issue have become entrenched habits.

We have acquired accompanying body habits as well. The most noticeable one is the inappropriate smile discussed in the previous chapter. The more we try to cover our anxiety about saying 'no' with an appearance of graciousness, the more often our smile and whole body stance come across as ingratiating. What's more, it is often confusing for the other person, who is hearing and watching you say 'no' but with a tone of voice, gestures and manner of someone saying 'yes'. It is small wonder that messages get muddled.

The anxiety we feel when saying 'no' leads to another habit. Instead of refusing a request and moving away, it has the effect of keeping our feet rooted to the spot. After a clean, decisive 'no', it is often more appropriate to leave. Instead we hover and dither, thus reducing the effectiveness of our refusal and also risking the possibility that the other person will take advantage of our hesitation to try and persuade us to change our minds.

So there are some new habits to be acquired. Someone approaches you and asks you a favour. What happens inside you? What is the very first thing you feel? This provides the key:

Notice your immediate reaction As soon as someone asks something of you, your body will let you know how you feel about the request, often before you have opened your mouth to reply. The feelings can be easy to identify when they are very clear. If you want to respond with wholehearted enthusiasm, you may feel like jumping at the opportunity: you will be absolutely sure you want to say 'yes'. At the other extreme, you can experience a sinking feeling which indicates extreme reluctance and you know you definitely want to say 'no'.

The difficulty occurs when the feelings are not so apparent: when you are confused and unsure, uneasy or doubtful about how you want to respond. Your body will still give you some signals to indicate what you are feeling if you listen for them but sometimes we need to listen carefully for that inner guide.

Many women fall into the unfortunate habit of ignoring this immediate guide. Instead of recognising it and following through, they dismiss it because of the pressure of what is expected, what is wanted and what they assume will avoid displeasure. We attend more to managing the outward impression than to the internal need. And it all happens so quickly. We know what happens: we agree or half agree, and then, hours or even days later, we are agonising about how to get out of a situation or kicking ourselves for saying 'yes' when we really wanted to say 'no'.

So the first step is to watch for the guide. Never ignore it. If this is a definite 'yes' or 'no' then you can say so. If you find yourself hesitating, even slightly, try the next step.

Say 'I don't know. I need more information.' This is an invaluable bit of advice. Do not be pushed. You do not have to make an instant decision. Acknowledge your uncertainty and confusion and give yourself time by asking for more information. This helps in two ways: it gives an opportunity for a necessary mental breathing space which allows you enough time to think for yourself. A simple phrase, such as 'I need to think about it' gives you the time to unhook yourself from the automatic pattern of answering *before* you think. You may need no more than a few seconds to identify what it is you want to say. Or you may need several days, depending on the circumstances. Take as long as you need but remember your first reaction is often an infallible guide as to how you honestly want to respond.

The second way this helps is by giving you answers to questions that may be genuinely relevant to your eventual decision: for example 'How long do you want me to babysit?', 'When could I expect the money back?', 'Are you really just inviting me to dinner?', 'If I were to take on this position, what would be my responsibilities?' You may provoke a surprised reaction in the other person. People often get defensive, especially if they are expecting you to say 'yes' automatically or if their intentions are less than honourable. It forces them to be straight and clear themselves when making the request, which not everyone welcomes. A lot of people prefer to shuffle about in the half light of inexplicit statements and assumptions in which they can hide away from responsibility. Have courage in persisting if it is important to you.

This brings us to the actual practice of saying 'no'.

Practise saying 'no' without excessive apology or excuses
Be clear for yourself about the difference between an explanation and an excuse. Ask yourself whether you are explaining because of your own anxiety or because you genuinely want the other person to understand your reasons. Are you genuinely sorry not to be able to help? Are you *really* disappointed not to be able to accept an invitation? It is not always helpful to embellish a refusal with all sorts of gratuitous protestations of regret.

Also practise saying the word 'no'. Many women find it surprisingly difficult to force this one small word through their reluctant lips! Saying 'no' nicely usually entails avoiding the word altogether. If you believe, mistakenly, that you will spare someone else's feelings by letting them down gently, then consider who you are really protecting. Much of the indirectness that muddies an assertive refusal is a way of avoiding a clear acknowledgement of responsibility. It can simply be a way of avoiding disapproval: the underlying messages are 'Please don't dislike me', or 'It's not my fault' or 'Don't be cross with me for saying "no" '.

If you have ever felt embarrassed and uncomfortable at the receiving end of one of those long-winded refusals, all plumped up with excuses and nonsense, you will appreciate the value of a plain, straightforward 'no'. At least you know where you stand.

When making a refusal, try accepting responsibility for doing so. You do not need to blame someone else or pass the buck. Changing 'I can't' to 'I don't want to'; changing 'They wouldn't like' to 'I don't like' are simple yet surprisingly effective changes of phrase.

Despite our tendency to associate the two, refusal does not *need* to be a rejection. A lot depends on the way you refuse. The following illustrations offer some examples:

> Jenny and Sheila have been friends for a couple of years. They were colleagues in the same office until Jenny left but they still keep in touch and have lunch together from time to time. On this particular occasion, Jenny tells Sheila that she is about to book a last-minute holiday in Goa. Sheila immediately jumps at the idea and proposes that since she also has a week's leave to take, they could both go to Goa. Jenny does not know how to respond. Her immediate feeling is uncertainty: they are friends but she is not sure whether they could successfully go on holiday together and the truth is she is actually looking forward to going away on her own.

How can she handle this? She can say 'yes' and then pull out later. She can put aside her fears and tell herself that it will probably be all right and then risk ruining her week away. Or she can make an assertive refusal as follows:

1.

Jenny: I don't think it would be a good idea.

Sheila: Why on earth not? We both like sitting in the sun and lazing around, don't we? And I could do with a break.

Jenny: Yes, that's true but I must say no because I do actually want to go away on my own.

Sheila: I don't understand. It seems a great idea to me.

Jenny: Look Sheila, I value our friendship very much. I enjoy meeting and talking to you but I just don't feel ready to go on holiday together and I had planned to go away on my own. That really is what I want to do.

Sheila: Well, I'm sorry I asked.

Jenny: Don't apologise. I'm sorry. Do you feel I've rejected you now?

Sheila: Well, I feel a bit upset but I guess it's best for you to make the right decision now. It would be awful to go away and then find you'd rather be on your own.

Jenny: Thank you for understanding. I do value our time together but I know this is the right decision.

2.

Maggie is dreading going home for Christmas. She knows her mother expects her to stay there for the holiday period as usual but she really doesn't want to go. She wants to spend the time on her own, seeing her friends at home. But as she isn't married with a family, her mother finds it impossible to understand what reason Maggie could have for not going home.

Maggie telephones rather than waiting for the inevitable invitation from her mother.

Maggie: Hello, Mum

Mother: Hello, dear. We were wondering when we'd hear from you. We're looking forward to seeing you up here soon. When will you be arriving?

Maggie: Well, Mum, that's what I was phoning about. This is really hard, Mum, but I've decided that I am going to spend Christmas on my own at home.

Mother: You can't spend Christmas on your *own*.

Maggie: Yes, I can, Mum. That's what I want to do.

Mother: But your Dad and I have been so looking forward to it. It won't be the same . . .

Maggie: I know that, but I want to spend Christmas in my own home.

Mother: It will be very miserable for us without you. I mean, I know there's nothing much for you to do but I thought you always liked coming home and being looked after.

Maggie: I do like seeing you but I really don't want to come up for Christmas.

Mother: Well, your Dad's going to be very disappointed, you know.

Maggie: I know he will and I know you are too, Mum. Try and understand that it's not you I am rejecting. I love you both very much and want to come and spend time with you but I do want to spend this Christmas on my own here.

Mother: Well, I don't understand but still, you're a grown woman now. I suppose you've got to lead your own life.

Maggie: Thanks, Mum. Having said that, I would like to come and see you over the New Year weekend. Would that be all right?

3.

Sally met Ian at a party. At the time, she enjoyed talking with him so she agreed to his proposal to meet for a drink during the week. When they meet and spend the evening together, Sally realises that they have very little in common and that she isn't interested in spending more time with him. During the course of the evening her discomfort steadily grows as she becomes aware that he is feeling very much more attracted to her than she is to him and that he obviously wants to extend their relationship. She knows she doesn't want this. She could agree to see him again, knowing that she would cancel the arrangement later or she could state her decision clearly there and then. How can she do that without rejecting him and hurting his feelings? As they are about to leave, Ian asks if she wants to go and see a new film together the following week:

Sally: Ian, I really don't think it would be a good idea for us to meet again.

Ian: Why not? I didn't think there was anyone else.

Sally: I don't have anyone else, that's true, but I would rather be clear now than risk being dishonest and more hurtful later. I have enjoyed our evening together but I don't want to make another date.

Ian: You certainly know how to hit below the belt, don't you?

Sally: I'm not hitting below the belt but I know that it must sound very abrupt and hurtful to you. It's just that I've learned the hard way that if I don't make a clear decision at the start, then everything gets very messy.

Ian: But your feelings might change.

Sally: Well, they might but right now that's how I feel.

Ian: Well, there's not much more to say, is there?

Sally: No, I suppose there isn't. Thank you for an enjoyable evening.

4.

For the second year running Monica has been invited to give a series of lectures in Manchester. Last year, she wrote to her longstanding friend, Penny, saying that she was coming and Penny was delighted to offer her a room in her house. Although Monica was happy to spend time with Penny, she found the household of four children a little too boisterous. It had been difficult to prepare her work because of the constant interruptions and the general mayhem of a large family atmosphere conflicted with her need for tranquillity and solitude. She has just received an email from Penny inviting her to stay again this year. Monica is unsure how to tell Penny that she wants to stay in a hotel. She could just say nothing and hope she doesn't bump into her. She can 'take care' of her friend's feelings and stay in her house, denying her need for privacy. Or she can explain assertively. She calls Penny:

Monica: Penny, it's very kind of you to offer me hospitality again but I have decided to take a room in a hotel this time.

Penny: But why go to all that expense when you can stay here for free?

Monica: I know it would be cheaper to stay with you but I need some peace and quiet to prepare my work and I think an anonymous hotel room would be better.

Penny: But the twins are very happy to move out of their room for you. They've been excited about your visit for weeks.

Monica: That's very kind of you but I know I'd be better in a hotel.

Penny: I feel terrible. You should have said last time if they were bothering you.

Monica: They weren't bothering me, Penny. You were very kind and hospitable. It's just that I need to get away from everything at the end of the day and it's easier to stay in a hotel.

Penny: Well, we'll be sorry not to see you.

Monica: I'll be sorry too but I know it's the best decision for me. There is one thing though. I'd really like to see you all while I'm there. Could I come round for a meal one evening? Would that be OK?

Sometimes it is appropriate to offer a compromise. Maggie and Monica offered a compromise which felt right because it did not negate what they had decided. On the other hand, Sally needed to leave right away because there was no point in drawing it out any further. It is important to follow through on your refusal. Back-tracking weakens your position and confuses everyone concerned. If you stand firm, people know exactly where they stand with you: this encourages respect even when you are turning someone down.

This means challenging a deeply held assumption that a refusal is always a rejection of the other person: this is not necessarily so. When you say 'no' you are refusing the request, not rejecting the person, although this doesn't mean that a refusal will never be *experienced* as rejection or that you have not felt rejected when someone said 'no' to you. There are bound to be occasions when the other person may well feel rejected by your refusal, even if assertively handled. This reaction can be used to manipulate you into changing your mind but, when there is such a response, it puts you in the front line of the tension between conflicting priorities. Only you can decide what is important enough for you to risk saying 'no' for – prioritising time on your own, privacy, spending your social time with people you want to be with – and only you know how important the decision is on each occasion.

The aggressive 'no' I remember that one of the repercussions of women being reminded about their right to say 'no' when I first started teaching assertiveness training was a pendulum swing in the opposite direction. Class members would arrive for the following session and proudly relate how they had said 'no' to their children, 'no' to their husbands and 'no' to their colleagues: clearly on a roll and making up for lost time. However, there was a problem in that the tendency was to say 'no' (which was good) only by excluding consideration of the other person (which was aggressive). When you say 'no' while blocking out the person's request, there is no equality in the interaction: by over-ruling anyone else's right to ask – or their right to respond – we are, in fact, behaving aggressively.

This kind of 'aggressive' refusal is most frequently used by those who say 'I don't know what the problem is – just say NO! They soon get the message!' It has become the norm in so many contexts that we assume wrongly that this is assertive. If you don't want to shut out the other person and pretend they don't exist, then an assertive refusal entails a different dynamic: it entails negotiating in an equal manner. It means listening to the request first. Once you feel assured that you have made the right decision for yourself, you can acknowledge that someone is angry or disappointed or upset without immediately trying to appease your own guilt. Nor do you have to make excuses but accept that this is your decision and stand by it.

A refusal does not have to be heavy, aggressive or hurtful. By clearly taking responsibility for your decision, you can also give the other person equal space to express their feelings. This allows the other person to feel acknowledged even though you are saying 'no'. They do not feel their needs have simply been over-ridden or ignored.

Equality applies both ways. It is also important to consider your part in failing to set limits when deep down you want to: this is the down-side of doing something for someone only because you feel sorry for them or because you tell yourself they couldn't survive being told 'no'. Submerging your own needs when you want to refuse is not necessarily charitable: it can be invalidating and demeaning for the other person. Think twice before acting out of pity.

When you do not remain true to your own needs and wishes and you put aside a heartfelt 'no' for a half-hearted 'yes', don't kid yourself that it does not matter. The heartfelt 'no' will seek expression through some outlet. A refusal, if not open and direct, will always emerge in an indirect manner.

The indirect 'no' Have you ever sulked or bellyached your way through an evening because you did not want to be there? Have you ever left a job to the last minute, done a task badly or 'forgotten' about a chore because you did not want to do it in the first place? Have you turned up late to a meeting that you did not want to attend or lost an address when you didn't want to arrive there? Sometimes we use our bodies to say 'no': headaches and backaches appear with miraculous timing when they can provide an unimpeachable excuse for not attending a function to which we could have said 'no' in the first place.

If you've ever been on the receiving end of an indirect 'no', you'll also understand how infuriating it is when someone cancels at the last minute with an excuse you know is fake or when someone has agreed to help you and then lets you down by not turning up. Most of us have responded with surprise, disappointment and frustration with people who did not say a clear honest 'no' *at the time*. There is a security in knowing that you can trust someone to say what they mean: that they will say 'yes' when they mean 'yes' and 'no' when they mean 'no'. Instead of feeling guilty for accepting someone's help, you can allow yourself the pleasure of knowing they are free to choose.

Finally, it may be helpful to remind yourself that you have the right to change your mind. It can act as a half-way house while you are still learning to say 'no' effectively. We have become so unaccustomed to thinking for ourselves and to knowing what we want that an assertive and immediate refusal takes a lot of practice. A commendable compromise, and one that many women have found helpful, is the following: you do not have to suffer for an unassertive decision. If you realise you really wanted to say 'no', instead of avoiding someone, ignoring a phone call or trying to concoct all sorts of acceptable excuses, try taking the initiative and communicate your change of heart in a firm and assertive manner.

This right includes the responsibility to communicate your change of heart and not leave it to the last minute: you could risk facing a reaction of disappointment or frustration but taking time to acknowledge the other person's feelings is often a better alternative to feeling trapped and resentful in the aftermath of your own indecisiveness. The advantage of saying 'no' assertively is that you have more time to spend on things you want to say 'yes' to instead of wasting time trying to extricate yourself from various unwanted commitments.

There is, of course, one remaining issue we haven't yet dealt with: how do we cope with feeling guilty when we say 'no'? This is what we address in the next chapter.

9

Self Disclosure

This is a new chapter. Although self-disclosure was included in the original, it is given more prominence this time because, although it sounds simple, I know from teaching this skill over many years, first, how supremely effective it is, second, how amazed people are when they get the hang of it and third, how very difficult it is to learn. This essential skill could be called the jewel in the assertive crown. It is not to be confused with a heart-to-heart dialogue or a chance to confess everything once and for all. It is not complex or sophisticated: it is a simple expression in words of the truth of what you are feeling.

Difficulties in putting our feelings into words arise from the following anxieties going round in our minds:

If I say what I feel, I'll give them more power over me; I'll be more vulnerable – I'll be labelled hysterical Although it is true that there are certainly occasions when it is wiser to keep quiet and probably more appropriate to do so, most of the time this anxiety is based on the cultural dismissal of 'emotional' as 'weak' and in the workplace, for example, tradition requires that feelings are excluded from all interactions. Even in a professional context though, it is important to distinguish between, on one hand, naming specific feelings to make our communication more truthful and more effective (self-disclosure) and, on the other, being 'over-emotional' and incoherent (messy collapse). It is entirely possible to acknowledge anxiety or annoyance and remain competent at the same time: it all depends on the way you do it.

I might get it wrong Fear of looking foolish discourages us from listening to our emotional wisdom and makes us reluctant to address feelings that might show us in a bad light. It also means that we tend to hold back until we imagine we are absolutely in the right which quickly translates into being in a superior position: a guarantee that the other person will respond defensively.

I can't find the words Understandable, but practice really does help.

If I don't say anything, the problem will just go away Highly unlikely! In reality, when we avoid paying attention to what we are feeling for any length of time, it is probable that when we *do* decide to say how we feel, it is often when things have gone past a comfortably manageable level. We tend to defend ourselves against vulnerability by relying on self-righteousness and blame. So the understandable mistake we make when beginning to use this skill is to *appear* to be expressing our feeling while, basically, issuing statements which hold the other person responsible:

'I feel that you have no right to say that'
'I feel you shouldn't do that'
'You make me feel miserable'
'I feel that you're wrong'
'You intimidate me'
'I feel that you're insensitive'
'You make me feel really small'

This can be contrasted with authentic self-disclosure:

'I feel very uncomfortable when you make that kind of comment'
'That makes me feel very angry'
'I feel pressurised'
'This isn't easy for me to say . . . '
'I feel intimidated'
'I feel very warm towards you'
'I feel a bit anxious about bringing this up . . . '

Self-disclosure lies in assuming *responsibility* for our own feelings which entails recognising that whatever you are feeling cannot be blamed on someone else. This is why it is so difficult to do. It involves a profound shift in awareness as it goes deeply against the conditioned grain to accept that what you are feeling is what *you* are feeling and that nobody has *made* you feel like that.

Individual responses to perception of another's behaviour vary so much that we cannot simply attribute a feeling to a cause even though we find comfort in doing so. If someone treads on your foot, you might have a case for arguing they had caused you pain, but even then, your response would vary from others' responses to the identical action. If you are predisposed to see someone's action as 'deliberate' or 'accidental', 'clumsy' or 'malicious' you will perceive it in exactly that way and respond accordingly.

The skill of self-disclosure lies in being clear and honest and upright.

Being clear Naming your feelings as specifically as possible improves with practice. At first, you will find that words like 'upset' come more easily than angry, that 'confused' hangs around for a while until the fog begins to clear and that you will almost certainly understate the intensity of what you are feeling. Blanket terms of 'rejected' or 'stressed' or 'guilty' tend to block your ability to be more specific and express yourself more effectively.

Being honest There is no point in saying you are 'a bit upset' when you are furious or hurt when you are angry. Nor is this skill about saying what you think the other person wants to hear or what you imagine will prevent someone expressing their anger towards you. It is simply about conveying your emotional truth as far as you can see it at the time. That is enough.

Being upright Ultimately fault and cause and blame become irrelevant. The aim of self-disclosure is to verbalise what you are feeling in response to your perception. Communicating your feelings without blame allows the other person to hear more clearly and the possibility of an *exchange* becomes far more likely.

Putting your feelings into words need not involve blame or apology. Self-disclosure is a way of taking responsibility for what you feel, simply stating the truth, without the need to be right or wrong. We often do get it wrong but the only chance we have of sorting emotional issues in relation to another person is by communicating without blame and in the spirit of *informing* the other person. We can never make pronouncements with anything approaching absolute certainty. Emotional articulation is relative and remember that, as a medium, emotion is always in motion and is in response to a perception which may be inaccurate or may conflict with someone else's perception. When you state your feelings, you have a chance to compare perceptions and then evaluate your own feelings in light of this exchange.

Eventually feelings can be included as just one part of your ordinary communication, even at work, as unselfconsciously and as naturally as you communicate your ideas, your opinions or thoughts. Self- disclosure is useful at the actual time of awareness of the feeling or in the longer term, when talking about past events or when wanting, for example, to clarify misunder- standings in any relationship.

In the previous chapter, we looked at the difficulties of saying 'no' assertively. Self-disclosure is helpful in avoiding an aggressive refusal while at the same time helping you deal with your own feelings of anxiety or guilt. Often women tell me they are able now to say 'no' but ask 'How can I say no without then having to feel guilty afterwards?' The answer is that no magic bullet exists to exterminate guilt or indeed any other feelings which we would rather not have. All feelings arise because we are human, whether we like them or not, but what helps is to put these feelings into words.

First of all, how do you feel about making your refusal? Remember the significance of acknowledging hesitation when someone makes a request of you. If you know that you want to refuse but are worried about doing so, you'll probably review your decision and possibly agonise about how, when or where to communicate your refusal. This is why the skill of self-disclosure is so appropriate at the beginning. For example, all four dialogues illustrated in the previous chapter could have begun with a statement such as:

'Sheila, I feel really anxious about saying this . . . (*refusing to go on holiday*)
'I'm not sure about the right moment to tell you, Mum . . . '
(*refusing to go home for Christmas*)

'Penny, I'm feeling a bit awkward but . . . ' (*refusing to stay at a friend's house*)
'This isn't an easy thing to talk about, Ian . . . ' (*refusing to meet for another date*)

If you're feeling guilty, then *this* is what you put into words:

'I feel guilty at having to say "no", but I must refuse'
'I don't like having to say "no" but on this occasion, I must'
'It's really hard for me to say "no" to you, but I have to this time'

And if you are genuinely regretful, you could say that too:

'I feel really bad about this but I have to say no'

Self-disclosure impacts on your body language. By acknowledging what you feel – in other words being truthful – your body and your words are acting in unison: they are matching instead of conflicted. So you relax a bit more, the tension subsides and you become a little stronger in your resolve to say whatever it is you want to say. As soon as you are relaxed, you will automatically deepen your breathing: this affects your voice which, with your gestures, can now convey a *totally* coherent assertive message. The importance of this particular skill cannot be over-emphasised.

Karen wanted to practise asking her friend, Myra, not to let her dog jump up on her new leather sofa when she came round. Myra had asked if it was OK but Karen hadn't said anything because she never knew how to handle it. When she role-played the first time, she managed to say 'no' to Myra but it sounded stilted and uncomfortable. The second time, she started off by saying, 'You know I feel really awkward saying this but I would prefer you not to let Smoky jump on the sofa. I'd prefer him to stay on the floor.' As soon as she disclosed what she was feeling she was more comfortable in making her request and the tension and stiffness disappeared.

The spinoff from being more relaxed and less defensive yourself is that you become more able to see the other person as an *equal*: that they have also have a right to ask or to expect or to assume something of you. This kind of dynamic makes it easier to put across your message without hostility.

Ruth's sons, Robbie and Tom, were 11 and 9. They were constantly nagging her to buy new trainers, a new Ipad, a new game, a new this, a new that and she resented having to say 'no' all the time. She couldn't blame them for asking but she had very little money to spare. She did three jobs as it was and she found it really difficult to cope with their demands and felt guilty about not being able to afford to buy them more.

She knew she was being aggressive in her refusals. She was feeling so frustrated that she resented them even asking her because she didn't want to have say 'no' to them: so it all came out in yelling at them. She decided they were old enough to have a discussion about it and so she got them both one afternoon to turn everything off and sit at the kitchen table.

Ruth: Look, boys, I want to say something to you. (*Their eyes open and they stare at her, knowing from her tone of voice that something is coming*) When you keep asking me for new things, I have to say 'no' all the time. And I hate having to say 'no' (*self-disclosure*), I really do. It's just that I don't have enough money and I hate that too.

Robbie: It's OK, Mum. We know that.

Ruth: I feel bad about not being able to get you what your friends have.

Robbie: We know.

Tom: It's OK . . . well, sometimes it would be nice . . .

Robbie: So you don't want us to ask for anything?

Ruth: No, I'm not saying that. Of course you can ask but you need to know that I'm likely to say 'no'.

Robbie: That's OK.

Tom: Is that it?

Ruth: (*smiles*) Yes, you can go now. How about we have a pizza tonight? (*The boys get up from, the table.*)

Robbie: (*grins at his mother*): You're sure we can afford it, Mum?

This helped Ruth to keep saying 'no' when she needed to but without the aggression that came from her own guilt and frustration. She didn't need any more to blame herself so much: by understanding her own feelings and expressing them, she was able to be more relaxed.

None of this is easy. I know myself that even after saying a clear and assertive 'no' to someone, I've often agonised about whether or not I made the right decision over an important issue, maybe not immediately, but some hours later. At this point, it helps to speak to someone who knows you and cares for you, with whom you can share your fears and who can help reassure you that you have done the right thing. You can also remind yourself that the level of guilt you feel after making a significant refusal is an indicator of how hard it was for you to do, so give yourself a pat on the back.

Following on

You can combine the learning of these past two chapters. Take situations from your own list or use the following suggestions to practise saying 'no', but using the skill of self-disclosure whenever you start:

a. Several colleagues are going to have a drink after work: you don't want to go but there is a pressure to join in. Practise making a refusal without inventing an excuse.
b. Your child asks for some more money to buy some sweets.
c. You are exhausted and have looked forward to a weekend of rest and solitude. On Thursday evening the telephone rings: an elderly relative wants to come and stay.
d. A friend asks to borrow some jewellery for a party. You do not like lending out your jewellery because it always seems to get damaged and so you want to refuse.

Checkpoints Invite comments on your body language. Can you look the person in the eye as you say no? Do you smile inappropriately as you say 'no'? Is your voice assertive or aggressive? Do you speak firmly or does your refusal contain a question? Can you say 'no' without being too apologetic?

10

The Compassion Trap

Guilt is sometimes part of a more general syndrome. When I first started teaching assertiveness training, it soon became clear that women in very different contexts and of varying nationalities identified readily with the concept of the compassion trap. This is usually defined as a sense of obligation that, as a woman, you should put everyone else's needs before your own *all* of the time: you should always be available and accessible to others. Consequently it is easy to feel guilty about failure, faults and weakness; guilty about letting others down; behaving uncaringly; being a disappointment; being selfish and above all, guilty when you *don't care.*

The compassion trap is deeply rooted in a psycho-social legacy inherited from our mothers, grandmothers and no doubt many generations before that. This inherited image is of the archetypal woman as a central, nurturing powerful force in the family. She is the focal point of the family. She is at home, bearing children: her task is to make sure that there is food on the table, that her husband's needs are anticipated and met. It is her function to be a homemaker with whatever slender resources are available and to keep the family together at all costs. She is the emotional centre, the heart of the family, while the men busy themselves with work and industry and moneymaking in other spheres. It is to her that the children turn first, with problems, physical and emotional bruises, tears to be kissed away by her. It is to her that the man turns for consolation and relief. She sees herself as a tower of strength, a refuge for those she loves.

According to the archetype, a true woman's life reflects the success and failure of her husband and her children. Her life energy is expressed in this love and devotion which nourishes her family. In turn, her own sense of pride and satisfaction depends on the knowledge of giving this to them all, of feeding and watching them grow, taking their strength from her. This is believed to be her fulfilment.

It's not hard to see that such expectations might appear quaint and out of step with the younger generation of women who have rebelled against them quite vehemently with the result that current norms seem to have swung in the opposite direction. We are a generation along from the time this book was first written and many women have grown up to expect to have it all: a career and a family, a partner and independence. It is considered a little old-fashioned nowadays to stay at home to look after one's children and those women who continue to make this choice sometimes feel that they have to justify their decision.

Despite a change in attitudes among individual women, institutional attitudes appear to be still attached to the archetype: this means that 'having it all' comes at a cost.

Some women clearly prefer the stimulus of work to the 'drudgery' of child care and domesticity but if they still decide to have children, a lot of money is paid for child care to enable them to continue with their careers as soon as possible after the child is born. Whether women decide to keep working out of personal ambition or financial necessity, or whether they take a break and then start back in their careers as soon as their children are of school age, all will tend to find themselves handicapped by a woeful provision of childcare facilities or family-unfriendly practices in the workplace.

It also appears that several young women have children when they really don't want to: they don't feel any great maternal instinct or desire to be mothers and yet they do so because it is still considered socially unacceptable to assert your right to be regarded as a 'whole' woman if you are not a mother.

Although it would be wrong to assume the family has represented complete fulfilment for *every* woman in the past, it is probably safe to say that it is more acceptable to articulate this openly in modern times. Women want more because they want what men have: they want to be able to succeed in the same way and on the same terms but are rarely prepared to lose out on anything. I see two sides to this kind of ambition: one is affirmative of feminism in the sense that no woman should be stifled or held back simply because she is, by gender, a woman. The second side, though, is less affirmative because achievement of this ambition appears to depend on down-playing or even denying some of the gentler aspects of femininity. Compassion, tenderness, accommodation, sensitivity, inclusiveness and softness are examples of qualities that are downgraded, even repudiated, as if they are only associated with passivity and a failure to be equal, reminders of an old and downtrodden past that is best consigned to history programmes on television.

So in these 'we can have it all' times, is the compassion trap still relevant? I think it may be.

As you read through the list below, see if you can recognise yourself or other women (of any age) in these examples.

Situations with strangers The patient who does not want to persist in bothering the over-worked nurses with a request for medication to relieve her own considerable pain; the customer who realises that others have been waiting a long time so she does not take the time to get what she really wants; the woman who doesn't complain about a new haircut because she doesn't want to make trouble for the trainee stylist.

Situations with friends The woman who consistently makes excuses for a friend's behaviour rather than mentioning it directly; who has sex with her boyfriend because he is turned on and she feels sorry for him; who is afraid to refuse a friend who wants to come and stay at a thoroughly inconvenient time, because she knows her friend has been recently divorced and needs someone to talk to; who feels guilty if she does not offer a lift to a friend because she is the only one with a car; who lies when asked directly by a friend for her opinion about the new shoes she's just bought because she doesn't want to hurt her feelings.

Situations at home The woman who has sacrificed her whole career to look after her invalid parents; the wife who feels too guilty about leaving her disabled son to have an occasional day off because she feels she is the only one who must look after him; the daughter who does not like to tell her elderly father that he really should not drive any more as his sight is failing because she knows he will take it very badly; the working woman who feels guilty about not spending more time with her children so does not ask for the help that she needs at home; the woman who does not ask her tenant to pay rent arrears because he's going through a tough time and she doesn't want to make things worse.

Situations at work The woman who will not move to a more rewarding and stimulating job because she is convinced that this would leave her team 'in the lurch'; the doctor who keeps covering for colleagues who have 'other commitments'; the young woman who tolerates her middle-aged manager treating her as if she were his daughter because she doesn't want to disappoint him; the older woman who will stay late at the office, correcting the work of junior colleagues because they are young with busy social lives to lead; the assistant who will not tell her boss he has made a mistake because it might deflate his ego.

How might our four characters respond to being caught in the compassion trap?

The Compassion Trap and a Passive, Aggressive, Indirect and Assertive Response

Dulcie's nineteen-year-old student nephew asks her to lend him some money to go abroad. It means giving him some  of her hard-earned savings intended for her own holiday but she feels sorry for him and a little sensitive about being considered selfish: after all, she only has herself to think of as she doesn't have children of her own and so she gives it to him. She swallows her disappointment but feels a lot of resentment when he doesn't even bother to thank her. Even his parents don't show any real appreciation of her gesture!

Agnes will often let her resentment build up to a tremendous outburst instead of appropriately saying 'no' beforehand. She eagerly takes up the cause of a less fortunate friend who needs her help to make an entrée into the world of her own business. She rushes around giving her advice, generously giving time and energy and suggestions, always being available when her friend phones. Somehow the friend never really expresses enough appreciation and Agnes begins to feel more and more used. Finally she erupts in fury, tells her friend in no uncertain terms what she thinks of her and then drops her like a hot brick.

Ivy's way of dealing with the compassion trap is similar to Agnes's but her strategies tend to be more hidden and indirect. When her next-door neighbour's husband walks out, Ivy feels very sympathetic and listens to endless post mortems and all the ins and outs of their previous married life together. But after a few weeks she becomes frustrated that the neighbour won't do anything except moan. Ivy, unable to express her feelings directly, simply pretends not to be at home or, as soon as her friend appears, finds an excuse for going out.

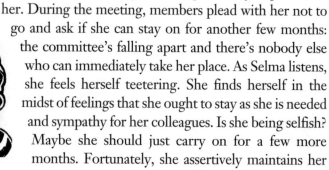

Selma sits through her last committee meeting having decided after a lot of consideration to resign from her position as chairperson. She feels that an awful lot of her time has been given to chairing meetings and she wants to conserve some of her energy and spend some time on things that are personally important to her. During the meeting, members plead with her not to go and ask if she can stay on for another few months: the committee's falling apart and there's nobody else who can immediately take her place. As Selma listens, she feels herself teetering. She finds herself in the midst of feelings that she ought to stay as she is needed and sympathy for her colleagues. Is she being selfish? Maybe she should just carry on for a few more months. Fortunately, she assertively maintains her

decision. The others realise she is adamant and, with regret, have to accept. She leaves and is satisfied that she has done the right thing for herself.

When you feel 'sorry' for someone, the interaction is always in danger of becoming unequal: there is a fine line between compassion – the real human quality – and the compassion *trap*. Being sensitive to others' needs and feelings is an attribute traditionally associated with the female gender. Because this open-ness can become a trap, the only protection seems to be to shut off completely: to determinedly close your eyes and ears to someone else's plight. When we do this, we risk becoming self-centred and ruthless as if the only way we can attain our own goals is by excluding any other consideration.

In competitive activities like sports or business this is requisite behaviour: you must stay focussed on your goal and nothing else can matter. As I have written earlier, this aggressive response has spilled over into personal relationships as well. The key to retaining our compassion, without getting trapped in it, is what assertive behaviour can achieve. It is a balancing act and a difficult one but it can be done. It means examining a little more closely how we get into this trap. How do we fail to set limits when we need to and when is it the right time to do so?

Setting limits Setting limits means calling a halt *before* you drop dead with exhaustion. Instead of waiting to the bitter end, you can look at ways in which you can ask for help, for support and for care from others. You can set limits on how you spend your time. You can give yourself time to rest, to replenish your energy. You can allow yourself to be vulnerable like everyone else. Your needs are not necessarily more important than anyone else's needs – nor are they less important – just *equally* important. Letting go of the image of being a tower of strength gives everyone a chance to breathe a sigh of relief: you are seen to be human as well.

If you have ever caught yourself sulking or resentful because someone wasn't sufficiently grateful to you for efforts you have made for them, then you can count yourself as playing the role of martyr. Consider whether anyone can ever be appreciative *enough*. It is likely that when we play the martyr we expect some reward for all our devotion. Have you ever caught yourself secretly wounded or annoyed because someone did not notice the trouble you had taken or the sacrifice you made? Even in these more egotistical times, many women still fall into this trap.

Setting limits also means looking to see whether you are taking your responsibilities too far. There is a fundamental difference between taking care of someone's practical needs and someone's emotional needs. Of course there are times in everyone's life when they are practically dependent on another person's care but if those limits are not recognised, then dependency slips into dangerous areas. Authentic care degenerates into compulsive care which usually entails subtle oppression. Oppression begins when you start assuming total responsibility for someone's emotional needs as well; when you deny them equal rights of interaction or consultation; when you take other people's decisions for them and organise their lives on their behalf because you assume they could not manage on their own.

There are two complementary roles. If someone is to play the role of the *inadequate*, then the other person can play that of the *powerful*. Many women are reluctant to relinquish this power, especially if they do not feel powerful in any other area of their lives.

As women take more and more power for themselves assertively, they are more and more willing to relinquish this strong manipulative power and claim real equality.

I would like to finish this chapter by reminding readers that compassion is undeniably a wonderful human quality when it is freely chosen.

Take two examples: one of Mandy's incessant grumbles was that she felt obliged to have tea with her elderly Uncle Stan every Thursday. It cut into her day, she complained, it prevented her from making other arrangements and she felt it was an inescapable burden. Once she had explored other options instead of moaning about it – refusing his invitation, reducing the visits to once a month instead of once a week or asking a cousin to take over some of the visits – she finally decided that she was really very fond of her uncle and that he wasn't going to live forever so she really wanted to continue her visits. This was her *choice*. The arrangement continued to give him pleasure at seeing her and to give her the pleasure of being able to brighten up his day.

Molly's life revolved around her work. She had convinced herself that listening to other people's problems was a waste of time. She feared getting too entangled and that everything would end up eating into her precious time. She knew that one of her colleagues, Judith, had been going through a bad time since her husband had walked out on her but Molly kept right out of it, even when she saw Judith's work deteriorating. One evening, she met Judith in the corridor on the way home and it was obvious she had been crying. Molly greeted her but walked straight on, as usual, but then hesitated and turned round: 'Judith, look, you can say no if you want, but I'm going to stop for a drink at Mario's on the way home. Do you fancy joining me for a quick glass of wine?' Judith was slightly surprised but accepted and the two of them spent a good couple of hours talking together. Molly was pleasantly surprised to find that not only was it not a big deal but it meant there was much better energy between them in the office.

If a woman feels compelled to put another's needs before her own, compassion becomes sterile: if she makes a conscious choice, the rewards are rich.

11

Expressing Your Feelings

We started to look at the relevance of expressing of feelings as an important aspect of our communication with the skill of self-disclosure. This chapter follows on from there. Handling feelings has always been integral to the model of assertiveness training that I've used, partly because this dimension has enormous potential to either distort and undermine our communication – even when we get the words right – or enrich and make it far more meaningful and effective.

Self-disclosure requires you to put feelings into words, but first you need to learn to notice and acknowledge to yourself what is going on. This of course presupposes that you have some awareness of what you're feeling which is often not the case. Most men and women are unfamiliar with the whole emotional realm and, as a consequence, feel very much at the mercy of their feelings. We approach our own and other people's feelings with the same mixture of awe and apprehension with which, if we were cast out on to the ocean in a small sea-going vessel, we might view the rise and fall of the threatening waves around us. We have learned that there are currents to avoid and are watchful for imminent storm clouds on the horizon. Alert to some unexpected turbulence and drama, we are tense and vigilant. We know that ultimately we have no control. The best we can do is to guide our frail and inadequate craft over the water, often getting splashed and occasionally capsizing, and always immensely thankful for a period of calm.

If you have ever felt at the mercy of your feelings or struggled to control them for fear they might overwhelm you, you will recognise the importance of being able to handle them effectively. Competence in managing feelings first requires some understanding of what feelings are all about. This chapter is especially relevant to assertive communication because you need to know how to *identify* your feelings first in order to know how to acknowledge them in words.

What causes feelings? We generally accept that some kind of emotion is to be expected when a significant event occurs in our lives, such as the death of a loved one, falling in love, redundancy, the shock of a bad car accident or the birth of a baby. But we tend to ignore the feelings triggered by minor events in our lives: ordinary, everyday interaction with other human beings gives us plenty of scope to experience all sorts of feelings.

Feelings are related to human needs. Let's start with the need to give and receive love. If this need is fulfilled, we respond with feelings of closeness, harmony, intimacy, belonging, together-ness, warmth and affection. If the need is not met or comes to an end for some reason we feel sadness, pain, longing, emptiness, rejection and loneliness: we feel the grief of loss and separation. A second need is to make choices, to be self-directing in our lives: feelings connected with this need when it's fulfilled are power, strength, enthusiasm, determination, energy, fulfilment, satisfaction and elation. If this need is blocked, we react with frustration, impatience, helplessness, irritation, fury, outrage and anger. A third need we have as humans is to understand and make sense of our environment: it moves us to enquire and seek information and to communicate. Satisfying this need makes us feel safe, secure and gives us a feeling of belonging. When we feel understood and recognised, we feel valued, acknowledged, a sense of belonging, confident and accepted for who we are: we feel trust. If we do not understand or cannot make ourselves understood we feel unsafe, anxious, confused, panicky, isolated, fearful, mistrustful and afraid.

The depth and quality of our feelings can vary widely. The ending of a wonderful holiday makes us feel sad but the ending of a close relationship makes us grieve intensely. An affectionate letter from a friend makes us feel warm; a spontaneous hug from a child touches a deeper level of love. If we are in a hurry and the tin-opener won't work or the traffic lights are red, we feel impatient and frustrated. But if we are cheated out of money due to us or fall victim to bureaucratic stupidity or racial discrimination, our anger will strike a deeper chord. The satisfaction which follows the mastery of a new skill or the pride in accomplishing a difficult task illustrates how we can feel when we are in command. The security that comes from knowing exactly what you are doing, the delight in talking with someone who is on the same wavelength or the relief of an important insight are all ways of experiencing the satisfaction of the need to understand. When we are vulnerable and unsafe, we feel fear: this can range from anxiety about getting lost in unknown territory to alarm if your child is late home or dread if you discover a mysterious lump in your breast.

One single event can affect a range of needs at the same time. Take, for example, a young child whose mother dies. She will feel grief through separation and the loss of her mother; she will feel frightened because she cannot make sense of the meaning of death and does not know what will happen to her; she will probably feel angry with her mother for 'leaving' her in this way and so feel helpless in these new circumstances.

Exploring our feelings can be a useful start to unravelling the complexity of what and why we feel the way we do.

Feelings are physical Expressions such as 'I don't know what came over me', or 'I wasn't myself', or 'I was beside myself with rage' suggest that feelings are vague, ethereal presences which exist *outside* our bodies: that they descend and take over, that they catch us unawares. In fact, what we experience as a feeling is a combination of sensations produced by physiological changes *inside* our bodies. Something occurs to stimulate the brain to signal the release of chemical substances through particular organs. These chemicals produce a change in our bodily systems, preparing the body for appropriate action.

This is a very simplified and incomplete description of a highly complex chain of events. The important piece of information at

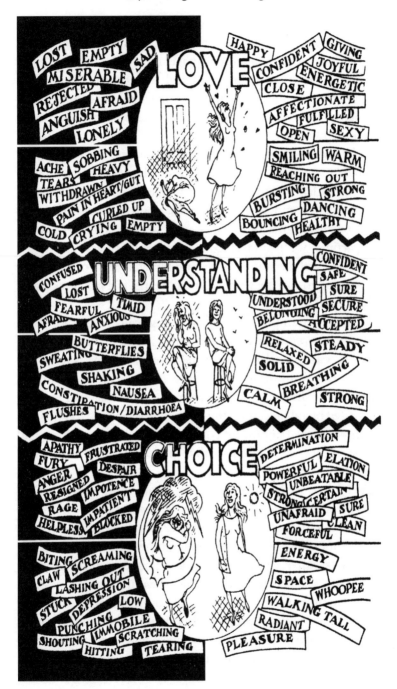

this point is that a feeling is not something which can be dismissed as imagination: it is a real, physical, internal response. If you look at the diagram on page 107, you'll see that every feeling is represented by a physical sensation in our bodies. Although individual variations are inevitable, we can usually recognise the types of sensation which accompany a particular category of emotion.

The bodily sensations associated with loving and being loved include the rush of love and affection, a bursting heart, an urge to sing, to dance or to bubble over with energy; feelings of head-to-toe vitality and energy, lightness, a warm glow; feelings of well-being, sexiness or radiance. And with the physical wrench of parting, we may feel cold, tired and listless; sadness is expressed with light tears or deep sobbing; a sense of emptiness or wanting to curl up; we ache in our hearts, feel pain in our guts and we feel heavy.

Elation, triumph and joy are physically experienced as extremely powerful: walking tall, feeling unstoppable, a sense of massive energy, a larger-than-life momentum. When we are angry, this same immense energy makes itself felt through sensations of heat, a pounding heart, sweating, muscular tension, increased blood flow, sometimes literally 'seeing red'. When this energy is turned inwards, it converts into a depressive force and the consequence is often apathy, immobility, heaviness and a need to withdraw.

When we are confident and secure, our muscles are relaxed, our breathing regular and energy is flowing easily. If we are confused and fearful, we feel shaky, sweaty; we may respond with 'butterflies', goose-pimples, a tightness in our stomach and shoulders; other symptoms include a pounding heart, clammy hands, nausea, diarrhoea, trembling, shivering or numbness; we can sometimes feel paralysed or quite overcome with weariness.

These physical symptoms will be familiar but on the whole, we remain fairly ignorant about our feelings and the essential link between our minds and our bodies. Feelings are rarely given due regard and consideration: they come in for quite a battering and are usually regarded as childish, ridiculous, weak, shameful, unfair or even crazy. If unleashed they are alleged to cause unseemly or undignified behaviour; emotions are approached with suspicion and distaste and, most reprehensible of all, emotions are judged to be *unreasonable*. So, most of the time, most of us try to hide what we feel, even from ourselves. Unfortunately, denial of feelings will sabotage any attempts we make to communicate or behave assertively.

Have you ever denied what you felt because, on the surface, it seemed illogical? Or reproached yourself because you felt guilty or ashamed or stupid for having certain feelings? Have you ever tried, for example, to dismiss the rejection you felt when you were criticised by someone on the grounds that they did not matter to you anyway? Or pretended you didn't feel jealous when your partner was attracted to someone else because you wanted to appear laid back and 'cool' about it? Have you tried to reason your way out of the feeling of frustration by counting your blessings instead? Or felt ashamed of wanting to hit out angrily at a helpless small child because you felt so frustrated? Have you ever denied feeling hurt because you thought you were simply being too sensitive? Or felt too embarrassed to admit feeling afraid or lonely and ask for comfort and support?

If your answer is 'yes' to any of the above questions, you'll recognise the unhelpful cultural legacy of dividing feelings into 'positive' and 'negative'. We are taught to believe that negative feelings – anger, sadness, hurt, anxiety, envy for example – are bad: that they are unpleasant, reflect badly on you as a human being and should not be felt at all, let alone put into words. On the other hand, we are constantly encouraged to feel happy, confident, fearless, in control and loving.

This simple division has an enormous effect on us psychologically. Time after time I have witnessed individuals struggling painfully with the conflict between wanting to deny 'negative' feelings and daring to admit to them. Denial of what we feel – even acknowledging the truth to ourselves – causes untold problems: eventually keeping them hidden will make them much harder to manage. Feelings accumulate and, after a while, reach levels which threaten to be uncontrollable. Once you can accept that your feelings are real, despite them being difficult to admit to, and even though they may not make much sense, you can begin to identify what it is you feel. By eliminating the initial mental censorship, you can learn to recognise any feeling *for what it is* without judging it: I'm feeling nervous; I'm feeling excited; I'm feeling wary; I'm very irritated. This process of recognition and acknowledgement is first of all for your own information. No one else need be made aware of it. A private acknowledgement can help you change your behaviour accordingly: you can leave the room, change the subject, breathe deeply, relax or whatever seems the right thing to do in the circumstances in which you find yourself.

Once you have acknowledged what you feel, you can then consider the next step of putting this into words. For instance: 'I feel nervous coming to talk to you about money but I want to ask for a raise' or 'I find it difficult to ask but would you help me with this problem'. The *immediate* effect of this is to reduce your anxiety. It allows you to relax and take command of yourself. Everything starts flowing in the body again: you feel looser and stronger. Identify what you are feeling and then make a similar simple statement.

A deeper level of expression Despite wishful thinking, feelings do not simply go away when we ignore them over time. However much we hope they will disappear, however much we repress, deny, pretend or hide them away, feelings will find expression *somehow*. Taking a deep breath and counting to ten can help temporarily: so does the practice of self-disclosure. However, when we let things build up to a point where they begin to interfere with our normal functioning, other measures may have to be considered. Various methods of stress-reduction can be helpful to a point: strategies for relaxation, meditation and exercise enable us to deal with some levels of anxiety and frustration in our lives. It is unlikely, though, that we can eliminate *all* stressful feelings in these ways. Unexpressed emotions will push for expression through another outlet. A pattern of physical and psychological symptoms often emerges in response to long-term suppression of feelings: for example, constant low energy and fatigue, depression, withdrawal from contact with loved ones, headaches, vaginal infections, cystitis, backache, bowel problems or skin irritations.

What holds us back from exploring any deeper expression is a major inhibition stemming from a fear that for an adult to express feelings openly is childish and shameful. This fear is endorsed by our experience with other adults. Instead of compassion and acceptance, tears in an adult are usually met with alarm and embarrassment: instead of respect and compassion, they elicit pity, suspicion or a sudden urge to withdraw as if tears might be contagious in some way. As very young children we were able to express our feelings quite openly and spontaneously without shame. Although we have to learn to control our feelings as part of growing up – which is necessary – most of us have learned to over-control them to such an extent that we are now no longer aware of even having any feelings, let alone being able to identify and express them.

The ability to express our feelings and deal with situations *at the time*, or a short while afterwards, is important but, in reality, there will be many times when we fail to do this: we deny our feelings, we swallow them down and bottle them up for days, weeks and even years. The result is that most of us, as adults, have accumulated a backlog of unexpressed and unreleased feelings. This accumulation will make itself felt from time to time in our personal and working lives.

We recognise these moments as times when we feel particularly vulnerable, 'stressed' or under pressure. The combined demands and circumstances of our personal and working lives push us to a point that is intolerable and this means that something has to give.

Sometimes, a release of tension comes in the form of what I call an *avalanche*: we erupt, blow a fuse, spew out showers of aggression and hurt and resentment onto those around us. At other times, the tension is released through *subsidence*: we collapse, succumb to all sorts of aches and pains and illnesses, suffer mental and physical exhaustion and, in extreme circumstances, a breakdown of some kind.

We do experience some release of psychosomatic tension (in our minds *and* in our bodies) and the immediate crisis passes but, unfortunately, it is unlikely that we are any clearer afterwards about what exactly caused the accumulation and what our specific feelings were.

A further disadvantage of accumulation is seen on those occasions when we find ourselves over-reacting or under-reacting: even if we sense our emotional responses are somehow disproportionate and irrational, we don't understand why. For example, a friend comments negatively on your new sofa and instead of mild disappointment, you feel terribly *rejected*; instead of feeling a little anxious about approaching your boss for a favour you are filled with *dread*; your partner is a bit offhand and you respond with a childish *tantrum*; someone dear to you dies and you feel absolutely *nothing*; someone beats you to a parking place and instead of irritation, you are ready to *kill* the other driver. Although we remain convinced that we are responding *only* to the present, reality has become coloured by past events with the result that our perceptions are distorted because of a backlog of emotion: the result is a potent and confusing muddle.

Understanding this process and developing a longer term approach to managing emotion in our lives is beyond the scope of assertiveness training and is the subject of my book *Reconnecting with the Heart*. It can be extremely helpful to learn how to unlock and release the accumulated feelings from the past. Many of us store a lot of unexpressed emotions, some stimulated by recent events and others caused by events that affected us long ago in childhood. These feelings can undermine our relationships with others in the present without our realising it. Releasing past, unexpressed feelings can help us arrive at a better understanding of ourselves and can open the door to deeper self-expression and fulfilment.

Meanwhile, the first few steps – recognition, acknowledgement and verbal expression – are a tremendous help in gaining more clarity in our relationships. Apart from opening up the possibility for emotional exchange, self-disclosure is a vital part of short-term emotional management because it acts as a first and major form of release of tension. This is because until there is an acknowledgement and therefore acceptance of the feeling, whatever it is, the battle will continue between the body, which pushes to release, and the head which has learned to keep everything battened down. The greater the pressure for the feeling to be expressed, the greater the counter-effort of the head to control and prevent expression, the greater the tension, the greater the pressure and so on.

Self-disclosure acts in an extraordinary way to allow the mouth to articulate your feelings, forming a meeting point between the battling head and body: head and body become congruent, in other words acting *together* instead of against each other, the head finding the language to translate the physical sensations of emotion.

At this point the conflict eases. There is a felt release of tension, especially if the language conveys the feeling accurately. The arousal doesn't dissipate immediately if it is high but once the conflict between body and mind stops, once we acknowledge and name the truth of what we are feeling, the struggle subsides and the tension eases.

Without self-disclosure we continue to believe that we can hide from other people what we are feeling inside. Beware being over-confident in this regard. Although we *think* that with sufficient facial and vocal control we can mask what is going on, little tell-tale signs on the outside tend to give us away: the inappropriate smile which masks unexpressed anger or grief or anxiety; tiny eye movements, gestures, set of the jaw and especially the tone of voice. All these will betray our true feelings and influence our communication even in the absence of conscious awareness.

Often in the course of role-play practice, a woman will learn from other people's observations that her body is emitting all sorts of little signals indicating feelings that she knows to be true, but finds it hard to admit even to herself. Remember we are not to blame for whatever we feel: we rarely have voluntary control over what emerges. Although we can control how we *act* on their feelings and can take responsibility for what and when and how we express them, we cannot be blamed or criticised for experiencing the feelings themselves. What you feel is what you feel. It may be silly, groundless, irrational or something you may not like to admit to: but if you feel it, it is real. Acknowledgement helps you to take charge of your emotions rather than being at the mercy of them.

This ability to identify and acknowledge a feeling helps to solve another difficulty. Many women experience a considerable time lapse between an initial emotional response and the actual acknowledgement of it. We may register a flash of feeling at the time but it may take hours or days for the full burst of recognition to dawn. So we often end up sighing 'If only I'd expressed what I felt', or 'If only I'd followed my impulse' or 'Why didn't I say what I really wanted to?' We tend to agonise and spend a lot of time re-running the scene in our heads, enacting the part to perfection with the other party suitably impressed, intimidated or penitent! With practice, we can reduce the gap more and more until we are able to recognise our feelings in the moment. In this way, we can develop a more spontaneous approach, and whatever the feeling – whether resentment or affection, confusion or joy – we can express it and act on it if we choose.

The value of feelings As we learn to identify our feelings, we discover how valuable they are. Feelings can act as a vehicle of understanding the truth of what is really going on in a situation even though our heads may be telling us something different. It is easy to dismiss what we feel because we do not have concrete evidence.

Yet our feelings give us important clues. You may have met someone for the first time and sensing with an absolute certainty that this person could be trusted. You may have felt suspicious or uncomfortable with someone's request even though you couldn't put your finger on exactly what was wrong. You may have made a decision in your life because you knew it felt right for you even though you could not offer a satisfactory verbal explanation to anyone else, maybe not even to yourself.

These perceptions are not accompanied by any real evidence of the sort that would stand up in court. Yet you know what you feel to be true: you just *feel* it. Recent research has indicated that within the physical heart apparatus, neurons have been identified within the cardiac muscle, referred to as 'the little brain'. Information obtained in this manner can complement what we can learn through our powers of reasoning and logic. When we cut ourselves off from what we feel, we cut ourselves off from our emotional intelligence and thus from an essential source of personal insight and guidance.

I should add that although I used this exact phrase in my original text for this book, 'emotional intelligence' is now a far more widely-used and familiar phrase, thanks to Daniel Goleman's book of the same name. In this context, I mean something a little different. I do not believe the subjective experience of emotion can be reduced to scientific measurement: obviously, research into the physiology of emotion is helpful but personal discernment of emotion is affected by other, less straightforward factors.

A checklist of indications of anger, for example, overlooks our profound reluctance to acknowledge this emotion because of its negative connotations; it ignores the consequence that many people feel symptoms of fear when they are angry and many women are likely to *cry* when they are in fact feeling anger.

Understanding emotional intelligence as a linear and rational set of attributes reduces the significance of the fact that every one of us carries around a personal emotional ragbag of a million memories from the past: some good, some not so good and some extremely traumatic. In the normal course of our psychological histories, some memories are repressed forever in the unconscious but many hover in the sub-conscious layers of our psyches. Their presence accounts for those occurrences I described earlier where we over- or under- react. The arc from stimulus to response is not nearly as straightforward for humans as it is for mice: the potential for distortion is ever present. Finally, the effect of accumulation is not given much prominence and yet this phenomenon exerts a huge influence on what we perceive and how we respond to those perceptions.

Emotional intelligence, in this context, refers to a facility that incorporates the skills already described in this chapter but also involves aspects of our being that are more complex and probably impossible to measure. When we say, for example: 'I am in two minds about what to do but, in my heart, I know the answer,' we allude to the essential difference between the rational and emotional realms.

Attitudes to feelings have changed in some ways. The need to address feelings in the aftermath of traumatic incidents is considered more relevant than thirty years ago. However, the underlying associations of emotion with *negative* occurrences – for example, abuse, natural or man-made disasters, terrorist violence or traffic accidents – are more deeply reinforced than ever. The emphasis is on recovery through professional help – like a physical illness – and although such help can certainly be beneficial in these circumstances, I believe there is an equally important role for emotion to be seen also as relevant to normal, everyday relationships. Negativity surrounding certain feelings remains: unwanted feelings are still as unwanted as ever. Even though we don't surgically remove parts of the brain to eliminate them any longer, we suppress them (on a frighteningly colossal scale) with, for instance, Ritalin, HRT and anti-depressants.

With the information in this chapter and with practice in expression, we can learn to trust our bodily cues and feelings and to see and enjoy them as an invaluable and reliable source of information and learning.

Instead of insisting that the head rule the heart, I believe that we would do better to foster a productive collaboration between the two. The use of self-disclosure acts as a bridge between short-term emotional management and a longer term approach. Its practice puts us very much in touch with our physical sensations and helps to correlate these sensations with a nameable feeling or emotion.

Choosing to 'have it out' with the person concerned, talking things through with a close and trusted friend or even arranging to do this with a professional are an important and vital part of emotional management and can help us move on from a place where we've previously felt very 'stuck' as we'll see in the following chapters.

12

The Two Faces of Anger

Of all our complex and powerful emotions, anger remains the most misunderstood. Whereas love is regarded as beautiful and enhancing, anger is considered ugly and degrading. We associate anger with the baser side of human nature which appears dark, sinister and threatening: a side we would rather not see or talk about. We control angry feelings in whatever way we can and we encourage others to do the same. It is because we neither acknowledge nor understand our anger that it remains for many men and women the most difficult of all the emotions to address and handle assertively.

In the last chapter we saw that the range of feelings connected with frustration and anger was connected to the energy for survival and self-direction. In order to understand this in more depth, we need to look at two aspects of anger: a deep layer which exists as a powerful source of energy and a top layer caused by past and present hurts and frustrations. Look at the diagram on page 119. Try to imagine yourself on the inside looking for a way through the maze. The very fact that you *want* to find a way through shows that the first and deepest layer is operating inside you. Without it you would give up, lie down and die. But with it you feel a wish to engage with others and the world, to move forward, to develop, to change, to overcome difficulties and achieve fulfilment. This movement is fuelled by a very deep and fundamental energy which keeps you going.

You may not be aware of it as a force inside you but you will feel its effects from time to time. It provides the impetus to learn new skills: to master a complicated recipe, pass an exam or learn to communicate in another language; it pushes you to express yourself in writing or singing or painting and it can push you on

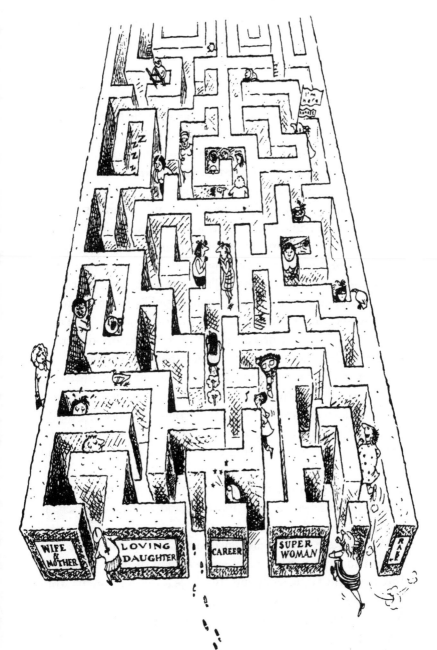

in a career or to some goal that you see as fulfilling. This anger helps you survive crises, disasters, set-backs, illness or handicaps. You may choose to read this book, to leave an unhealthy relationship, to take care of your body when it needs it, to set up a business, overcome a setback, write a poem, attend a class or to say 'no' or 'yes' for yourself. You respond to the frustration of a meaningless job by deciding to study for a new career: you know it's going to be tough but this energy will fuel your determination. You may protest or campaign against outside barriers such as cruelty, racism, inequality or injustice.

This anger, which I call *root anger*, has, at its source, the basic *you*, the person under all the roles and responsibilities you assume in your life. Imagine the figure in the diagram starting off through the maze. The signposts give an idea of the confusion of directions and conflict of goals ahead. Most of us use our response to the model represented by our mothers or other women as a starting point for our own journey. We may choose to follow suit or take a totally contradictory direction, depending on how we felt about what we perceived and experienced. But as you can see from the diagram, many of the choices can be self-limiting. The woman in the maze may feel that marriage and motherhood is the right direction for her to take and then find herself, a few years later, unable to move any further. Or she may opt for a career or intellectual status and still find herself unchallenged and unfulfilled. Or she may choose to go in more than one direction or follow the routes which promise status and approval and *still* find herself at another dead end.

Within these walls we also encounter the source of the second kind of anger: reactive anger. Our awareness of angry feelings of this kind will fall broadly into two categories: one stems from the desire to tear down the walls and the other describes the despair at feeling the walls are immovable. On some occasions we feel powerfully driven to engage and challenge: at other times we feel overwhelmed by the odds and sink into helplessness. We may find ourselves wanting to hit out at those walls, whatever they represent in our lives. We may see them as society, our parents, our children, our rivals, the government or maybe just fate: whoever we see as responsible for blocking our movement, impeding our progress, stopping us from doing what we want, holding us back and restricting our freedom and blocking our path. We want to break the obstacles down and destroy whatever stands in our way.

At other times, we get tired of banging away at those walls and feel very alone. We feel helpless, convinced that it is futile to keep trying; we lose heart, we stop fighting, become immobile and tend to sink back in despair and resignation. The world closes in.

Most of us alternate between these two extremes of aggressive or passive. Either way we remain ineffectual. A major problem is that reactive anger becomes entwined with root anger. Some of the stress we feel *enables* us to move forward: it motivates us to change our lives and we certainly don't want to lose an ounce of that energy. It becomes so bound up with wanting to hit out and blame and take revenge that, in fear of our violence, we can repress everything. The combination of the general taboo on the expression of anger in our culture plus a further discouragement, as women, from showing the more powerful facets of ourselves, has meant that many of us have lost contact with not only our destructive anger but also a fundamental source of energy and purpose.

What are your particular anxieties about expressing anger: do you fear losing control and showing some unpleasant and destructive side of yourself? Do you fear provoking a violent response in the other person? Is the emotion of anger a friend or stranger to you? Have you ever witnessed a woman expressing anger in a clear and effective but unaggressive manner, in a way that inspired you?

Teaching the skill of self-disclosure, I have many times witnessed the struggle to voice angry feelings: we even try to avoid the use of the word itself and opt instead for 'upset' or 'hurt' or 'surprised'. It always seems so difficult to pinpoint this particular emotion: we tiptoe around it as if it were some unpredictable and terrifying monster. I believe we are frightened because of our confusion between anger and aggression. Since we have all been on the receiving end of aggression in some form and inevitably on the issuing end as well, we end up thinking of anger as dangerous rather than informative. As an emotion, anger reveals our own (and others') emotional and physical boundaries. Anger signals to us (and others) when enough is enough; when a limit has been reached, when something in us says 'Stop!' 'No!' 'That's enough!'

As an exercise in understanding the relevance of this particular emotion in your life, consider the following questions.

What makes you angry? Injustice? Stupidity? Incompetence? Insensitivity? Lies? Bureaucracy? Snobbery? Untidiness? Prejudice? Waste? Cruelty? Hypocrisy? Corruption? Gossip? Being taken for granted? Being ignored? Being excluded? Not being listened to?

Who makes you angry? Do you feel most strongly affected by people close to you? Those in your immediate family? Friends? Parents? Relatives? People far removed from you? People in authority? Particular professionals?

What are the signs that your body gives you when you are angry? Do you feel hot? Does your heart pound? Do you feel sweaty? Tension in your jaw or shoulders? Do you feel like grabbing something or hitting out? Do you feel powerful? Frightened? Do you feel like stamping on something (or someone)? Are your fists clenched? Do you feel physically like breaking out? Needing air or space? Do you feel a rush of adrenalin? Restlessness?

When and with whom do you feel safe enough to express angry feelings? On your own, miles away from anywhere? With your family? A close friend? Your partner? Men? Women? Your cat? With no one? With a large amount of alcohol inside you? In a letter? By email? Never?

Before we look at the assertive expression of anger let's look more closely at the aggressive, passive and indirect approaches which are far more familiar. How do Agnes, Dulcie and Ivy handle their anger and frustration: how does it make itself felt in their lives?

Agnes uses aggressive tactics to express her rage. On the  receiving end, the effect is the psychological equivalent of being punched hard by a heavyweight boxer. You know exactly where it is coming from, you reel under the force of it: you may try and retaliate and protest or you may shield yourself from further damage. Agnes is quick to flare up: her resentment simmers just below the surface so the slightest provocation can trigger the actual eruption although the hurt and frustration has been accumulating inside her for quite a while. When someone moves out of line, says the wrong thing, makes a silly mistake or has a particular facial expression, she over-reacts and attacks before she can be hurt any more. She often goes over the top and then feels remorseful afterwards when she surveys the damage. She feels helpless, angry, hurt and guilty. Furthermore she knows that the other person did not really hear what she was saying so she continues to nurse her grievances. This confusion can tip her into a complementary Dulcie-like mood of despair and futility.

Dulcie wonders what the point is anyway. She has lost sight of her frustration. She does not have the energy to make much of a fuss any more. She still complains and moans about how she is treated unfairly but never to the person concerned. Dulcie's anger lies deeply buried like the winter earth under successive layers of snow. Occasionally she may lash out like Agnes but will then feel guilty and reinforced in her conviction that it is pointless to try and change things. Her unexpressed anger becomes a burden to  herself and a burden to others. Like a ball and chain, she drags her unexpressed anger along, clinging on to those around her, slowing down their progress in turn. Her anger is conveyed through her silence and she often closes off from physical affection or sexual contact.

The more her anger grows, the more Ivy tightens the reins of control on herself and others. Her unexpressed anger takes the shape of invisible poison darts: quick, apparently coming from nowhere, sudden, difficult to spot in flight but very painful on impact. They may appear as put-downs, be transmitted as 'a look that could kill' or feel more like a slap in the face. Her strategies of expression might include for-getting something important to you, not turning up  to an agreed meeting, betraying a confidence, making a fool of you in front of others, letting you know exactly how inadequate or disappointing you are in her eyes.

It should be emphasised that although this book is specifically looking at women's problems with anger, these kinds of strategies are not a female prerogative: men use the same tactics, with the same devastating effects. One tactic is to *disrupt* the status quo by making an apparently innocent remark or 'accidentally' letting slip a snippet of information which, very subtly, sows seeds of doubt and anxiety among others. Another is *sabotage*: finding the means to wreck well-laid plans or intentions, butting in on an enjoyable conversation between two other people, managing to spoil the moment with an ill-timed remark or gesture. Similar to sabotage is the behaviour of the person who feels compelled to make a comment that is guaranteed to *deflate* someone else's pleasure or sense of achievement. Finally, there are those who find a channel for their frustration by driving everyone else up the wall with their complaints until they are goaded to a point where *they* explode while the person who actually stokes the flames sits innocently in the background.

Before we look at the assertive expression of anger, I want to identify one very clear difference between anger and aggression because they have become synonymous in so many people's minds to the extent that they are very surprised to hear there is any distinction between the two. Given the potential for con-fusion, we start with a crucial distinction between aggression and assertiveness.

Aggression *always* requires an object. This is true whether the aggressive behaviour is overt . . .

> Violence (physical or verbal)
> Revenge
> Blame
> Punishment
> Humiliation
> Cruelty
> Murder

. . . indirect . . .

> Sarcasm
> Constant criticism
> Sabotage
> Put-downs
> Malicious gossip
> Covert cruelty
> Second-hand criticism

. . . or even passive, when the object is no longer external but internal and we attack ourselves:

> Self- blame
> Self-harm
> Withdrawal
> Self-destructive behaviours
> Depression
> Addictive behaviours
> Suicide

Once you understand this, it is easier to tell the difference between aggression and anger because aggression, in all its forms, exists only in relation to a target: it entails attacking something or somebody (including oneself). The object will vary enormously but the dynamic is always the same: aggression cannot exist in a vacuum.

On the other hand, anger is an emotion in response to the real or perceived transgression of our physical or emotional boundaries. It is like an eruption upwards, a volcanic response to internal pressures when defences and controls have to give way: it does not require an object for expression and release. It is often a very dynamic force, shocking in its energy but *it need not do any harm.* Anger is more an expression of self in response to frustration, unfairness or invasion; to being ignored, overlooked or trapped; to the experience of oppression and repression in all their forms.

Aggression actually belongs in a different category of emotion altogether. Fundamentally it is rooted in anxiety and fear: it is very much associated with the ladders of power and status described earlier and is completely embedded in a perceived need to win (rather than lose), to crush (rather than be crushed), to succeed (rather than fail) to gain or regain status (rather than face the prospect of demotion).

Bearing this distinction in mind, how do we ensure we express our anger without getting caught up in the habit of aggression? The following guidelines will help.

The assertive expression of anger

Assertive expression has to be addressed in two parts because there are two separate dimensions: the need to release the energy physically and reduce the stress level in your body and the second, equally important need to communicate your anger. It makes no difference in which order they come but it is imperative that you *don't* attempt both dimensions at once for reasons which will soon become clear.

Physical release We recognise when we are angry from body signals. We feel hot, we go red in the face, we want to stamp or jump up and down. However anger can rise up in us without such obviously dynamic signals: frustration and pressure also have the effect of causing us to feel hemmed in and stifled, of feeling inert and blank. Learn to identify what happens in your own body. Once you detect the physical sensation, you can recognise what you are feeling and then respond appropriately. Obviously it may not be possible to do so at the time when you recognise you're angry: you're unlikely to want to erupt in an important meeting or yell at the boss or hit out at your children or have a tantrum in the middle of the supermarket. You can choose to control this in the short-term and find a way of calming down and regaining composure for the moment: going for a short walk, focusing outside your distress or counting to ten, whatever works for you. However, in the longer term, it is important to make a mental note to give yourself some uninhibited 'release time' as soon as possible.

The following ways of 'release and letting go' are among those recommended by course participants: driving with the windows closed and yelling or screaming at the top of your voice; scrubbing the floor; kneading bread; slamming doors; going for a long run; punching cushions; singing loudly; stamping or jumping up and down; strangling a towel; biting hard into a towel or screaming your head off; hitting the wall with an old tennis racket; breaking old crockery; writing an uncensored letter of rage (but not sending it!). You may have your own personal way of letting off steam: choose whatever works best for you.

The more often you allow yourself this space when you need it, the less you accumulate tension and rage; the more accustomed you become to dealing with events as they happen, the lower and more manageable you will keep the internal pressure. The other advantage is that it becomes easier to admit to being angry, at the time, assertively and clearly without precipitating an avalanche of stored-up tension. With the information about what is happening inside you, you can allow yourself to decide what to do in a particular context, whereas simply denying your feelings makes life much more difficult.

Communication The reason for separating release from the dimension of communication is that it is not humanly possible to communicate assertively when you literally 'see red'. None of us can be clear enough when feeling any intensity of emotion, whether extreme fear, grief or anger. High emotional arousal will trigger all sorts of chemicals to surge round the body and these will affect the function of the brain: as a consequence our perceptions are distorted. Our mental capacities cannot function properly during a state of high emotional arousal which is why we need to have enough distance from strong emotion if we want to say something *clearly*.

Even though some people believe themselves to be articulate and focussed when they are angry, assertive communication requires you to be more specific than simply conveying your feelings. And it's also useful to remember that anyone on the receiving end of someone else's outburst will automatically become defensive and mentally shield themselves: their own anxiety will impair their ability to hear what is being communicated even if you're convinced you are being crystal clear in your message. You need to have sufficient distance to be able to follow three steps:

Express your feelings appropriately: in other words, match what you say to the level of what you feel. This can range from mildly irritated to absolutely outraged.

Describe the reason for your feelings: in other words, identify the behaviour that is causing you to feel this way and, if you want to avoid aggression, you will have to discipline yourself to let go the habit of blame. It is always tempting to hold the other person responsible for causing you to feel in a particular way but it is important that you resist this temptation because the moment you resort to accusation or blame (even indirectly), you set yourself on an aggressive path and the other person will respond in kind.

Request a change: This may be as simple as asking the person to stop whatever it is they are saying or doing or it may be more complex. Either way you need to be specific.

These steps are relevant whether you are expressing anger on the spot, when you confront someone immediately and also when you look at a relationship from a longer-term perspective and decide to approach someone to talk about their behaviour in the past.

A congruent message

Given the resistance I've already described among women to acknowledge their anger, simply getting the phrase 'I feel angry' out of one's lips can feel like a daunting challenge. But it is important to give yourself permission to do just that because, in using this phrase, you are stating that you have had enough, that your limits have been reached, that you don't like what is happening, that someone has crossed a boundary, all of which is very much part of establishing genuine self-esteem.

Our body language often reflects our ambivalence. We may grit our teeth or end up in tears instead of getting angry. To make matters worse, as I mentioned earlier, we usually smile: the kind of smile which stems from nervousness and a desire to placate. This confuses everyone because of the double message. If you want to be angry with conviction you must first be aware of your smile and try and lose it.

Your voice and body need to match the content of your speech so that that you make a clear, unequivocal impact. You may need to practise raising your voice level. Often we have become so unaccustomed to using our voices that raising the volume seems at first physically impossible. However, sometimes we need to push through our controlled and reasonable tones. Strength and conviction do *not* include sarcasm: this is where you need to be careful. A slight inflection of contempt or a sneer will undermine the assertive nature of your expression. Once it tips over into hostility, the expression becomes aggressive rather than assertive.

Hitting the right note has a lot to do with relaxation. When we are faced with a confrontation we are often paralysed by anxiety. Anxiety restricts our breathing: the throat tightens and our attempts to shout end only in producing a high-pitched squeak. Practise increasing the volume of your voice and learn that you can still have control of it. If you deepen your breathing, you will deepen the sound so that the tone of your voice will be more effective.

Gemma was standing next to two male colleagues in the bar

after the first day of a conference. The men got into discussing Mac, their immediate boss and an unlikeable man who was unpopular with most of his department. Ron, one of the two, was relating an anecdote about Mac's latest exploit and said, with some feeling, 'He is such a cunt, that guy . . . ' The other man, Jim, nodded in agreement. Gemma was phased for a few moments. Her instant response had been to wince: she hated that word used in this way. Although she wasn't really part of the conversation, they'd been aware she was there.

She thought about it a few moments and then said: 'Look, guys, I have to say something. I really hate it when you use that word with such contempt. I mean, I don't like Mac any more than you do but it makes me so angry when this is the only word you can use.' (*There is an awkward pause*). Gemma continued: 'Can't you find another one?' she asked with a bit of a smile. (*The tension lessens*) 'How about 'dickhead'?' said Ron. 'Would that be more acceptable?' To which Gemma's response was 'Absolutely.'

Gemma had been able to indicate a boundary crossed: without blame and without getting into a whole sexist debate. By moving the conversation on, she was able to help restore 'normality' to the dynamic among the three of them. Expressing anger without aggression is an essential part of developing self-esteem because we can draw strength from knowing what we are willing and unwilling to tolerate.

Marsha is gay and while she makes no secret of it, she believes her private life is exactly that – private – so she doesn't thrust her lesbian identity in everyone's face. There's a bit of friction between herself and a colleague, Amjad, and she suspects he's uncomfortable with her but has never bothered to clear it. One morning, Amjad is conducting an unofficial poll in the open plan office about whether or not a particular TV celebrity is attractive: he asks the women to vote and then the men: he is counting them up. 'So the guys are yes, the girls say no . . . ' and when he sees Marsha, he quips 'What about you, Marsha? You're an undecided, are you, keeping your options open?'

There is a brief, awkward silence and then everyone goes back to their screens.

Marsha is left fuming but makes the wise decision not to confront Amjad right there in what would be a public arena. Her decision is wise because it is very hard to avoid an aggressive outcome when the person you are talking to feels 'on display'. So she asks him a few minutes later to meet her outside the main office.

Marsha: Amjad, I want you to know that I felt very angry about what you said in there just now.

Amjad: It was a joke . . . I thought you were cool about it.

Marsha: It wasn't funny to me. I'm proud of my sexuality but for me it's something private and I would like you to respect that.

Amjad: I think you're over-reacting.

Marsha: Amjad. I'm *serious*. Just cut it out.

He realises she means what she says. She recognises that it is time to end the conversation and goes back into the office, leaving Amjad to sort out his own response to her challenge. He may have been surprised, genuinely taken aback or secretly knowing he had been goading her: what mattered is that there was no aggression in Marsha's words but she was clearly angry and when she intensified the level of expression, he got the message.

Taking the aggression out of your expression does *not* mean you have to simper. We often have difficulty in matching the tone and facial expression to the strength of what we are feeling: the distinction between expressing your anger with clarity and revealing it in all its forcefulness is an important one to learn. If the other person doesn't respond the first time or take you seriously, you may have to repeat your statement or request, like Marsha, to get your point across unequivocally.

Fear of our own anger spills over into fear of others' anger, especially as it is usually expressed aggressively which leads to uncertainty as to how to confront someone who is yelling at us. Sandra worked as a social worker and frequently had to deal with hostile clients. She wanted to know how to do this more effectively so she practised dealing with a particularly volatile individual who had stormed into her office one morning.

She had first to practise raising her voice which meant battling through several layers of self-consciousness. We tend not to be familiar with the power of our own voices but we have to master this if we want to interrupt a diatribe issuing forth from the other person. You need to get their attention before you say anything and this requires you to *match* the volume of your voice to theirs. So first of all, use a simple phrase like 'listen to me' or, preferably, the person's name: call and repeat the name. As soon as the person pauses – because they will if you persist and look them in the eye and match their volume – then you say something simple like 'I want you to listen to me.'

This is how it went for Sandra:

She is in her office at her desk when the door opens with a bang and John Simmons is in front of her. The surprise, not to mention shock of someone's entrance like this, is hard to move away from so this does take practice.

John: (*at full volume and very agitated*) I'm glad you're here for once. I have been leaving messages for you and you never respond. Why don't you ever get back to me? You know they're going to take her away soon.

Sandra: Mr Simmons

John: (*continues*) I'm absolutely sick of this. Why did you bother to say you'd help?

Sandra: Mr Simmons (*a bit louder*)

John: (*continues*) You're just like the rest of them . . .

Sandra: Mr Simmons (*louder this time and she stands up to establish better eye contact. John pauses for two seconds then continues*) You don't have any idea of what it's like.

Sandra: Mr Simmons (*she remains standing and raises her voice a bit more. He pauses this time for three seconds.*)

John: What?

Sandra: I can't respond to you when you're shouting at me like this. Please lower your voice.

John: Why should I?

Sandra: (*reduces her own volume*) Mr Simmons. I understand you're

very angry and I'd like to help but I want you to stop
shouting at me so we can have a proper conversation. (*This
time she gets through to him.*)

Sandra: Please have a seat.

Matching the volume, making eye contact and repetition will usually get someone's attention however wrapped up they are in their own feelings. Once they look at you, hold their attention. Follow through immediately with a short phrase, whatever you want to communicate: for example 'I know you're angry. We'll talk later when you have calmed down' or 'I know you're angry but I'm frightened when you're behaving like this'.

If you follow through straightaway the other person will hear you and then you have a chance to communicate.

When you practise this in role-play (and it is essential to practise this beforehand) you may find that, being generally unfamiliar with the power of your own voice, you are quite startled when the other person stops, so you back away, dumbstruck. Practice will help you to follow through at that vital moment. One final point: if you try and it does not work and the person continues regardless, then remember you always have an option to walk away.

One final point in this chapter is challenging aggression, not in a one-off situation like the above example, but when it is a pattern, especially in someone you're close to. Steph lives with Paul and they have been together about four years. Things started going wrong when Paul lost his job six months ago. He became morose and although he's looked for other work, his whole manner has changed. Steph is still working – and enjoying it – but she can't talk about it at all because it will always provoke an aggressive outburst. Her response has been to sit tight and wait for it to pass and she doesn't know what to do. She feels a mixture of fear and anger: she has become scared of him but also has had enough of feeling she has to walk on eggshells in her own home.

What does she want to change? She wants his aggression towards her to stop.

Steph decides to talk to Paul when they are sitting at home after dinner. He is watching TV but nothing important.

Steph: Paul, I want to talk to you about something.

Paul: What?

Steph: Just something I want to say to you. *(Paul's eyes are still fixed on the screen.)*

Steph: Paul, I need you to *listen* to me.

Paul: *(looks at her)* I am listening.

Steph: I'm feeling awkward about this, Paul, so I'd rather turn the telly off for minute.

Paul: *(surprised)* What's the matter?

Steph: Can we turn it off? *(Paul picks up the remote and turns it off.)*

Steph: *(clears her throat)* I'm feeling really nervous about saying this, Paul, but recently . . . since you lost the job . . . you've become really aggressive and moody and I hate it basically.

Paul: You don't have to take it personally.

Steph: Well, I do take it personally. You shout at me for the slightest thing. I can't mention my work at all 'cause you jump down my throat and . . . I know it's not me that's making you angry and that it's really hard for you, but I hate it. It's making me not want to come home in the evenings.

Paul: *(now a bit alarmed)* Why didn't you say so before?

Steph: I don't know. I didn't want to make things worse. I want to support you, Paul, but I am just getting too tense myself. You really scare me. You shout and then you storm off . . . I hate it. I need to feel welcome when I come home, not just cope with your resentment. *(There is a silence between them.)*

Paul: So what do you want? Greet you with a smile and a bunch of roses every evening?

Steph: Don't be daft. I want you to stop taking it out on me. I want to help you if you're willing to be more open but if you'd rather deal with everything on your own, then stop shouting at me. Can't you understand that?

Paul: *(shrugs his shoulders)* I don't know what to say.

We've reached the point when it is time to close the conversation. Paul needs time to think things over: unlike Steph he hasn't been aware of her feelings accumulating for six months. Steph also needs time to recover: this kind of important conversation always leaves us a bit unsettled even when we know we've said what we wanted to say.

> *Steph:* That's fine. We both need time to think. Look, put the telly back on . . . I'll go and make some tea. (*Gets up and goes to the kitchen.*)

While these various guidelines can help you to defuse another person's anger or aggression, don't imagine they are mechanical techniques. You can get the words right and the voice right but there is something else at the heart of this kind of communication which is essential for it to be truly effective. If you speak from a position of judgement or disapproval about the other person's feelings; if you ignore or negate their anger; if you imply that they have no right to feel what they are feeling, this will come across as an open invitation to get into a fight.

Sandra's acknowledgement that Mr. Simmons was angry – even though she may not have understood exactly why – was a major contribution to defusing his tirade. Steph didn't criticise Paul for being angry: she understood why and sympathised. What she wanted was for him to stop taking it out on her. The process of accepting and understanding your own anger – without disapproval – will make you more able to respond to anger in others without negating their feelings. Once again we see how equality is at the core of assertive communication.

13

How to Handle Criticism: on the receiving end

Few of us welcome criticism with open arms. If caught unawares by a critical comment we can feel stung; if we are anticipating a criticism, we feel anxious and defensive. Our current adult response to criticism is usually based on our reaction to being criticised in the past: a week ago, a year ago or even many years ago in childhood.

Childhood experience of criticism can provide an important insight into achieving an assertive response: both how to respond to someone's criticism of you and also how to give critical feedback to someone else. It is a very sensitive area and an element in the training programme that many participants find difficult to handle. It means looking at the vulnerable places within each of us which we may prefer to avoid. But avoiding criticism is what most of us try to do already. It's easy to stop ourselves from saying what we want to say, doing what we want to do, living how we want to live, being who we want to be, all to avoid the possibility of real or imagined criticism and disapproval.

Why does criticism hit so hard? Why does the very word 'criticism' have such a nasty ring to it? Pause for a while and review your recollections of being criticised, especially those from childhood and see if you can identify with any of the following: being made to look foolish when making a mistake; the ominous comment on a school report about being lazy or a bad influence; being scolded for getting dirty or shouting back; being punished for being jealous and spiteful; being ridiculed for something beyond your control like getting low marks in a subject or being overweight or clumsy; belittled for being childish because you were afraid of the dark and did not want to be left alone.

The first, almost universal, element in our experience of criticism is the use of *labels*. Few parents heed the principle that it is far more effective to criticise the behaviour not the child. So we tend to associate criticism with a label of some kind: 'you're stupid', 'you're hopeless', 'you're a nuisance', 'you're a show-off', 'you're deceitful', 'you'll never be as good as your sister', 'you're selfish', 'you're a real burden to your mother'. It was not simply that you had done something silly or said something unkind: the label implied that you were fundamentally stupid and bad!

The second element is that many of us interpret criticism as *rejection*. When someone criticises us, we tend not to regard this as stemming from loving intentions designed to benefit us but as disapproval, punishment, a withdrawal of affection and love and occasionally total annihilation. In fact, we are often correct in perceiving criticism as negative and unloving because that is exactly how it was and still is communicated. Our anticipation of criticism as rejection is based on childhood memories and later reinforced by more recent criticism given to us as adults. Obviously we are no longer as vulnerable as when we were children but past and present tend to become quite muddled in our emotional reactions.

Both giving and receiving criticism tends to be handled very badly. To get a better idea of how childhood perceptions affect your adult reaction to criticism, consider how you respond to criticism now. See if you can identify with the six-year-old thoughts and feelings of the following three little girls:

'You wait!' . . . an Agnes in the making: 'How dare you call me stupid? I'm not stupid. You're stupid. What's wrong with it anyway? Ouch! I always get hit. That hurts. You just wait until I get bigger. Then I'll get my own back. I'll hurt you more. I'll make you sorry. You'll see. Just because you're a grown-up . . . you wait!'

'It's not fair' . . . an Ivy in the making: 'It wasn't my fault. He started it anyway. You're just picking on me. It's always *me*. You never see the good things. What do you mean, take that look off my face? I just hate you. Still, I'd better look as if I'm sorry. But I'm not really, it's not fair . . . '

'I just can't help it' . . . a Dulcie in the making: 'I can't help making mistakes. I can't help being clumsy . . . how was I to know it was so important? I can never seem to do the right thing. You're always getting at me. If I weren't here, *then* you'd be happy. You don't love me anymore. Why is it always me? I just can't help it.'

You may recognise a little of yourself in all three examples. Some of the same thoughts and feelings of the young Agnes, Ivy and Dulcie emerge as adults. We can often end up struggling to manage criticism as an intelligent adult, yet inside experiencing feelings and reactions more appropriate to the six-year-old child.

The problem with all three strategies is that none of them includes *listening* to the criticism. The adult Agnes will remain impervious. She regards criticism as nothing but an attack and since she spent so much time in the powerless position, she now has to make sure she wins. Consequently, she tends to retaliate immediately with 'How dare you!' or 'It's your fault'. She will not hear of being at fault herself. All the past helplessness wells up in her and she has to prove herself the winner when under threat in this way.

The adult Ivy will also refuse to let in the truth of the criticism because her sense of unfairness is stirred up. Although she may adopt a suitably penitent expression and silently 'suffer' accusation, she will get her own back. She won't forget and will retaliate with a subtle barbed or loaded comment later on (sometimes *much* later on) when her critic is least expecting it.

And Dulcie? She does not really listen to the criticism either. She immediately crumbles: too readily she agrees with the critic that she is at fault, she is no good or she really is a failure. Anything valid and specific that her critic is saying is likely to sink without trace in the broad swamp of self-pity and self-reproach.

As a result of such conditioning, most of us have developed the habit of feeling defensive when faced with someone who criticises us. We anticipate an attack: we expect to have to defend ourselves and so the minute we suspect a criticism is coming, psychologically we arch our backs. We are also very suspicious about the slightest possibility of one-upmanship, alert to the possibility that the other person is trying to demonstrate superiority over us in some way: this means that by acknowledging the truth of what they are saying, it automatically means that we have 'lost' and they have 'won'. This is why criticism is such a sensitive area: a veritable minefield.

These difficulties are perpetuated by the manner in which most adults continue to give criticism to each other. Most critics – whether our friends, partners, parents or employers – will still use labels and often consider themselves as self-appointed judges of our behaviour. But even though you cannot demand that others hone their skills in giving criticism, you can nevertheless learn to respond assertively to criticism yourself.

An Assertive Approach to Criticism

It will make a difference to your response whether or not the criticism is true or untrue. This means we have to listen to what is said before responding appropriately. Too many unspoken challenges and too many kneejerk apologies combine to make us so confused and oversensitive about the issue that even when someone says something true and potentially helpful, we cannot hear it and instead are prone to hate the critic for having dared to voice a personal opinion.

Valid criticism is criticism which hits home. You can't deny that it's legitimate. You *did* make a mess of that job; you *have* arrived late too often; you *did* forget an important instruction; you *do* change your mind a lot; you *are* putting on weight; you *are* fussy . . . whatever it is, you know that it is true and does apply to you, even if you would rather not admit it.

Handling such criticism requires the skill of *negative assertion* which helps you to respond either when it's constructive and meant to be helpful or even when it's hostile and aimed at making you feel small. Whether the critic has your own interests at heart or is simply out to attack you is less important than whether or not what is being said is *true*.

Negative assertion is learning how to agree with the criticism, if it applies to you, and to recognise it as valid: 'yes, I am untidy'; 'yes, I agree, I did make a mess of that last piece of work'; 'you're right, it was a stupid decision'. You do not have to melt into a pool of self-deprecation and abject apology. Nor do you have to round on your critic and prove them wrong. You can simply acknowledge the truth in what your critic is saying. Then you can feel less defensive and more accepting of yourself.

When most of us have spent a lifetime ducking criticism or being hurt by unfair criticism (that we failed to challenge), we need to acknowledge this is going to be a tricky path to follow. However, once we begin to listen to criticism without instantly feeling demolished, it makes an enormous difference to our behaviour. It frees us up to be more impulsive and to take more risks: in other words, it gives us more self-confidence. It may take a while but it is really worth practising these skills.

Listen first and then agree if you know it's valid. Try to curb the childlike tendency to follow up automatically with excessive apology or statement of intent to improve your shortcomings. Sometimes you may be sincere in your apology: at others, it may be enough to let it go. But even if someone takes the trouble to point out to you a fault which (in your eyes) is not that serious or perhaps even a quirk you rather like about yourself, remember the guideline of equality: leave the door open to negotiation.

For example if you are habitually scatter-brained and chaotic, there would be no point in offering profuse apologies. Clearly nothing is going to change. So instead, while you acknowledge this trait as your own, you can, at the same time, genuinely acknowledge that it must be irritating or frustrating for your colleagues or friends. See if you can negotiate as equals. For example, you might say 'Yes, I know . . . being disorganised is a real problem for me. It must drive you mad. Is there any way we can work around this?'

Invalid criticism brings up a whole new area of difficulty. There are few of us who – at some time in our lives – have not withheld a retort or protest in response to being criticised unfairly. These unspoken protests have an effect as they accumulate and we become extremely sensitive to the relative fairness or unfairness of what is being said.

Throughout my years of teaching, I have become convinced that, over time, failure to challenge unfair criticism has a devastating effect on lowering self-esteem. It often goes back to childhood when we felt unable to protest for fear of making things worse: but even as adults, we continue to keep quiet instead of voicing our disagreement.

In such circumstances, not only do we build up resentment but we also lose the sense of ourselves as an anchor point. When the past mixes with the present, we can hear someone's criticism and *know* it to be untrue but then, instead of speaking up, we hesitate and wonder. 'Was I?' 'Did I?' 'Maybe he has a point'. Even, for instance, if you're accused of being mean and you know that, in general, 'meanness' is not one of your failings, you'll probably remember the last two occasions when you failed to be your usual generous self and this will be enough to justify holding back from disputing the comment. In other words, we risk giving more credence to the other person's perception than our own. This is why it undermines our self-esteem so much: we lose the ability to balance others' perceptions of ourselves with our own, making us ever more dependent on others' approval.

If the criticism does not belong to you, you do not have to work hard to try and make it fit! Try saying something like 'That's really not true! On the contrary . . . ' or 'I don't accept that at all'. Of course, changing a life-time's pattern is not easy but you have the skill of self-disclosure at your disposal. This, as always, is the key.

First, if you know immediately that the criticism is wrong, then you can say so: 'I really must disagree with you' or 'you are quite wrong to say that of me' or 'that criticism is completely unjustified'. This takes courage and, furthermore, it takes a determined choice *not* to get into battle with your critic. Your critic has a right to speak their mind: you can challenge the criticism while *at the same time* treating the other person as an equal. These are some examples:

> 'I really must disagree with you. The responsibility for that particular task was not mine but anyway, you're obviously disappointed so let's talk it though and find out what happened . . . '

> 'I'm really taken aback. You are quite wrong to say that. I am never disloyal to my friends. What on earth has given you that impression?'

> 'That criticism is completely unjustified and hurtful. I put an enormous amount of effort into this evening and was never 'half-hearted' as you accuse me of being. Please can we talk about this without you attacking me?'

In each example, the door is left open for the interaction to continue but without declaring war!

A further problem presents itself on those occasions when the criticism is preceded by 'always' – or 'never' – because we are not sure whether to agree or to disagree. Whether a criticism comes in the form of an outright attack or hidden within a put-down, you may feel there is a grain of truth in it and yet you're not comfortable agreeing with the whole damning label. For example, you may have been inconsiderate to a friend last Wednesday but this does not mean you are *completely* selfish; you may have been short-tempered with your child going to school but you are not *always* grumpy; you choose not to go to the pub with your colleagues but this does not mean you are *antisocial*.

Responding effectively to a criticism which is partly true means agreeing with the partial truth while refuting the label. Sorting out the particular from the general helps you to feel more equal in relation to criticism. In other words, instead of being caught out and defensive, you can start to listen to what is being said, sift through it, see what is true, partly true or not true at all.

Put-downs One final dimension of criticism is how to handle put-downs which are made trickier by their very nature: instead of a direct comment or label for you to focus on, put-downs are very slippery. The criticism is implicit rather than explicit and comes in the form of veiled comments, innuendoes, pauses in speech, gestures or even facial expressions. You sense something unpleasant but cannot put your finger on exactly what.

The time lapse already described between emotional reaction and response is very pertinent to the delay in reaction to hearing a put-down. Perhaps you do not register at the time but then wake up in the middle of the night, thinking 'What the hell did she mean?' Even if you *do* register that you are angry or hurt by a comment and venture to say so, you're met with retorts of 'You're imagining it', or 'Why do you have to take everything so seriously/personally?' or 'The trouble with you is you've got no sense of humour!'

These comments end up effectively as double put-downs. They hook into secret anxieties that you really are over-sensitive, that your feelings are bizarre, that you are over-serious and that you do not have the intelligence to hear what you hear or see what you see. In other words it's your fault! Often in a class, participants are invited to contribute to a put-down parade: this has the effect of enabling people to see that they are *not* imagining things and they can draw reassurance and support from other to establish that they are not simply neurotic or paranoid.

Some people recommend that the best way to deal with put-downs is by a clever and cutting remark that will instantly demolish the speaker. Although there are some very brilliant and amusing examples often quoted and re-quoted, not all of us have that talent. I also believe that encouraging women to cap one put-down with another is more competitive than assertive so is less relevant in this context.

Using self-disclosure as the starting point, you can voice your feeling without accusation: this is the most effective way of holding your ground. Then whether you have a sense of humour or not, whether you are hyper-sensitive or not, even whether you are right or wrong ceases to matter. Start with your *own* response: if you (psychologically) keep your feet on the ground, you can ask the person for more clarity or to stop this behaviour if it is offensive or unkind.

Ingrid was German and had lived and worked in England for over ten years. During a meeting at work, she made a proposal about a particular project and this prompted a comment from one of her colleagues, Gary, who quietly but audibly muttered 'Ve haf vays of making you talk' in a mock German accent. At the time Ingrid said nothing: she didn't know how to respond. Racist comments of any kind tap into a vast reservoir of feeling from individual and collective experience and it easily feels too 'big' to deal with. In a training session, she asked to practise a way of handling it.

First she had to identify what she felt. In the practice role-play, she said she couldn't really believe what she was hearing: she had been so shocked. She tried out her new response 'I don't believe you said that, I feel really shocked' but then didn't know how to continue from there: in a group meeting, there would be an air of embarrassment and awkwardness and the one thing to avoid was getting into a fight in public with her colleague. This meant learning how to defuse the situation. She tried a second time:

(*Gary makes his comment.*)
Karen: (*looking directly at him*) I'm really quite shocked, Gary. And hurt actually.

She then immediately looked away from Gary to the others who in the meeting. Changing her tone of voice, she addressed the rest of the group:

'I've made a proposal and I'd like a response. Do any of you agree with my suggestion?'

After a few practices Karen learned to handle this comment with authority and dignity, much to the delighted applause of everyone in the workshop.

Whether criticism is valid or invalid or a put-down, you will probably recognise that some areas are much more difficult to handle than others. And there are some which we would prefer not to mention at all. These are what I call *crumple-buttons*. This term describes those chinks in our defensive armour where each of us is most vulnerable. We all have them: words or phrases which are so highly sensitive that the mere mention has the effect of making you crumple instantly inside. You may feel utterly defeated, or hurt, or you fly off the handle: it may be a reference to your appearance and general manner; your hair, weight, dress sense, breast size or accent. It may be a reference to your background: class, race, education, accent, talents, qualifications. If may be a comment on a particular area of competence: as a mother, a lover, as a cook, an intellectual, a driver. It may be a specific word: such as selfish, over-bearing, hard, stupid, aggressive or tight. It may even be some area of sensitivity that nobody has actually voiced to you but you are terrified they might!

Whatever the word or phrase, you will recognise its impact. It does not matter if the same word or phrase leaves everyone else unmoved. They may not make *sense* but notice your own vulnerable areas.

One way of learning to handle crumple-buttons assertively is by making them a little less sensitive. The following exercise is specifically designed to reduce this sensitivity. I often use it in training but it can be done at home with a friend.

First of all, write down two lists; one of valid criticism – that is, things that you know to be true about yourself – and a second list of invalid criticism: labels or epithets which really do not apply to you. Don't fall into the temptation of making everything stick as this will hinder you making your list of invalid criticisms. You may believe that there is nothing that is not true at *some* time but it is important to persevere: make use of adjectives like dishonest, immoral, dirty, or personally inappropriate words like domineering, if you know you are very timid or lazy when you know you work very hard.

When you have written your *two* lists, with up to ten words in each, check and see which are your crumple-buttons. Put an asterisk by each one. When you and your friend have your lists ready, exchange lists, sit facing each other and proceed as follows (I'll give the two women the names Mary and Jane): Mary will alternate valid and invalid criticisms from Jane's list.

> *Mary:* Jane, you're so selfish.
> *Jane:* Yes, I am selfish. It's important to consider my own needs at times.

It is essential to include the actual word – to say 'Yes, I am *selfish*' not just 'Yes, I know I am'. In this way you desensitise the actual word or phrase.

Mary gives feedback on how Jane is coming across: on her gestures, her eye contact, her voice, her tone. It is important not to convey apology or defensiveness. They keep repeating the phrase in the same way until both Mary and Jane agree that Jane's reply and manner are assertive.

Then they proceed to a criticism somewhere on the invalid list.

> *Mary:* Jane, I think you're insensitive.
> *Jane:* That's quite untrue, I'm really shocked by that. I'm actually an extremely sensitive person.

It is important that Jane's voice expresses conviction and that she looks at Mary with a steady gaze as she rejects the invalid criticism. It is no good using the words with an apologetic tone or smile. Then Mary goes back to one of Jane's list of valid criticisms. This continues right through to the end of both lists, after which Mary and Jane swap roles and repeat the process with Mary in the 'hot seat'.

This exercise needs about thirty minutes to do effectively (about fifteen minutes each, maybe a little longer). It may take a while to rid oneself of a lifetime's sensitivity but it really does help to take these criticisms out of the psychological closet and, by sharing them with someone else, the words become less 'loaded' and easier to handle. It is a valuable way of illuminating people's reactions to criticism and also of identifying the source of much of the resentment and helplessness attached to some of these words.

Once you gain a little confidence in walking through the minefield of your relationship to criticism, you can begin to take more risks. This means you can even invite criticism when you think someone is trying to tell you something that may be useful feedback. Here you can use the skill of *negative enquiry*. This helps you take the initiative: you ask if there is something critical the other person would like to say to you.

Negative enquiry helps you to prompt criticism either to learn from the information if your critic's intention is to be con-structive or, on the other hand, to expose it as manipulative or vicious and then disregard it. If it is constructive, you can give the other person an opportunity to express honestly what they feel which will help to improve communication between you. You are then able to invite and receive criticism from a position of equality rather than disadvantage. Here are some examples:

Have I behaved insensitively to you?

I'd like to know how satisfied you are with the quality of my work

Do you feel intimidated by me?

Do you think I could have been more supportive?

Do you resent me being successful?

Do you feel rejected by my refusal?

Are you disappointed with the way things have turned out between us?

If you ever feel pushed by me into doing things you don't want, you must say so.

Are you angry that I'm late?

Are you worried that I might let you down?

You can also use negative assertion and negative enquiry

together. This is a very powerful way of enabling someone to feel secure enough to express feelings to you that they may find difficult. It also helps you feel secure enough to listen to what is being said. You will not necessarily like what you hear but at least it can be said directly and there is a chance that the way will be open to a frank and truthful exchange of feelings between you. Here are some examples of how both techniques could be used together:

> I find it difficult to handle the question of money. *(negative assertion)* Do you think I'm too aggressive about it? *(negative enquiry)*
>
> I've been very preoccupied lately. *(negative assertion)* Have you been feeling neglected? *(negative enquiry)*
>
> I talk a lot when I'm anxious. *(negative assertion)* Do you get irritated? *(negative enquiry)*
>
> I know I'm inconsistent. *(negative assertion)* Does it drive you up the wall? *(negative enquiry)*
>
> I'm very inquisitive. *(negative assertion)* Do you mind my asking you so many questions? *(negative enquiry)*
>
> I know I feel things very intensely *(negative assertion)* Does it bother you? *(negative enquiry)*

If you use the combined skills of negative assertion and negative enquiry, you'll find that people do not think any the less of you for acknowledging your faults and mistakes. On the contrary this kind of approach can generate a lot of relief all round: because you are inviting criticism, it puts you in a much stronger position to handle it. You choose the moment so you are not caught off your guard. Instead of responding defensively you can relax, breathe and listen. Once you've listened, you can then sort through what is valuable to you and what is not.

Choose your time wisely to ask the other person. You cannot expect a considered response if you pounce on someone just as they are rushing to a meeting or totally preoccupied with something else or once they are already in mid-delivery of a general stream of abuse about you. You need a few minutes of privacy and calm and probably you'll need to reassure the other person you really want to listen to their reply: everyone, after all, finds criticism hard to handle.

The more often you survive hearing something you do not like about yourself, the easier it will be to deal with criticism – both invalid and valid – when they occur unexpectedly. The ability to use these skills will stem from the strength of your own self-esteem. With practice you can hear the criticism without sinking into the 'poor me' Dulcie pattern or rising to the 'Who? Me?' Agnes reaction.

The crucial difference in how you respond will have a lot to do with how you handle your own internal critic. Many of us suffer from listening to the endless critical ramblings of an internal voice which is much more damning than anything we hear from the outside. With or without the help from others, our internal critic can condemn us to the psychic stocks where we sit, waiting passively for confirmation of our low self-worth. Instead of feeling stuck in that position, it is possible to get up and walk away: these skills help us do this.

It is possible to use criticism wisely: that is, to listen and *weigh up* what is said. There is no need to rush around in a panic, making desperate and futile attempts to achieve a complete personality make-over. Nor, on the other hand, do we need to block our ears completely to what others say. We do not live in a vacuum and other people's perceptions and comments, precisely because they come from outside us, can be illuminating and helpful. This, after all, is part of the purpose of interaction with other human beings: to exchange ideas and perceptions and learn from each other. I have come to value enormously the observations of others who often challenge and surprise me and make me reassess my own assumptions.

We started this chapter looking at the common experience of criticism as rejection. When being criticised means being bad and unlovable, we feel helpless in the face of it. When criticism is an exchange, however, it is not the same. We don't have to take on board everything that everyone says: we can consider and contest it. If we disagree, it doesn't have to be a battle in which there is a winner and loser.

When you can assertively disagree at the time, your boundaries are strengthened and you become more flexible. Does the criticism fit? Does it worry you? Rather than feeling helpless, you learn that it is not the essential *you* that is wrong. Instead of feeling unloved, you can begin to view criticism as a gesture of regard rather than attack. You can understand that criticism need not stem from someone's low opinion of you: on the contrary, it can stem from respect or compassion, from a wish to reach out and make contact, from a desire to improve communication and deepen understanding. Criticism can provide a demonstration of someone's clear and loving regard for you as a person in your own right. It can be empowering and enriching to hear and accept a criticism clearly and cleanly. In fact, you may be about to discover that criticism can be a *gift*.

Following on

1. Make a list of your own crumple-buttons and try the exercise described in the chapter between Mary and Jane.

2. Just in case you get too immersed in the negatives, give yourself a lift: write down a list of ten positive qualities about yourself. Try not to use words like 'good' but be specific. For example, instead of a good mother use a specific word like loving, patient or affectionate; instead of a good teacher use competent, clear or sympathetic: and instead of a good friend – use loyal, humorous or understanding.

3. Consider whether you have done or said anything which you suspect upset someone. Is there a general aspect of your behaviour which you think irritates or disappoints or angers someone else? Write down the behaviour and who you feel is affected by it. Write down what you would say to this person if you were to use the skills of negative assertion and negative enquiry.

14

How to Handle Criticism: As the Critic

Learning to handle criticism on the receiving end will give you a much better idea of what makes it possible for any criticism to be heard: this, in turn, will help to improve your ability when it comes to giving criticism to others when you either need to or want to. The problem most of us face is distinguishing between challenge and confrontation. The latter is associated with an aggressive encounter where either winning or losing are the only two outcomes: consequently, those of us who do not enjoy confrontation try to avoid it.

Every single one of us, at some time in our lives, is faced with situations which present us with a dilemma: how do I express difficult feelings in a way which allows the other person to hear what I am saying without them feeling hurt or attacked or rejected? How can I avoid getting into a fight which risks causing unpleasant and lasting repercussions?

We first need to understand why some feelings are regarded as difficult. Difficult feelings usually refer to those that are labelled as negative: annoyance, hurt, irritation, anxiety or embarrassment for example. Second, precisely *because* we find such feelings difficult to communicate, we find ways of not doing so with the result that, if and when we do decide to speak, we will have acquired a backlog of 'unspoken' feelings which make clear and assertive communication an even tougher proposition.

Consider what happens now. How do you express what you consider to be a legitimate grievance or problem you have with someone? How do you express resentment or hurt or disappointment? How do you go about criticising someone else, whether in a personal or professional context? Do you tend to avoid direct confrontation altogether like Dulcie but moan to everyone else *about* the person concerned? Do you find yourself going in like Agnes, with a sledgehammer and send the other person reeling away with an ear too thick to hear precisely what you are saying under the general tirade? Or like Ivy, do you make snide remarks, communicating your resentment indirectly, leaving the other person feeling put-down and vaguely guilty but without knowing exactly what your point is? All these approaches have one thing in common: the message will not be heard either because you have actually said nothing, or what you have said has been delivered in such a way that antagonises the other person or because you leave them confused and uncertain as to the message you were trying to get across.

Look more closely at a typical passive, indirect and aggressive approach as Dulcie, Ivy or Agnes might use.

Dulcie is a nervous passenger. Her husband fancies himself as a second Jeremy Clarkson; he is a fast and aggressive driver and, what's more, prides himself on his driving ability. Every time they go out in the car together, Dulcie holds on tight to the edge of her seat, feeling tense and uncomfortable.

Dulcie: Why don't you slow down a bit?
Husband: There's nothing to be frightened of. I know exactly what I'm doing.
Dulcie: Do we have to go this fast?
Husband: It's quite safe, don't worry.
Dulcie: Why don't you slow down?
Husband: Look, it's all right. *(Impatiently)* I do know what I'm doing, you know. *(Accelerating)*
Dulcie: Yes but . . .
Husband: Look, close your eyes or something. Leave the driving to me. *(He accelerates to overtake: Dulcie is too terrified to say any more.)*

Ivy is under a lot of pressure at work and finds it difficult to cope with the chores at home. She wants to ask her son to help her clear the kitchen.

(*Ivy comes into the kitchen.*)

Ivy: (*in a critical tone*) Look at this mess.

Son: (*on the defensive*) For heaven's sake, stop moaning.

Ivy: (*sounding pained*) Well, I'm always the one who has to clear it up.

Son: Nag, nag, nag.

Ivy: Don't start being cheeky. If you were more considerate in the first place, I wouldn't have to keep on at you. (*Son gets up and walks to the door.*)

Ivy: Where do you think you're going?

Son: Out. I can't stand this place any more. (*Goes out and slams the door. Ivy is left feeling defeated, resentful and bursts into tears.*)

Agnes comes home from work at 7 o'clock to find her two children still not ready for bed . . . again. This has happened several times and she hasn't said anything because she couldn't be bothered to have another argument after dealing with aggravation at work all day. She tells herself that this has gone far enough and that she has every right to complain to the au pair.

In her mind, Agnes builds up an array of legitimate grievances against her: she is paid well to do her job, she has a lovely room and Agnes has *always* been more than generous to her. Agnes makes a decision to tackle her before she goes to work the next morning.

Next morning, they are all in the kitchen, the children playing and Livia, the au pair, is preparing their breakfast.

Agnes: By the way, Livia, I just wanted to say that I did not appreciate coming home last night and finding that the kids were still not ready for bed. You are paid to do a job and I really have enough on my plate without having to chase you as well. (*She glares at Livia*) Do you understand?

Livia: (*apologetically*) I'm sorry. I just forget about the time . . .

Agnes: (*raising her voice a little*) That is no excuse, Livia. You are paid to do a job and I'd like you to do it. I don't want to have to *tell* you to do it.

Livia: I said I'm sorry.

Agnes: (*feeling dominant now and wanting to reinforce her position*) And while we're talking about it, I also noticed Adam's trainers were left out in the garden last week . . . what *are* you doing now? He doesn't eat that kind of cereal. You should know that by now.

Livia: (*Feeling defensive, her voice slightly louder*) There seems to be nothing I can get right this morning!

Agnes: Don't be sarcastic with me. Just remember your position here. (*Sees the clock and realises the time*) I've got to go. (*Goes to kiss the children goodbye*)

Each of these scenarios illustrates a particular problem about giving criticism which we will look at in turn. First, consider the common denominator: a build-up of feelings. Each scenario represents the latest in a sequence of similar occurrences when most of the time we have said nothing or, if we have tried to get some words out, they have probably been vague, understated and indirect.

What makes us hold back? Why is it that we let things build up to a point when feelings, which may have been minor in the beginning, eventually take on major proportions?

As we have seen, the first obstacle is that what we are feeling is judged to be negative and since the whole area of criticism has acquired such negative connotations, a whole host of reasons for *not* saying anything come into our minds.

We find all sorts of plausible justifications for holding back and keeping quiet. Do you recognise any of the following 'good reasons' for not expressing your feelings?

It's not their fault: 'He's just in a bad mood'; 'She didn't know what she was doing'; 'He can't help it'; 'She's going through a bad patch.'

It's not important: 'It's too trivial'; 'I'm being over-sensitive'; 'It's just not worth making a fuss about'; 'Nobody's perfect'; 'Who am I to judge?'

The need to protect someone else: 'She's over-tired/too sensitive, too ill, too young/too old'; 'He couldn't take it'; 'She'd feel terribly offended if I told her how I felt'; 'He'd be devastated if I said anything.'

There's no point: 'He'll never listen'; 'She won't change'; 'It won't make any difference'; 'Some things you just have to put up with.'

Fear of the consequences: 'Maybe he'll criticise *me*/maybe she'll lose her temper'; 'He could get really nasty'; 'How will she react if I say something *now*, after all this time?'; 'I don't want to rock the boat'; 'I may be fired'; 'He'll leave me'; 'It'll open a can of worms.'

Fear of making a bad impression: 'If I'm wrong, I'll look stupid; 'I don't want to make a fool of myself'; 'I don't want to look petty/unreasonable/ungrateful.'

It's not the right moment: 'We're all having such a lovely time . . . it *is* Christmas after all'; 'I'm in someone else's home'; 'it's the middle of dinner'; 'I can't make a scene in front of all these people'; 'I can't bring it up now'; 'It's too late to say anything.'

What is interesting about these excuses and rationalisations is that most of them revolve around the issue of relative power. If you look again at what we say to ourselves in justification for doing nothing, you'll see the phrases cluster around one of the two aspects of perpendicular power. Because of our past experience of criticism, reviewed in the previous chapter, we associate criticism with handing down something from on high: in other words from someone on a higher rung on the ladder to someone on a lower one. When we identify with the higher position, our fears tend to be focus on the aggressive and hurtful power of criticism, regarding it as a weapon which can cause harm: hence those concerns about others' inability for one reason or another to cope with its damaging effects.

On the other hand, if we identify with the lower position on the ladder in regard to the other person, then our concerns revolve around our own ability to survive. We fear being wrong or made to look stupid; we fear retaliation and unpleasant consequences of daring to speak 'above our station'.

Whichever position we're in, we anticipate that criticism will have negative repercussions. The problem is that when we shy away from saying something important to us, the resentment and the hurt are only temporarily shelved. Instead of speaking up while our grievance is still small and manageable, we store it up. Eventually the pressure builds up and we explode, often at someone who is close to us who either doesn't deserve it at all or, if the criticism is legitimate, they become a target for all the unexpressed frustration we've been carrying around towards everyone and everything else. Suddenly, whether or not someone volunteers to make you a cup of tea becomes a life and death issue. A scratch on the paintwork, the top left off the toothpaste tube, your hair moved slightly out of place, a flippant remark, one abrupt email: some tiny event can assume huge significance.

Stored-up resentment distorts what we feel and what we say. We start with an attempt to make a simple statement or request but, in the confusion, things get out of control: we lose our grip and we grab at anything that we know will hit home to help regain some control of the exchange. A small remark escalates to pitched battle with both people fighting it out, establishing the dynamic of an *arena*. Here is a sample piece of dialogue you might hear in such an arena:

A: That was a stupid thing to do.

B: I wouldn't have done it if you hadn't suggested the idea in the first place.

A: I suggested it because you didn't have any ideas of your own, as usual.

B: Well, the last time I had an idea, you never stopped moaning.

A: Me moan? You didn't stop whining about how crowded it was when we went to the show last week. You never do anything but whine or complain. You're such a drag.

B: Well, you're not exactly hot stuff yourself. Life with you is about as exciting as a used tea bag.

A: Oh, so you're bored, are you? Well, let me tell you something, sweetheart, if it weren't for you, I could have made something of my life . . .

Arenas are appropriate for contests: you view the other person as an opponent and one of you has to win. Arenas are fine for having a good fight which can be exhilarating and stimulating: they can also be exhausting and a waste of time. The intense feelings will also distort the listener's ability to hear what you are saying. In fact, neither person is saying anything much at all: just an exchange of general vindictiveness. There are many fragments of past hurts and frustrations flying around which make easy weapons but any potential clarity gets lost in the exchange of missiles. If it is clear communication that you want, if you want a dialogue, if you want the other person to *listen* to you and understand you, then you will need to establish the more civilised atmosphere of a *forum*. Then you can proceed in a way which promotes mutual self-respect. You can say your piece and also listen to the other person. The aim, as ever with assertiveness, is clear, equal and effective communication.

How can you establish the climate of a forum to express negative feelings assertively? If you want to criticise in a way that will encourage the other person to hear what you are saying, without scoring points or acting as a self-appointed judge, you'll find the following guidelines helpful.

The very first challenge is to ask yourself the following three questions: *only* when you have clear answers to these questions need you bother to go any further. With aggression so common-place and acceptable in our culture, it's as if the default position is set for the arena: without these answers considered before-hand, you won't be able establish the alternative of the forum.

- What is happening?
- What do I feel about what is happening?
- What do I want to be different?

This little bit of homework will make an enormous difference to the outcome of your conversation.

What is happening?

What is the person doing or not doing that you are unhappy with? This may seem obvious but you'd be surprised how often general resentment obscures the specific behaviour we would like the person to change. Constructive criticism is not the same as a general pronouncement about right or wrong. Simply saying 'you're boring', 'immature', 'stupid' or 'selfish' is not helpful. Similarly, it is unlikely to help if you start giving unsolicited advice about how other people *should* behave. However well-intentioned they are, statements like 'You should be more under-standing', 'You shouldn't be so sensitive' or 'You should be more sociable' sound judgemental and are again likely to provoke a defensive reaction.

What do you feel about what is happening?

Identifying what you feel in relation to the specific behaviour will not come automatically. Once you work your way through the habit of blame, you can learn to detect specific feelings of hurt, annoyance, anxiety. Consider the difference between these two statements:

'You're such a bully, always trying to belittle me in front of others'

and

'I feel belittled when you imply in front of others that I don't know what I'm talking about.'

The first labels the person and suggests that the effect is intentional. The second simply expresses how you *feel* about the behaviour and the effect it has on you.

What do you want to be different?

You may wish for a total transformation but this won't happen. To find the answer to this third question, you have to focus on one specific change. Once again this constitutes a personal challenge. We become lulled into thinking others should know what we want so it goes against the grain to have to spell it out. If you embark on this process of giving criticism, *without* knowing what you want or having any specific focus of what you would like the other person to do instead, then you might as well forget about trying to handle it assertively. It is this *one* feature of assertive criticism that distinguishes it from aggressive criticism: the specific request for change makes it constructive.

Being specific is crucial because the responsibility for the transaction is yours, not the other person's. In the same way that acknowledging your feelings without blaming the other for causing them means you take responsibility for your own feelings, specifying the change you want in someone's behaviour is your responsibility too. It is not up to the other person to read your mind or work out what might satisfy you. Do not assume that the other person is inside your head and will know automatically. Stating the change you would like clearly and directly is what distinguishes constructive criticism from an attack or complaint. Constructive criticism is an equal interaction and most individuals are willing to respond if they are given a clear and specific instruction.

So how might have a consideration of those three questions altered the approaches used by Ivy, Dulcie and Agnes?

Ivy considers the questions.
What is happening?
Her son is not doing his share of household chores.

What does Ivy feel about this?
Fed up, frustrated, resentful

What does she want to be different?
She wants him to help but this will not be enough to communicate. It takes a while but Ivy eventually settles on one chore: cleaning up the kitchen at the end of every day.

Ivy: I want to talk to you about helping me in the house.
Son: Oh no, not that again.

Ivy: *(firmly)* I know we've been through it before but I wasn't very clear. Now I'd like to talk to you calmly about it.

Son: What do you want? *(Grudgingly but listening)*

Ivy: I've been under a lot of pressure lately and I just can't cope any more. I get resentful *(feeling)* when you leave all the clearing up to me. *(Current behaviour)* I'd like you to clear the kitchen once a day. *(Specific change)*

Son: It's not my job to do it.

Ivy: I know it's not your favourite occupation but I need the help. I'd like you to clear the kitchen once a day.

Son: I can't do it every day. I've got my exams . . .

Ivy: I know you have commitments but you're old enough to take some responsibility: all I am asking you to do is one task and while you live here, I'd like you to agree to that.

Dulcie considers her situation.

What is happening now?

Her husband is driving too fast for her comfort.

What does she feel?

Anxious, but after consideration, she realises it's closer to terror.

What does she want to be different?

She wants him to drive more slowly when she is a passenger.

Dulcie sensibly approaches her husband when they're at home, rather than trying to do it while they're in the car and she's already scared stiff!

Dulcie: Jack, I want you to listen to me. I feel so anxious when you drive that I'm a wreck by the end of the journey. I would like you to drive more slowly when I'm in the car. *(Specific change)*

Husband: I know what I'm doing.

Dulcie: I realise you know what you're doing, but when you drive so fast *(current behaviour)* it terrifies me *(feelings)*.

Husband (looks a bit surprised): I didn't realise you were that frightened.

Dulcie: Well, I didn't say so clearly before, I know that, but I just can't stand it. I know it sounds silly but that's what I feel. All I'm asking you to do is drive more slowly when we're in the car together.

Agnes' questions and answers:

What is happening?
Livia is not getting the children ready for bed on time.

What does she feel?
Irritated and frustrated.

What does she want to change?
She wants the children ready for bed when she gets home from work.

 Agnes' particular problem challenges her to reconsider her perspective on power. Giving her employee legitimate criticism means she has to add a specific request, something she failed to do in the original scenario. She didn't because she thought it was obvious. Like many others who offer legitimate criticism in this way, especially to sub-ordinates, she didn't give a thought to this third step. What seems important instead is to reinforce one's position and status: in other words, we use the leverage of the perpendicular power with which we find ourselves to give weight to our criticism. As a result, equality never figures and the usual format consists of:

- An overall complaint, rather than addressing specific behaviour
- The tendency to pile on one thing after another (while you've got the upper hand)
- Absence of a specific request for change (more of a generalised allusion to the need for improvement)

Sometimes there is a final reprimand to the other person for actually responding to your aggressive criticism ('Don't you get angry with me' and so on).

161

With some reflection, Agnes decides to try and handle her perpendicular power (as an employer over an employee) in balance with a respect or consideration for Livia as a human being (and therefore as equals)

Agnes: Livia, I'd like a word with you.

Livia: What is it?

Agnes: I was very annoyed (*feelings*) when I got back last night to find the children still not ready for bed (*current behaviour*). I'd really like you to make sure they are ready when I come home (*specific change*). It's important to me.

Livia: I am sorry. I took them to the park and forgot all about the time.

Agnes: Well, it's happened before but I haven't said anything. We're happy with your work but I must insist that you come back earlier or do whatever you have to do to make sure they are ready for bed by seven.

Livia: Of course, I'm sorry

Agnes: Don't worry. I'm glad we've been able to talk about it. (*Time to close*) I've got to go. (*Goes to kiss the children goodbye*).

These three dialogues show how each woman has expressed her feelings, described the behaviour and asked for a specific change. The guidelines outlined above allow you to establish a forum and to regard the other person as an equal, even if you are higher or lower than them on a hierarchical scale.

The ladder or perpendicular power is so all-pervasive and engrained in our psyches that criticism (both receiving and giving) appears always to be associated with this inequality. If we are uncertain about how to criticise, we tend to revert habitually to a conviction that we need to gain or regain the 'upper' hand.

Even where there is no actual differentiation in power we try and achieve this by using labels, which imply some kind of moral superiority on the part of the critic. None of us likes to be told we are immature or lazy or inconsiderate or dull. It rankles and the immediate reaction will be defensive. Expressing your feelings allows a statement *without* putting yourself in a position of dubious authority. A straight statement of feeling does not come across as superior so there is more chance that the other person will listen to what you are saying.

These steps also help to avoid the trap of blame: in a forum we can use the opportunity to inform the other person how we feel in response to their actions. This is a whole new approach because we tend to assume that we know exactly what the intentions were behind someone's behaviour. When we say, for example, 'How could she have done that? She must have known it would upset me', or 'He obviously did it to annoy me', we are interpreting from our personal perspective. Although we *may* be right, there is always the chance that we can be mistaken when we use our own behaviour as the sole reference point for interpreting everyone else's actions and intentions. It may just be that the other person was not deliberately trying to hurt or attack: informing them of the effect of their behaviour can therefore come as a revelation to them.

People do not always know how deeply a remark can hurt or offend you or how important something is. They do not always know what you need or want. Furthermore, if you have successfully hidden your feelings in the past, it can come as quite a shock to the person to know what your true feelings were and still are. Rather than jumping straight in and accusing, you can give them the benefit of the doubt. If, after you have done this and knowing quite clearly what offends or hurts you, they repeat the behaviour, then you are dealing with a new situation. But first, try stating how you feel about the person's behaviour and letting them know *honestly* how it affects you, without assuming it was a deliberate injury: give the possibility of an *exchange of communication* a chance.

Next we will look at how to put all of this into practice.

15

The Art of Assertive Confrontation

What follows is the entire sequence of assertive confrontation. It may strike you as a bit formal but there are good reasons for this. There are so many ways in which a process like this can go wrong and although it is actually very simple, we need safeguards until we become accustomed to how it all fits together. The following guidelines act like stepping stones to help us move across turbulent waters without losing our balance.

Before we embark on this process – based on face-to-face conversations – it is relevant to return to the issues raised by using other forms of communication. Most people believe that email or text is the only way to communicate because of convenience. However these methods bring three problems to the fore in terms of assertive interaction. First, clarity is diminished, as I explained in Chapter 7: we cannot be completely accurate in our perceptions of what is being written or in the recipient's response because we are unable to pick up the totality of a message, including all the signals conveyed with our body language.

Second, it is tempting to opt for sending an email if we feel in any way anxious about what we want to say and, as there *is* so much anxiety about giving criticism, it is understandable that email offers a more remote and therefore easier way to deliver what you want to say than having to face someone directly. Directness takes more courage and it means taking responsibility but this is what being assertive involves: treating the other person as an equal human being.

The third problem is that emails and texts provide a very convenient way of avoiding having to deal with the repercussions of our communications. When institutions inform employees by email that they have been fired or when an individual uses email to break off a relationship, it is easy to see how convenient remote communication can be in this regard.

In assertive terms, this behaviour belongs to the category of indirect aggression whereby you deliver your (often hurtful) message and then make sure you are unavailable to deal with the response. By not dealing with the consequences of your actions, you manage to avoid any responsibility.

For these reasons, the following process assumes a willingness to deal directly with the person concerned. There is no disputing that it is difficult but this is the reason for the following guidelines.

1. Setting the scene

Choose your time and place prudently. If you do, you will be in a much better position to express yourself clearly. If you want to confront someone, don't wait until it happens again. It's always tempting to kid yourself that *next* time you'll be better equipped to speak up. When the next time comes around, your feelings will be just as strong, maybe stronger, and you risk making a mess of it again: either you'll bottle up everything once more or go over the top. So if you feel at all uncertain about confrontation and even if you don't, give yourself an easier start by setting up the time in advance. A simple statement is enough: 'I'd like to make some time to talk to you about something important'. Be realistic about the time you need: five minutes, an hour, whatever you want. The other person is then prepared and so are you. This way you will have the opportunity to establish the climate of a forum rather than an arena.

It will feel very odd doing this especially if the other person is a friend or family member. It will seem formal and unlike how you would normally behave which is precisely the point. You are going to try and do something which you do *not* normally do – confront the other person assertively – and to give yourself the best chance, you need to establish a time and space outside of any normal activities. This means avoiding tacking your dialogue onto any other activity like watching television or perusing emails, in the middle of a meal, a party, making love or during a meeting at work. Arrange time out of everything else both for your sake and that of the other person.

2. Self-disclosure

The time has come: you've made the arrangements and someone is there waiting for you to speak. Whether this is your partner, employee, neighbour or friend, the wisest way to start is with an expression of how you feel. Right now. How do you feel beginning this conversation? It's a safe bet that there will be feelings of awkwardness, anxiety, embarrassment, dread or nervousness: this is entirely normal and natural and if you pretend at the outset that you are *not* feeling any of these things, you are likely to start off on the wrong foot. It doesn't require an intense focus on your fears – just a simple statement – and then you begin and go on to the next steps. For example:

> 'I'm feeling really silly about this but there is something important I want to talk about . . . '
> 'I don't find this easy but I want to discuss something with you . . . '

The idea is to be truthful.

3.

Then you move to the answers to your three questions developed in the previous chapter and proceed with these three clear points.

- Describe the other person's behaviour
- Express your feelings in response to this behaviour
- Request the specific change

4. Ask for a response

At this stage, bearing in mind this is intended as an equal inter-action, pause and ask the other person to respond. This may be to clarify understanding or check their reaction and under-standing of your request.

5. Closure

At this point there is a great danger of getting stuck. This whole process has been initiated by you: you have opened the door, as it were, to this dialogue and now you must take responsibility for closing it. This helps both you and the other person. Your own anxiety will probably be high: this is not an easy conversation for either of you (which is why you have spent so long avoiding it). This means that it is wiser to bring it to an end. Depending on who it is, you can call the meeting to an end, get up from your chair, leave the room or if you are going to stay in the person's company, you can signal closure by switching the topic of conversation to something completely neutral.

This also helps the other person. It is likely that they have been unaware of what you've been feeling and they may be surprised, startled, even uncomfortable. We are all sensitive when it comes to criticism and, even if you have handled it assertively, others too have past responses and need a bit of space – physical or psychological – to let the information in.

You'll find this point invaluable to remember whenever you have summoned up your courage to challenge someone in any circumstances. It allows you, as speaker, to deal with the emotional fallout from having spoken out: even if it's visible to nobody else, we all tend to feel residual symptoms of anxiety for a while after the event. Equally important is that, by ending the meeting or changing the subject, you help shift any lingering tension and awkwardness between the two of you: you both then have the opportunity to let the impact of what's been said sink in.

Consequences

Occasionally you may have to reinforce your request for change by spelling out the consequences. This does not have to be a 'do-it-or-else' threat. In fact you may never have actually to spell out the consequences in so many words but it is important that you have worked out for *yourself* what the consequences are. These can be positive or negative consequences. It may be easier to express the positive consequences: what will happen if the other person co-operates. Ivy, for example, might feel that a positive consequence of her son's help would be that she would feel less harassed and more agreeable towards him: the atmosphere in the house would be better. Dulcie might add that she would stop being so tense and irritable and enjoy going out with her husband more. Agnes might have said that she would be more able to enjoy the short time she had with her children in the evening.

The negative consequences are more difficult to articulate without being threatening but sometimes, they have to be considered:

Emma worked for a large internet provider as a supervisor in the sales department. She had been aware for a while that one of the staff, Luis, was letting through too many mistakes in the advertising copy: there were spelling mistakes, the quoted prices were sometimes too high and key words were not checked.

She had returned his copy a couple of times and – by email – tried to suggest that he checked his copy but there had been no improvement. After learning these skills, she arranged to see him when he came in for a meeting.

Emma: Luis, look, this isn't easy but I've got to say that you need to check your copy.

Luis: I do check it.

Emma: Well, it really isn't good enough.

Luis: Maybe my English isn't perfect but surely it's OK, isn't it?

Emma: I want you to check your copy and spelling, prices and key words in particular. Do you understand?

Luis: Of course I understand. I just think you're making a bit of fuss.

Emma: I'm not. I don't want to have to chase you all the time and we don't meet often but I want to know if you will agree to be more thorough in checking your copy.

Luis: I think it is good enough.

Emma: This is quite serious, Luis. If you don't improve the quality of your work, I shall have to refer it to the Head of Department (*spelling out consequences*).

Luis (sighs): OK. I still think it's a lot of fuss about nothing.
Emma (gets up from her chair): Thanks for coming in, Luis. I'll see
    you later.

In a personal relationship, even though there are no clearly defined consequences as in a professional or contractual context, there are also occasions when we are confronted with difficult decisions. If your neighbour refuses to stop making your life hell, the only option eventually may be to move house; if your partner won't stop drinking heavily your ultimate decision may be to split up; if your friend will not stop lying to you, the only option may be to stop seeing her; if your boss refuses to pay you more money, you may have to find a new job. All these are major steps and ones which you may not want to take. But at least having realised this, you can look at what you will settle for at the moment.

If you have taken the trouble to express *exactly* how strongly you feel to the person concerned, you will still feel better because you are not secretly harbouring the resentment inside. Choosing to stay with a given situation despite its limitations is not the same as feeling a helpless victim of circumstance. Obviously these decisions are very personal: we all have our individual limits. However often we look from the outside at someone else's plight and say 'I don't know s/he puts up with it, I'd have left ages ago', each person will take what they want and decide on their own limits. We move on if and when we are ready.

Be gentle with yourself and others: since we handle criticism so badly in our culture, we need to remain sensitive to the impact this sort of confrontation can have. Take another example. Nicole and Debbie are friends. Nicole is pleased to have Debbie to stay for a few weeks but it's niggled her for a while that Debbie hasn't contributed more to the housekeeping. She would have liked her to have bought a little food, taken her out to a meal, offered to pay for something, maybe contributed a couple of bottles of wine. However, Nicole has not actually *said* anything directly up until now.

Nicole: Debbie, I've been meaning to say this but I'm resentful about you never having paid for anything while you've been staying.

Debbie (shocked): You never mentioned money. I thought I was a guest.

Nicole: Well you are a guest, but you could have bought a bottle of wine or paid for something. (*Implied judgement 1*)

Debbie (hurt and defensive): You're saying I'm mean, aren't you? If you'd been staying with *me* . . .

Nicole: I'm not saying you're mean. And I take full responsibility for not saying anything clearly at the time. I should have sorted it out and been direct but I wasn't. I'm not surprised if you feel angry with me. (*Negative assertion 2*)

Debbie: Well, I am upset. And yes, I'm cross that you haven't said anything before. It doesn't say much for our friendship if you couldn't be honest with me.

Nicole: You're right. I accept that. I'm sorry.

Debbie: I could always find somewhere else to stay.

Nicole: Well, you don't have to for my sake. I love having you here, you're terrific company and you're been really supportive recently. All I want is for us to come to some arrangement that we both feel happy about. (*A little awkwardness hangs in the air.*)

Nicole: Are you OK if we leave it there? (*Debbie nods.*)

Nicole: Why don't we try the new curry place? I'm dying to hear how your meeting went today.

The key lies in the statements numbered 1 and 2. Number 1 is reproachful. Nicole is not taking responsibility for her own past lack of assertive behaviour but reproving Debbie instead. Number 2 is on the level and *equal*. She accepts responsibility and invites some criticism in return. This illustrates difference between assertive criticism and one-sided or aggressive criticism. The principle of equality remains throughout an assertive interaction: even if you are taking the initiative to confront, you are treating the other person as equal.

A word of caution: it is essential to discipline yourself to keep to one specific issue without trawling through the past. In any relationship which is long-standing, there is an inevitable history between you and the other person. Our memories function like archives which chronicle details of this history along with details of other relationships in the past. With remarkable accuracy we are able to recall incidents in detail along with our unspoken or half-spoken resentments and our unresolved battles. We remember unforgiven deeds and offensive remarks and keep them in the back of our minds: when we want to fuel current grievances and grudges, they come to the fore. One small occurrence can set us sifting through the backlog of a lifetime, particularly when we feel under threat ourselves, such as when we are being criticised or fear being rejected:

A: You accuse me of being jealous! What about that party when you made such a scene?

B: That was *years* ago!

A: That's not the point. You were terribly jealous when I was dancing with that man who'd just come back from America because his wife had walked out on him . . . .

X: To think that for so long I've put up with all your unkindness . . .

Y: What do you mean?

X: Do you remember when I was in hospital and you said you were too busy to come during the week to visit?

Y: That's going back a bit . . . and you said it was OK at the time, I seem to remember. You said you understood, that it didn't matter.

X: Well, it wasn't OK. It *did* matter!

When we've tried and failed several times to talk about delicate subjects with someone we are loath to go back over old ground and end up in the same mess. It is hard to remain in the present when you have a history with a family member, a partner or a longstanding friend. Consequently we hesitate to try again when it always seems to end up as a fight and we fail to achieve any break through. It can be managed alternatively by following these steps so that, although you are aware that there is old ground, you can make a decision to go forwards instead of backwards.

Although I have emphasised the importance of requesting a specific change, there are occasions when, after reflection, we can't really specify what we want, not because we're being lazy or chickening out but because the problem isn't that specific in itself. Frequently in relationships you notice some general change in the other person: you pick up odd signals or notice a change in someone's manner or behaviour and you're not sure why. You don't know what outcome you want because it needs an actual consultation with this individual to give you more information. In such cases, the answer to the third question can be simply a request for time to talk, an explanation or clarification about an issue to give you the information you need.

Even when someone is reluctant to face up to things, the process of assertive confrontation can be really helpful in initiating an uncomfortable discussion and opening a door that the other person would prefer to keep closed. Sarah's husband, Geoff, has Parkinson's disease. Over the past three years his mobility has deteriorated but he refuses to talk about it. She understands why, of course, but she wants to be able to talk openly and directly about what plans to make and she wants to do this with Geoff, not for him. She has tried to discuss this in the past but it always degenerates into a row, with accusations of interference (from him) and of self-centeredness (from her) leading to the usual impasse.

She first tells him she wants to set aside time to talk about something important to her. He is inevitably suspicious and uneasy but agrees. They decide to sit in the garden.

Sarah: Geoff, I want us to talk . . . about the future and your health.
Geoff: Oh, for God's sake, I thought that's what it would be about (*gets up to go*)
Sarah: Geoff, please don't walk away from me. I realise it's *your* illness but I can't stand not talking about it anymore. I can't stand it! (*Geoff turns round and stops*) It is breaking my heart to see what's happening to you and I need to have some idea of what you want and how we, yes, *we* are going to manage everything.
Geoff: I really don't want to do this.
Sarah: I know that. Of course I know that. But I want you to stop

turning everything inwards and at least *think* about how you can let me in a bit. You don't have to answer right now but I'd like to be able to talk to you and not have you shut up in your own head. Will you think about it?

Geoff (*stays silent a little while and then looks at her*): OK. I'll think about it (*his tone is softer now*)

Sarah: Thank you. (*Gets up*) I'm going to the supermarket: do you want anything?

This is enough for now: the door has been opened and, at times, that is all we can do.

From teaching these skills over the years I have distilled four common pitfalls regarding the whole process of assertive confrontation:

Avoid trying to change something you can't

When you consider your answer to the third question – what do I want to be different? – be realistic. You can ask for a change in behaviour but not if you are secretly wanting a complete remould of someone's basic personality. However much you want someone to change, a basic introvert is never going to be the life and soul of the party; some people are never going to be good cooks; others are born chaotic and untidy so expecting a complete makeover is only going to end in disappointment. Be realistic in what you are asking.

Avoid asking for more than one change at a time

Once you have the person's captive attention, you suddenly feel you're on a roll: while you're about it, it is tempting to mention this and that and then another thing! Before you know it, the other person is completely overwhelmed and, once someone's back is against the wall, the only way to respond is to come out fighting. Keep to one thing and one thing only: this is what any of us can take at any one time. I find that most people are willing to consider and probably agree to a request for a single change as long as that one change is both specific and clear.

Avoid post-mortems

When you check for understanding, this is supposed to be brief. First of all, (unlike yourself) the other person has not been pre-occupied with these issues for a very long time so is likely to be taken aback. If you ask how someone feels, they may reply 'nothing': they may need time to reflect and let it all sink in. Avoid probing too deeply at this stage as a way of displacing your own anxieties about whether they will still like you/ love you/ talk to you/ respect you: give the other person whatever space they need. You will simply have to survive the uncertainty and let go the need to control the outcome. This is why closure is so important.

If you don't discipline yourself to close the conversation, you will be tempted to pick over what you have said and question the other person's response: extensive analysis will only end up undermining the effort you have made.

Avoid being under the influence

Start with a clear mind. Do not attempt to achieve clear communication when you – or the other person – is under the influence of alcohol or any other substance. Bolstering your own courage is tempting when you are nervous but you need to be clear-headed: avoid trying to communicate over a drink or during a meal. Remember the point about setting the scene: if you want the optimum chance of making this a successful interaction, avoid trying to communicate in the middle of any other activity.

A final suggestion is to end on an upbeat note. This does not mean ingratiating yourself with the other person to make up for what you fear could be an adverse response to your criticism: 'Well, you know I like you really/please don't take any notice of what I've just been saying/it's really nothing/it's not important.' Nor is this about 'sugaring the pill' which only comes across as patronising and artificial. This suggestion means finding a positive and genuine statement to mark the end of the conversation, for example:

'I'm glad to have had this chance to talk to you'
'I'm relieved we've been able to clear the air'
'I'm grateful to you for listening'
'I've enjoyed being able to talk about these things with you'
 'I was so anxious about bringing this up . . . I feel much better
    for having got things out in the open'

If appropriate, you can add a positive statement about the
other person. In the conversation between Nicole and Debbie,
once Nicole had requested some new arrangement, she
reassured her friend that she enjoyed having her to stay. You can
find some remark to balance the interaction, some small positive
comment which shows you genuinely value the other person
and are not only seeing the negative.

This brings us to an equally important skill in the next chapter.

16

Giving and Receiving Compliments

Curiously enough, we encounter similar difficulties when handling appreciative comments. Self-censorship results in many opportunities that slip by without grasping the moment to say thank someone properly, to tell them how much they mean to us or how special they are in our lives. It seems a pity that so many of us wait until someone is dead before we make the time and effort to find the words to express how much we value them.

This difficulty can be traced back to our reluctance to be direct and to risk surviving a moment of awkwardness or embarrassment with another person. Consider your own approach: if you want to say something appreciative to someone, how do you go about it? Do you ignore it? Do you feel embarrassed giving a compliment and find yourself mumbling something almost inaudibly under your breath or saying something very general, like 'You're brilliant/awesome/fantastic/great' or 'love you' which makes a start in conveying a positive message but falls short and leaves the other person unsure about what exactly you mean?

Overcoming your own awkwardness can be the first hurdle:

Rita, a single parent and forthright woman who had no difficulty expressing her feelings in other ways, found it impossible to tell her teenage daughter that she was impressed by her hard work and achievement at school. She wanted to tell her but didn't know how.

> Both Rita and Angie were in the kitchen.
> Rita: (feeling surprisingly nervous) Angie, I want to say something but I feel really stupid.
> Angie: (somewhat alarmed) What on earth is it?
> Rita: (pauses to find the words) I just want to say how proud I am of you.

Angie: Oh, Mum.
Rita: No. I'm serious. I really am proud of what you've achieved
         at school. It hasn't been easy for you without your Dad
         around and you've just got on with it all.
Angie: Well, you've made me respect myself, Mum. It isn't all
         down to me. (*Rita's eyes fill with tears*) Oh, come here,
         Mum. (*Goes to give her a hug*)

An assertive expression of appreciation involves a little effort and refinement of what you want to say. Instead of using a vague word like 'good', it is a bonus when you can be more specific, as in these examples:

'That was a very difficult situation: you handled it very
    sensitively.'
'I admire your persistence.'
'I really value the time and trouble you take to make me feel
    comfortable.'
'You look stunning in that dress.'

Being on the receiving end A similar kind of embarrassment around compliments tends to make us respond less than graciously when on the receiving end. We dismiss what the other person says in a variety of ways. For instance, someone compliments you on something you're wearing and you quell their enthusiasm with a retort like 'What? *This* old thing?' or you look quite incredulous, 'Elegant? I bought it ten years ago in a charity shop!' If someone praises you for a task well done, your modesty assumes exaggerated proportions and you deny any credit, ' No, it was nothing' or even 'Don't make such a fuss about it'.

Another defensive reaction to avoid is the automatic return: no sooner has the compliment left the other person's lips than you are straight in with a kneejerk and often insincere reply: 'Oh, but *yours* is lovely too' or 'I was *just* thinking the same about you!' This again stems from our own anxiety and too easily negates whatever the other person has said.

Quite unintentionally, our defensive reactions make their

gesture look inappropriate. Remember from your own efforts that when someone *does* take the trouble to give you a genuine compliment, they could be feeling vulnerable themselves.

Spot the difference If you've ever caught yourself thinking 'Now *what* are they after?' when someone gives you a compliment, it is probably because you are suspicious that a compliment is only flattery and is being used to manipulate you in some way. It is possible to discern the difference between true compliments and those with strings attached:

'But you did it so *well*,' you hear when someone is trying to make you change your mind and do it *again*.

'We feel you're exactly the right kind of person,' when someone is trying to persuade you to take on a job that nobody else wants.

'We can count on you to be understanding in the circumstances', you hear as they are about to cheat you out of your fair share.

'You're always such a rock,' they say, with a pat on the back when they are too uncomfortable to acknowledge that you are hurt and vulnerable.

It is true that compliments can be used manipulatively but, in our defensiveness, we risk throwing everything out indiscriminately. We learn to distrust compliments of *any* kind. A first step is to identify the duds and handle them in the same way as put-downs (Chapter 12). The second is to learn to receive assertively those which are offered in sincerity.

If you are not sure, ask the person to be clearer. If you are assured that a compliment is sincere, give a simple acknowledgement: a smile or simple 'thank you' is sufficient for the other person to know that their compliment has been received instead of dismissed or rejected. If you are sure that the intention is genuine but are not clear what is meant by 'amazing' or 'incredible', then again *ask*. Just a gentle encouragement helps the other person to make a little more effort to be specific. That effort can be much more rewarding for both of you.

You may want to go further and agree with the compliment. This does *not* mean an arrogant dismissal which implies that the speaker has stated something so obvious that it wasn't worth saying. It means agreeing with what the other person says:

'Thank you. I like this colour on me too.'
'I'm glad you like it. I think it suits me better this way.'
'I'm reassured that you think so. I wasn't sure if I'd done the right thing or not.'
'I'm pleased you noticed. I was quite proud of myself as well!'

Any comment that comes naturally to you, which allows you to show that you have heard what was said and that you liked it is all that's needed.

Small and simple, spontaneous and specific The danger with looking at compliments in this way is that you will feel even more embarrassed and self-conscious than before. It is important to practise. It then becomes easier and you can allow yourself to be more spontaneous.

Linda and Ben were sitting in the garden, exhausted after a day with her very extended family who had descended on them for the day and had not long departed. They weren't the easiest crowd and Linda was looking at Ben thinking how great he'd been. Instead of saying nothing or saying he'd been 'great', she took the opportunity to say something more heartfelt.

Linda: Ben, you know, I'm sitting here thinking that I really couldn't have managed today without you.
Ben (shrugs): it's OK.
Linda: It may not be a big deal for you but I really do appreciate it. You were so patient with the kids and made such an effort to make Roy welcome. I know you don't like him but I was very touched that you went out of your way. (*Ben feels a bit embarrassed and doesn't say anything.*)
Linda: It meant a lot to me (*gets up to give him a kiss*) I want you to know that.
Ben: It's OK. But I can tell you . . . I'm glad they've gone!
Linda: So am I!

Kivita has just been awarded a place at the university of her choice. She is absolutely elated and has texted all her friends with the news. She then remembers Mrs Robson, her physics teacher who has been such a support the whole way through. She decides to see her at school and finds her in the classroom.

Kivita: Mrs Robson, can I see you for a moment?
Mrs Robson (turns round): Hello, Kivita. How are you?
Kivita: I'm really good . . . I got my place!
Mrs Robson: That's wonderful news. I'm so pleased for you.
Kivita: I just wanted to say thank you. You were so helpful and you've been a brilliant teacher.
Mrs Robson: I was only doing my job.
Kivita: You did more than that. You really gave me confidence to keep going when I didn't think I could ever make it. So thank you.
Mrs Robson: Well, it's good of you to come in and tell me personally. I really value that.
Kivita: I'll let you get on . . . bye
Mrs Robson: Bye, Kivita and good luck!

It is so easy to forget to say to the people who are important to us that we value them: we buy elaborate cards, offer expensive gifts or send greetings with commercially clichéd phrases instead of using simple, heartfelt words of our own. We remember to say thank you for tangible presents at Christmas, maybe, but we often forget to say thank you on all those small but numerous occasions which do not merit a big production but which could easily be honoured with a simple word of appreciation.

With practice, you'll find yourself less afraid to speak out and be able to express appreciation simply because you feel like it. You will find it easier to respond immediately to people. We become so stuck in habits of comparison and competition that we forget how to reach out with a simple word or gesture of love or praise or acknowledgement just for the sake of it. A spontaneous hand-out that is sincere, heartfelt and absolutely free.

17

Women in the Workplace

Whether single or married, with or without a family, employed or self-employed; working to make a living, to make ends meet or to retain a measure of independence; whether established in a career, returning to work after bringing up a family or trying to balance motherhood and a career at the same time, there is nevertheless some common ground in the difficulties we encounter as working women.

Our concerns in the workplace are best understood from two angles: the external system – the culture and values of the organisation – and the internal problems many of us face in terms of self-doubt and uncertainty about handling authority which range from giving instructions, making refusals and correcting someone's behaviour to challenging the status quo or confronting someone's inadequate performance.

What we're up against

The workplace has changed radically in the three decades since this book was first published and is a useful focus because it serves as a microcosm of cultural values. A lot of what I have written for women in the workplace is based on the reality that their experience is different from that of men. To young women who have seen their mothers work throughout their own childhood, it is easy to forget that, historically, it is only relatively recently that women have been employed outside the home.

Though women are now far more in evidence in middle and lower management, it is evident that, despite attempts at positive discrimination, underlying sexist attitudes still prevent access for the vast majority of women to the highest positions in every nation. Among those in power in the fields of industry, entertainment, medicine, education, politics, business and local government, there are few women so when a woman *does* achieve a prominent position, it is sufficiently remarkable to never pass unnoticed in the media. Claims (in the western world) that women have achieved equality of professional opportunity with men are based more in wishful thinking than reality.

Sexism, like racism and ageism, does not simply disappear because the law has changed: attitudes (whether conscious or subconscious) and deeply entrenched resistance to change simply go underground but their chilling influence blows down every corridor of power. Greater awareness and subsequent obeisance to politically correct procedures have led to a decrease in the grosser forms of sexual harassment in the workplace but women continue to encounter more tacit and subtle forms, less visible but equally shocking on impact, a bit like walking straight into a glass wall.

While ageism in the workplace applies to both men and women, older women feel an additional pressure caused by emphasis on the preference for youthful attractiveness over wrinkles: a double whammy so to speak. Even younger women who have not been aware of sexist attitudes while at school or university are surprised in their first jobs to find themselves treated by senior colleagues either as young attractive things or as sweet little girls.

One colleague in her middle years and working in a very competitive field told me that younger men with whom she now has to engage in the course of her work simply don't know how to respond to her. Since, in their eyes, she is no longer viewed as sexually viable, they don't know where to place her in the scheme of things; how to deal with her obvious expertise and competence; how to relate to her. The problem is that we *know* this mind-set exists. Media coverage of protests by a few sacked female TV presenters doesn't shock: it merely confirms our direct or indirect experience of working within a particular culture which has been established over a very, very long time.

Internal thought system

Although one cannot do an awful lot about the external system – except not to deny it – a further stumbling block exists to the advancement of women in work: our own self-diminishing beliefs. When new initiatives are announced with the laudable aim of getting more women into parliament or executive positions within companies, the external barriers come under scrutiny. There are regular proposals for 'quotas' which always provoke the same controversy: surely women should achieve on their own merit versus the argument that unless there is a legal requirement, attitudes will never change.

Both sides of the argument tend to ignore the significance of our own inner barriers. Of course the availability of child care arrangements, for example, is a hugely significant factor for many women in terms of juggling day-to-day family and career responsibilities but our attitudinal and emotional difficulties tend always to be side-lined. It is as if we don't want to admit they exist.

But they do. When I have worked with women at various levels of seniority and even in countries where the infrastructure of child care provision is way in advance of the UK, it doesn't take long to find, when one scratches below the surface and provides a safe environment to talk, that women (middle-managers, executives and directors of companies) will still disclose an underlying lack of confidence. This may emerge as a tendency to work much, much harder than their male colleagues; to refuse no task that comes their way; to hold back from necessary confrontation or from speaking up in the minority; an inability to challenge an aggressive colleague or a reluctance to challenge the prevailing norms and values of the business culture in which they work. This uncertainty is certainly affected by external attitudes and stereotypes from others, but the point is, by denying a) that the system is there and b) that we feel unsure sometimes, we undermine our effectiveness to challenge it.

We cannot take on the entire bulwark of sexism but it is very much within our capability to challenge our own internal doubts. One of the first steps is to crawl out from under the suffocating weight of denial and recognise that being a woman at work means facing different challenges from her male counterparts. This is not to blame anyone in particular or to expect anyone else to do anything about it: it is simply to acknowledge what we're up against. Consider the following typical concerns brought by women who attend training programmes to learn how to be more personally effective at work:

'I'd like to deal with male colleagues who are not pulling their weight without being labelled a nag.'

'I want to confront workplace bullying and prejudice.'

'I want to be able to act on and express disagreement especially with senior male colleagues.'

'How do I deal with managers who are apparently unwilling to accept the real responsibilities of management? By this I mean developing a vision, leadership, setting priorities and team commitment.'

'In a male-dominated field, my ideas are often dismissed'

'I'm the only female lecturer in my department and I'd like to know how this affects my position.'

'I'm increasingly up against a very aggressive competitive male atmosphere: how do I cope?'

'Why do men in the workplace still think that women should be supportive of them and not criticise them?'

'How do I tackle male colleagues who are generally supportive and would be appalled at the thought of being sexist and yet are unaware that there is a conspicuous bias that informs their way of thinking?'

'I had to work for two years with a manager whose temper drove many staff to tears, including me.'

'I find it difficult to distinguish between problems that I have arising from my gender and those arising from my level of competence.'

These give some idea of the challenges many women face in a *normal* working environment.

The assertive skills we have reviewed so far in this book all come into play in the context of the workplace as you will see from the following illustrations. These explore key recurring themes: fear of disapproval; balancing the personal with the impersonal; setting limits; handling money; dealing with harassment. These examples have been set out in detail to show how practising these skills – in a safe and supportive environment – leads to significant learning for the women taking part.

A willingness to accept a measure of disapproval

In Chapter 6, we reviewed our rights. The last one – the right to act independently of others' approval – is especially pertinent here because one of most commonly revealed obstacles to our effectiveness at work is our unwillingness to tolerate being disliked. Many of us fear disapproval which interferes with behaving authoritatively when we need to: this fear leads to hesitation or overkill, depending on our perceptions of the other person.

Tessa wanted to confront a member of her team, a man who was attractive, popular and a good salesman but who would never get his end-of-month figures to her on time. She had asked him several times before but without success.

When we discussed the issue, Tessa admitted that she was insecure about asking because she felt a little undermined by him and had the impression that he wasn't really taking her seriously as his manager. This both irritated and worried her.

I suggested she took the initiative. This was difficult to arrange because he was hardly ever in the office but, as it was important, she knew she'd have a better chance with a face-to-face conversation. He was going to be in the office for a team meeting so she decided to ask him to meet her for ten minutes before the meeting started.

Practice 1

Tessa: Hello, Bob. Take a seat, thanks for coming.

Bob: What's with the formality then?

Tessa: I don't find this easy (*self-disclosure*), Bob, but the situation now is serious. Each month I chase you for your returns and each month you are late. This means I send them late to the head office. I'd like to have them in on time.'

Bob: 'So what does it matter if they're a bit late? My figures are good and that's what matters, not the admin.'

Tessa: 'I know your figures are good, but I still have to provide end-of-month team figures, whether I want to or not and I need yours on time, Bob. Do you understand?'

Bob: (*a little mockingly*) Yes, Miss.

Tessa: 'You don't have to take that attitude, Bob.'

Tessa's Learning 1

Does it *matter*? If she behaves assertively and clearly and does her job with authority, does it matter that Bob feels compelled to respond with sarcasm or mockery? If the answer is yes, Tessa faces a very arduous task ahead trying to smooth everything out, please everyone, keep them smiling and ensure a happy ending for all. If the answer is no, she can shelve her need to be liked and settle for being respected.

Practice 2

Tessa: Hello, Bob. Take a seat, thanks for coming.

Bob: What's with the formal meeting then?'

Tessa: (*not getting hooked by Bob's manner but staying more rooted within herself*) I don't find this easy, Bob, but the situation now is serious. Each month I chase you for your returns, and each month you are late. This means I send them late to head office. I'd like to have them in on time.

Bob: So what does it matter if they're a bit late? My figures are good and that's what matters, not the admin.

Tessa: I know your figures are good, but I still have to provide end-of-month team figures, whether I want to or not, and I need yours on time, Bob, do you understand? (*Repetition and reinforcement*)

Bob: (*a little mockingly*) Yes, Miss.

Tessa: (*taking a deep breath, anxious inside but with more external assurance*) I don't find this easy, Bob, but I'd like your figures by the end of the month and I'd like your agreement to this. This is not as a personal favour to me: it's for everyone else's benefit as well.

Bob: (*with a loud sigh*) Well, I'll see what I can do.

Tessa: (*getting into her stride now*) I need those figures on time, Bob.

Bob: OK. (*Tessa stands up to indicate an end to the meeting*)

Tessa: Thanks for coming.

Tessa's Learning 2

Tessa was convinced. 'It's true.' she said. 'It isn't personal . . . and it really doesn't matter.'

Tessa learned an invaluable lesson. Precisely because of the system – and as I mentioned earlier, women are relatively new-comers in the workplace – it is the system we have to contend with. When we encounter these attitudes and prejudices, we make the mistake of taking them personally which is completely understandable because they are affecting us personally: we get upset, hurt and frustrated. But, in a way, we are merely representatives of our gender in an extremely unequal and biased system. Men of all ages have difficulty with women in positions of authority and are likely to project all sorts of stereotypes onto us: we may be subjected to these equally from women employees as well. I've noticed an interesting tendency (among both men and women) to be far less tolerant and more critical of female bosses than their male counterparts which is further evidence that sexism hasn't disappeared from the bedrock of people's attitudes.

Balancing the person with the impersonal

It can help to stand back a little and see that what is happening is not necessarily to do with who you *are* as an individual female human being but also what you *represent* in the greater scheme of things. By diminishing your sense of being targeted as an individual, you gain sufficient emotional distance to help you realise that there may be very little you can do to change the wider picture in which you find yourself. What you *can* do, however, is determine what you want from a particular colleague or employee or boss and then go for it, clearly and specifically and directly.

If you can shelve your (personal) need to be liked and settle for your (professional) wish to be respected, handling your authority gets easier. Reminding yourself of this boundary is a great help: when you need support and understanding to counter the sense of isolation (which we all do from time to time) seek it from those who care for you and *see* you.

The need to be clear about the personal/work boundary emerges in other ways. Glynis was particularly unhappy about two women in the office where she worked, who persisted in asking her about her private life. Where was she going in the evening? What had she done at the weekend? Who was she seeing? Who was the man who had met her from work last week? And so on. She did not know how to handle it. When she role-played it in the group, she found she wasn't alone in finding it difficult to refuse to answer similarly intrusive questions without being aggressive. It took practice but Glynis was eventually able to convince them without being hostile that she did not want to answer their questions.

Lucy also wanted to maintain privacy for another reason. After ten years' absence from paid work and having a family, Lucy had started a job in an insurance office. The personnel manager emailed her to inform her that he was going to contact her family doctor to check details of her past medical history. She was so stunned that she did not reply to it. In fact, she was really anxious that the personnel department should not delve into her past: she had been in hospital twice for depression and suspected that this would be held against her. With the support and encouragement from others on the course, she went in to work the next day and made an appointment to see the personnel manager in person. She told him assertively that she didn't want him to write to her doctor as she felt this to be an infringement of her privacy. She believed she was taking a risk in that she might lose the job in doing so but her wishes were respected on this occasion without any negative consequences.

One of the criticisms leveled at women is a tendency to be 'emotional' and work is no exception. Being human, of course, means that we will probably be sensitive to feelings: we often pick up 'atmospheres' and unaddressed issues. Self-disclosure, once again, is an enormous help in expressing feelings in a way that doesn't interfere with our ability to function. A little emotional distance doesn't mean that you have to be unfeeling, heartless or robotic. You can still be human even when you are operating in a professional and authoritative manner. Being sensitive doesn't automatically translate into being able to address what we sense is happening: this step requires a certain degree of resolve and courage but whenever we decide to directly address an impasse or an apparently closed door of hostility, our inner confidence is boosted.

Sandra had been appointed to Head of Department in a large school and found herself having to work with Lena, an older woman, who had been at the school a long time and had applied unsuccessfully for Sandra's post. Sandra had attempted to build bridges between herself and Lena over the course of the first term but her overtures were met with a chilly aloofness. The problem was that there were only four in the department and they needed to collaborate. Unexpressed feelings very easily create an intangible gulf in all our relationships and, even at work, can adversely affect the ability to achieve co-operation.

Sandra had let things ride for a while believing there was nothing she could do. There were too many aspects that she couldn't change. She took the opportunity to practise in a training session. What did she want? What was her starting point? She decided she wanted at least to have a discussion and clear the air.

She arranged for Lena to come to her office.

Practice 1

Sandra: Lena, thanks for coming. I realise you're not happy with me being here but I'd like to find some way of working better together.

Lena: (*stiffly*) Is there something wrong with the way I work?

Sandra: No, I didn't mean that. It's just that we need to have a talk about things.

Lena: There's nothing to talk about.

The atmosphere between them tense and uncomfortable.

The learning here was twofold: more helpful to use self-disclosure to begin with and *not* to use the word 'we' in this context: this happens when we are anxious so it is a little manipulative, in trying to establish some false camaraderie. Phrases such as 'I thought we'd have a little chat' or 'we need to speak about what's happening' tend to make the other person suspicious and defensive which is not the ideal start!

Practice 2

Sandra: Thanks for coming, Lena. I've asked you here because I find myself in a difficult situation. I've tried to improve our working relationship but you don't seem to want to, so I'm frustrated. I'm not asking you to like me – I can't do anything about the circumstances – but what bothers me is that it is getting in the way of our working relationship. And that *does* matter to me. So I'd like to clear the air enough for us to be able to move on. Can you accept that?

Lena: (*paying far more attention*) What exactly do you have in mind?

Sandra: I don't have anything specific in mind – I'd like to talk more openly, that's all.

You've got a lot of experience in things that I don't and I have some in other areas. I'd really like to make this work but the decision is yours. Will you at least think about it? (*Lena shrugs her shoulders but the hostility has dissipated. They end the meeting there.*)

That's enough. Sandra cannot do any more but has given Lena a clear option. That's all she can do but even so, facing her anxiety about confronting the problem really strengthened her self-esteem: she didn't have to continue feeling helpless.

Two further problematic areas emerge time after time in training: setting limits on the time and energy we give to our work and also the topic of money.

Setting limits

A major obstacle to being assertive at work is the problem of establishing the limits of the job and your particular responsibilities. What are you expected to do? Do you feel you are asked to do more than you are paid to do? What do you demand of yourself? Most of us do not take the time to ask ourselves these questions and, as a result, we get into the habit of taking on more than we want to and stretching ourselves to the limit.

In Chapter 8, we looked at some of the issues facing us when we want to say 'no'. This time, in addition, the fear that our jobs are on the line constitutes a powerful inhibitor. Although there may be some truth in this, a lot depends on *how* we set limits and when. However, problems in this area are not straightforward: there is also an insidious emotional influence that is rarely addressed. This is the 'superwoman' stereotype often featured in the popular press. You'll be familiar with her features: the woman who is a highflying financial wizard, earning a six or seven figure salary, has five contented children who are all accomplished and doing well at school; a happy and supportive husband and, on top of it all, manages to look incredibly glamorous and elegant.

As a role model, 'Superwoman' elicits as much angst and despair as inspiration and encouragement. Which does it do for you? Of course there is nothing intrinsically wrong with high achievers but the worrying element is that this stereotype taps into an already existing tendency among many women to exceed their own limits to a point of self-detriment physically, psychologically and emotionally.

The effect of the 'superwoman' myth can be detected when we find ourselves thinking one or more of the following: 'being tired is a sign of weakness or at least admitting I am tired is a sign of weakness', 'I have to muster that last bit of energy from somewhere', 'I have to keep going to the bitter end'. With these thoughts to contend with, we end up becoming over-burdened and depressed, sometimes physically ill. We behave as if our energy and time and our resources were unlimited.

It can be easy to forget that we have the right to acknowledge our own needs for care. It goes against the grain to admit openly that we need to rest and replenish our resources. The urge to prove herself a match to the tireless superwoman drives a woman on and on: taking on extra work, working too late at night or at weekends, being ever accessible to clients and patients and family, coping with every crisis around her, anticipating everyone's needs with a headful of a-hundred-and-one things at a time will all eventually take their toll. The internal murmur 'what about me?' builds into a scream.

How do we express this exhaustion? Dulcie is always tired. Her shoulders are hunched, her feet move slowly. She punishes her body by going on too long. Her back aches. She may go and ask the doctor for something to keep her going. She may cry every now and again with exhaustion. Others suspect something is wrong and try to persuade her to take a rest but she refuses.

 Agnes pushes herself hard as well and everyone else around her. She is impatient with anyone who slows her down or does not do what they are supposed to do. She pushes others as she pushes herself, intolerant of frailty, feelings, mistakes, 'time-wasting', delay or anything that doesn't go according to her (very tight) schedule.

Ivy, as you might expect, expresses her feelings indirectly. She too is likely to feel resentful but will use guilt to make this known. She may even go out of her way to make some elaborate but quite unnecessary effort, imposing unsolicited care and attention on those around her. They may protest in vain: they don't know whether to feel grateful or guilty but they may certainly feel uncomfortable under the weight of some unarticulated but extremely heavy expectations.

An assertive approach starts with realising how hard it is to break the habit of what can potentially develop into a vicious circle: the more tired you become, the less assertive you feel and therefore you become less able to set limits and say enough is enough. Instead of calling a halt when you need most to do so, you can find yourself believing that just a little bit more can't make *that* much difference.

Many women adopt this pattern of behaviour which can become compulsive, even addictive: there is a lot of pleasure and satisfaction to be found in stretching yourself to achieve fifty goals where anyone else would only have achieved ten. And there is a curious pride we can feel in achieving what others deem impossible. Sometimes it is our very frustration which fuels a self-punishing frenzy of over-activity.

Breaking out of the circle needs to be done very gradually. Selma decided to start in a small way in her own life. Setting aside half an hour each day was a beginning – to do whatever she wanted – lie down, sit, walk, rest, whatever. It takes a mammoth effort of will because she could still find thirty things she 'should' be doing but she managed to allow her guilt to hover around her like a fog until it  eventually evaporated. When her phone went, she reminded herself that this was *her* time. She needed the time to review how she could begin to cut back on her other activities: where she could begin to delegate, ask for help and say 'no' to more.

This is what Fiona had to do. She worked as a nurse at night in a local hospital: childcare and housework filled up the remainder of her day, allowing herself virtually no rest and little sleep. She knew she was tired but what she had to do was first acknowledge her *need* to ask for help from her partner and then to see how she could get that help. By asking him to do some shopping and her sister to pick up the children from school, she was able to make a start.

Making the first step is difficult. It is easy to pretend that you can still manage and that things have not really got out of hand at all.

Jackie had been working for two years as a PA to a busy executive. Almost unnoticeably her job, which had started as eight hours a day, had taken over her evenings and most of her weekends. As the company was restructured, she was asked to do the administrative work for others in the department. The more competent she proved herself to be, the more she was asked to take on.

She did not once say 'no' but let everything accumulate until she found she had no time for personal life at all. Looking at why she always allowed herself to take on more and more, she realised that she didn't want to say 'no' because she feared she would lose her job if she appeared unwilling or unco-operative, so she failed to set clear limits with her boss. Jackie decided at this point that she needed to look at ways in which she could ensure sufficient personal free time while still coping with her job. For her, this meant taking the initiative, approaching her boss, arranging a meeting and exploring the situation together.

Practice 1

(*Jackie enters Ken's office at a pre-arranged time.*)

Jackie: Thanks for seeing me, Ken.

Ken: (*looks up*) So what's up?

Jackie: Well, I feel very awkward about bringing this up (*self-disclosure*) but I need to talk to you about how to restructure some of my workload.

Ken: Tell me about it!

Jackie: I know you're under pressure as well, Ken. But for a while now I've been aware that things are building up and I end up working late and at weekends I'm still working. I just need a bit more time for myself.

Ken: I sympathise – my kids hardly get to see me these days – but I really don't know what I can do. Things are just like that.

A good beginning but Jackie has learned again how hard it is to proceed with nothing definitive to aim for. This is a common omission and goes back once again to the difficulty of being specific: Ken is agreeable and sympathetic but Jackie isn't going to get anywhere without a specific request. This helps the other person focus on something concrete instead of floundering under a generalised complaint without much idea where to proceed. Remember, being specific is *your* responsibility.

Practice 2

(*Jackie enters Ken's office.*)

Jackie: Hi, Ken. Thanks for seeing me.

Ken: OK. What can I do for you?

Jackie: Well, I feel a bit awkward about asking this but I need to find a way – with your help – to restructure my workload so I get a little more time to myself.

Ken: I know what it's like. Believe me. It's tough for all of us.

Jackie: I realise that but you see, Ken, I'm taking home stuff in the evenings and at weekends and it's getting too much. I would like to find a way, with your help, to restructure my workload.

Ken: But what can I do?

Jackie: Well, there are a couple of possibilities. We could consider getting someone in to replace Jill which would help: that's my preferred choice. Or we could ask Jay to come in an extra day and take over a section of the marketing. (*Two specific options*)

Ken: (*ponders*) I'll have to check it out. I'm really not sure we can do much at the moment.

Jackie: Ken, I really like working for you. I believe I contribute a lot and want to stay. It's just that I'm not giving of my best. It's hard to admit it but there are limits. If we can restructure my workload, it will make a big difference. (*Repetition and reinforcement*)

Ken: (*sighs*) I know . . . look, Jackie, I'll have a word and see what, if anything, can be sorted.

Jackie: Thanks, Ken. I really appreciate it. I'll check up on when you get back from Denmark next week. (*She gets up and leaves his office.*)

Being amenable, friendly, committed and above all obliging may be important aspects of the image you want to project to others. But sometimes the expectation becomes a trap. You become known as obliging: people rely on you to be obliging, you can always be depended on to say 'yes' where someone else would say 'no'. This makes it increasingly difficult to begin changing the pattern. The first time you say 'no', your uncharacteristic response may cause a little consternation and this is often the crunch point: 'But you usually/but you always/but we've been able to depend on you in the past . . . ' are typical responses. Once you get over this hurdle, it gets easier and you'll find it possible to break the pattern, maybe not every time but enough to stop getting to a point of overload.

Judy found this to be true for her. As a teacher and single, she found herself constantly lumbered with various assignments or paperwork to complete after school and at weekends. She was then asked to be part of a team that accompanied a group on holiday over Easter. The staff assumed she would oblige, which of course she did. She felt she did not have the right to say 'no' as she did not have family responsibilities like the others. Once Judy admitted to herself that she did not want to take on all the extra work, she was able to exercise more discretion. She learned to define more clearly her dual obligation to herself and her colleagues and from that position could then choose to give up *some* of her free time after school hours but not all of it.

Negotiation and money

Since this book was first published, the economic scene has been irretrievably transformed. Neoliberal economic policies have taken over the world with seismic political and social repercussions, one of which is that instead of being a specialist preoccupation, the economy has taken centre stage in mainstream media with everyone, both men and women, discussing it on a daily basis. Women financiers and stockbrokers are now firmly installed and we are no longer hidebound by the attitude that it is unfeminine to know about, talk about or argue about money.

And yet, many ordinary women, who are not financial professionals, still find it hard to assert themselves when dealing with money: how to tell a client or student that they need to increase their charges, for example, or to ask for a raise at work or request a repayment of a loan they have made to a family member or friend. At the root of these difficulties remain vestiges of the belief that it is still not 'nice' to have to talk about money which infiltrate our interactions.

Maureen found it difficult to query a bill. She would always feel embarrassed and if ever she suspected she was being overcharged in a shop or restaurant, she did not mention it because she was embarrassed to do so.

Jo had planned to go on holiday with Virginia for two weeks. As the time approached, she realised that Virginia, who had a well-paid job, had a lot more money to spend than she did. Jo didn't want to cause an 'atmosphere' between them before they went away but neither did she want to spoil her holiday worrying.

Kathleen, too, needed some financial help. Her pension was very limited and she knew her daughter would be able and probably only too willing to help her but she felt it was undignified to talk about such things.

Margaret found it extremely difficult to ask for the return of £100 which she had lent her brother. It bothered her yet she felt too uncomfortable to ask directly. She told herself that she was being petty and that a hundred pounds shouldn't matter that much. She kept hoping that her brother would remember and suddenly produce it. When she did ask him, after practising in a workshop, she found he had forgotten completely and he immediately repaid the loan.

A similar discomfort presents difficulties when negotiating a price for labour. If you are not employed within a fixed payment structure, how do you arrive at a price? Do you pick a figure out of a hat? Do you settle on a price that you know is appropriate but then ask for less, get less and moan about all those people charging more than you and getting away with it?

If you hesitate to ask for money for whatever reason, you need to ask yourself if you feel comfortable with giving away your time and talent or are you selling yourself short? Pam was faced with such a dilemma: she had been a hairdresser before she married and enjoyed cutting hair for the women on the estate. But they were friends and did not have much money to spare. An assertive compromise for her was to exchange cutting hair for babysitting time which suited everyone. She was happy that her time and talent were valued and her customers, who could not afford to pay in cash, were happy to pay in kind.

Cecilia was Italian and made her living as a language teacher. When she role-played asking her fees for private tuition what emerged was her embarrassment at actually mentioning a price directly. It was important for her to practise saying what she wanted as an hourly rate.

Our anticipation of disapproval is often imaginary so it is useful to take the time to feel more comfortable with actually stating the fee and sticking to it. Of course we are still liable to meet *real* disapproval. I have learned over many years of freelance work that whatever I state as a fee will appear outrageously over-priced to some and a surprising bargain to others. The only way to cope with these fluctuations is to find a fee that you yourself feel comfortable with negotiating.

Discomfort with the mention of money can cause anxiety when asking for a raise at work.

Josie wanted a pay rise because her job as office manager had expanded over the last two months with one colleague leaving. She was happy with her work but it was beginning to irritate her that she wasn't getting paid a bit more when she was doing more. She also heard that a new colleague had started on a basic salary that was higher than her own. Although Josie knew what she wanted – more money because she was feeling undervalued – one of the traps we can fall into in this kind of situation is to be as vague as possible about the actual sum of money involved.

It is important to do some homework beforehand and to be clear of a figure you have in mind which represents a fair price in the circumstances of your qualifications, experience and responsibilities: your market price, as it were. Josie decided to ask for another £8000 before practising her approach to her manager.

Having made an appointment beforehand, she goes to talk to her manager, Rob.

Practice 1

Josie: Hi, Rob, is it OK if I come in?

Rob: Sure.

Josie: Look the reason I'm here is that I'd like to ask for a pay, rise . . . I'm thinking of £8000. I don't know if you think that's too much but that's what I came up with (*a little uncertainty in her tone*).

Rob: (*also uncertain*) That's a bit of a jump. I don't know whether we can pay you that much. What's prompted this?

Josie: Well, with Tom going, I've landed up with two people's work now and I thought . . .

Rob: I know that, you're right but I just don't know if we can afford it. Things aren't at their best.

Josie: (*imagining this to be her winning card*) Well, Rob, I happen to know that Jason started at more than I'm getting now . . .

Rob: (*shifts uncomfortably*) I really can't discuss anyone else's salary with you, Josie. It wouldn't be right.

Josie: (*feeling awkward now as well*) What I meant was . . .

Rob: I know what you meant. Look, I'll get back to you, OK? (*Josie realises the meeting is over.*)

A useful lesson to learn is that once you introduce someone else's salary into the conversation as leverage to help your own case, you immediately lose out on the equality of the interaction. Suddenly it isn't you and your boss negotiating but an invisible coercion which tips the balance and easily makes the other person feel cornered. It's wiser to avoid direct comparisons with another person and stick to asking for what you want exclusively on your *own* merit.

Another point to learn from this kind of conversation concerns the problem of leaving an inconclusive meeting. There are many times when someone legitimately cannot give you an answer there and then. They need time to consult or consider and, though this is understandable, it can present problems when you leave in this open-ended manner: you'll probably not know the right time to come back or how long the person needs to think. This raises anxiety about being too pushy while at the same time not wanting it all to be forgotten. To avoid this, endeavour to get some answer to these questions before you leave the room (or before you end the conversation, if it is over the phone).

Practice 2

Josie: Hi Rob, can I come in?

Rob: Yes, sure. Have a seat.

Josie: Rob, I feel a bit awkward asking you this but I've given it a lot of thought and I'd like to ask for another £8000.

Rob: Wow – that's quite a jump!

Josie: I know it may be a surprise but the reason I'm asking is that the way things have panned out since Tom left, I've basically been doing two people's jobs so that means I've got twice as much responsibility. Do you agree with that?

Rob: I can see that you're doing more now.

Josie: Well, that's why I decided to ask for an increase. What do you think?

Rob: I don't know, Josie. Things aren't great right now. I'd have to ask the board. (*This time Josie avoids any reference to anyone else and reinforces her own merit.*)

Josie: I'd really like you to consider it, Rob. I think my work is worth the extra.

Rob: (*taking her more her seriously*) Well, I can't give you an answer right now, Josie.

Josie: I realise that. So when might you be able to? Would it be OK if I got back to you in a week, say, next Friday?

Rob: Probably, yes, that should be long enough.

Josie: (*Stands up*). OK, thanks Rob, I'll get back to you on Friday then. Bye.

The common denominator in these scenarios is the importance of speaking up: although we can't guarantee the outcome in our favour (this would be coercion), we give ourselves the best chance when we are clear and specific. Each time we do this, we are refusing to stay locked in anxiety or stuck in helplessness and blame: each time we take this kind of step our self-esteem is strengthened. This helps to build psychological 'muscles' for those times when we have to draw on internal personal resources if we need to confront harassment or bullying.

Harassment

In many women's experience at work, visible harassment is far less conspicuous than an intangible feeling of being different, a feeling of alienation. This is both because we are women at *work* and *women* at work. In other words, we can feel alienated from the culture of the workplace and we can also feel out of place because, as I described before, women at work are a relatively new phenomenon.

In the past three decades it has become more politically incorrect for a man to pinch a woman's bottom or make some verbal comment about her anatomy but we are now faced with more subtlety. Every now and then the newspaper headlines inform us of ongoing harassment suits usually lodged by a high-flying female executive who has been cheated of millions in salary or bonuses because, for example, she took maternity leave. Big sums of money make for big stories but what gets lost in the sensationalism is the vicious and hurtful nature of both sexist and racist intimidation within a working environment.

Sometimes harassment is quite obvious: feeling more permission to look at or touch a woman's body is embedded in the particular power structure in the world at large and therefore is not going to disappear, regardless of any legislation regarding political correctness.

Harassment can also appear in more vague, implicit, and subtly patronising forms. Rosie was called in to her boss as part of the monthly review in the department. She was told she needed to produce more material and that, although her work was good, she needed to pull her weight a bit more. She did not enjoy the criticism but accepted it and knew it was valid.

Later that day, before going home, her boss came into her office. He suddenly announced that he realised he had been a bit hard on her and could he make it up by taking her out to dinner that evening. Rosie was horrified. Suddenly she felt no longer treated as an employee, capable of receiving criticism, but as a potential sexual object. She did not know what to do. She did not accept the invitation but expressed nothing of what she felt because she didn't know how to handle it. This kind of dilemma is not uncommon and aggravated by silence.

It is useful to place sexual harassment in a context of general harassment, in a context of the values that dominate not only in the workplace but also in the world at large. We can see harassment as part of an entire syndrome, consonant with attitudes to women, to women at work especially, in the conditioned and sometimes unthinking responses of men, who would not dream of actually physically harassing a woman.

Tina was nineteen and therefore the youngest in her department, a fact that Barry, a colleague in his early thirties, never missed an opportunity to point out. Conversation was peppered with 'Well, you wouldn't remember that, Tina . . . before your time' or 'How are you going to feel when the new guy comes? He's almost as young as you are.' At one level, Barry was being just a regular pain so what should Tina do? Ignore it? Mutter under her breath? Shake her head and raise her eyes? The problem was it *irritated* her. It irritated her that whatever she suggested or proposed was countered with some reference to her youth.

In her first practice, Tina tried to come back at Barry when he made a typical remark. It proved to be too difficult mainly because when you try this kind of thing in public, it will fail. All of us – every single one of us – are defensive in front of others and given assertiveness is about equality, you can't achieve this when you're on display. Consciously or unconsciously, we all feel more defensive when being criticised in public and therefore aggression is almost certainly the outcome.

Practice 2

Tina decided her best option was to say something in private. She located an empty room and asked Barry if she could have a word with him.

Tina: This won't take long. Barry, you know you do keep going on about my age. I don't know why. Do you have a problem with me being nineteen? I can't do anything about it, you know. Anyway I'd like you to stop.

Barry: I don't always go on about it.

Tina: You do, Barry. And it's beginning to get on my nerves so I'd like you to stop. Could you agree to that? I would really appreciate it. *(Barry looks completely surprised. He shrugs.)*

Tina: I'll take that as a 'yes' then. Thanks. *(She leaves the room.)*

Keeping it short and sweet is the key to this kind of interaction. She doesn't need to initiate a deep and meaningful conversation but to get the message across as she did: it was important to end the conversation by leaving the room. This allows Tina to recover and Barry to digest in private what she has said to him.

Less obvious examples of discrimination can also occur in the form of:

- Put-downs by colleagues
- Intimidation by using threatening gestures or language
- Exclusion from decision-making
- Being asked to fulfil trivial and demeaning tasks
- Being denied credit from bosses for work achieved
- Your expertise and credibility undermined by a colleague/boss in public

The realisation that there is a gender difference and that it is not in our imagination doesn't mean that we are always right in our perceptions. Sometimes we hear a put-down when there isn't one or wrongly attribute someone's criticism to a sexist or racist attitude. Of course we make mistakes but we can forgive ourselves and take responsibility knowing that reality is a lot more empowering than denial. The reality of sexism and racism in the workplace, as elsewhere in life, is undeniable.

One of the things that hold us back is that these issues are such minefields that we fear getting lost in such hazardous territory. This reinforces the need to have a specific request before you start and also to both initiate and close the conversation so you can keep it within the limits that you are ready and prepared to handle.

Viv worked with six male colleagues. She liked them and they worked well together. The problem was the continued banter about the time of the month, being emotional, her hormones and so on. This was often said with humour but it was incessant. Up to now, she had told herself she was being over-sensitive but had withdrawn more and more until she realised that she had reached the point when she felt unable to contribute to the team as she wanted. How could she deal with the situation without coming across as too 'heavy'?

Practice 1

This provides another example of when *not* to wait until it happens again before you tackle it, which is what Viv had imagined herself doing. Instead, she took the initiative, asking everyone to a short meeting at the coffee break.

> *(Six colleagues seated at or near the table, all eyes on Viv.)*
> *Viv*: Look, I've asked you to meet because there is something I want to talk about. It's not easy but you keep putting me down, referring to my hormones and so on . . .
> *A*: It's only a tease, we don't mean it . . . '
> *Viv*: I know it's a joke but I get fed up with it.
> *B*: We're like that with everyone, you shouldn't take it seriously.'
> *Viv*: I know you are . . . but *(losing heart and losing her way through the dialogue)*

I asked her what was happening and she replied that this was exactly what happened: she would try to make a serious point and it would be dismissed, all good-hearted banter but still dismissed. She was keen to try again, using self-disclosure.

Practice 2

Viv: I'm feeling very anxious about saying this (*self-disclosure*). (*All eyes now on Viv and paying attention.*) I've called you to a short meeting because there's something I want to talk to you all about. When I say something serious, you tend to dismiss it with a flip comment or a remark about my hormones . . .

A: Playing up now, are they . . . ?' (*there are a few smiles*)

Viv: You're doing it *now* . . . it makes me really angry.'

B: You shouldn't take it so seriously . . . '

Viv: 'Well, I do take it seriously because I'm fed up with it . . . (*tears well up in her eyes*)

A: You don't have to get upset.

B: You always look as if you can take a joke.

Viv: (*regaining her composure*) Look, I haven't said anything before because I didn't want to spoil the 'team spirit' and all that. I don't know whether you've noticed but I don't contribute as much as I used to because I don't feel able to be myself . . . every time I open my mouth to say something, you make some comment about me being a woman . . . (*not a joke to be heard, just a slightly uncomfortable silence . . .*) so I want to ask you to ease off a bit. I don't want to be po-faced about it . . . all I'm asking is for you to make an effort to consider what I'm saying before you make a joke. (*She could sense the atmosphere had changed so she moved away from the subject.*) Thanks for listening. We'd better get back to work. Rick, do you have the number of the technician?' (*Closing the conversation and moving to a neutral topic.*)

Viv learned that you can lose your way and regain it again while you're talking. She also learned the importance of stating her anger clearly instead of blaming and to ask for a specific change which, in this instance, was to stop.

When faced with these issues, part of the problem is doubt as to whether they are real or imaginary. Abena worked as a technician in a laboratory concerned with cancer research. Twice in three years there had been the possibility of her moving to a higher position and she had begun to wonder if she was being overlooked, and if so, why. She did not have the easiest of relationships with her boss, Philippa, but decided to talk to her. She knew this would be a difficult conversation so did her homework beforehand and found answers to those three key questions: what's happening, how do you feel and what do you want to be different? Her three points were: I am concerned about being overlooked for promotion; I am disappointed; I'd like to know what is going on. She made an appointment to see her.

Practice 1

Abena: Thank you for seeing me, Philippa. I'm wondering if you could tell me why I wasn't considered for the senior research post last month.

Philippa: You were considered but there was someone more qualified.

Abena: Excuse me saying this, Philippa, but this has happened twice now and I'm beginning to wonder if you have a problem with me . . .

Philippa: (*narrows her eyes*) What exactly are you implying, Abbie?

Abena: I am not implying anything. I just want to know if you have a problem with me being African.

Philippa: (*defensive and a little hostile*) I hope you're not accusing me of anything, Abbie.

Abena: I wasn't accusing you, I just wondered . . .

Philippa: I really have to get on now. This meeting is over.

Abena could just leave it there but she is unconvinced. Philippa never gets her name right, she talks across her at staff meetings. She even grimaces occasionally when she is speaking as if she finds it impossible to understand what Abena is saying, so much so that she checked this out with other colleagues but they said they didn't have a problem. She decided to try again and be more definite in her request.

Practice 2

Abena: Thank you for seeing me, Philippa. (*She sits back in her chair and looks at her directly*). I don't find this easy to say but I have a feeling you may feel a little prejudiced towards me.

Philippa: Don't be so ridiculous!

Abena: I get the impression that you are uncomfortable with me being African.

Philippa: You are talking nonsense, Abbie.

Abena: My name is Abena, you know. I don't want to accuse you of anything but I wonder if my colour makes you blind to my abilities as a scientist. (*Philippa looks distinctly unnerved.*) It does happen very easily, you know.

Philippa: What do you mean?

Abena: I would like to know if you have a problem with my work, Philippa. Do you find my work satisfactory? Are you pleased with it?

Philippa: Your work is fine.

Abena: Well, then, I'd like you to seriously consider me for promotion when the next opportunity arises. Will you agree to do that?

Philippa: (*a bit perplexed by now*) Yes, of course, Abbie.

Abena: (*quietly but firmly*) Ab-e-na

Philippa: Sorry . . . Abena.

Abena: (*stands and smiles*): Thanks you for your time, Philippa. (*She walks out of the room.*)

This kind of gentle forcefulness is a true hallmark of personal power. No attack, no weapons, just a persistent and unswerving conviction of your own perception and, at the same time, treating the other as an equal. Communicating assertively allows a space for exchange, for seeds of real change to be sown.

This chapter has been concerned with addressing some of the problems encountered as female employees in the workplace. Many women however feel alienated within a work culture, not because of sexism *per se* but because of the general value system which affects both male and female employees. The following chapter addresses the question of handling authority within a system of perpendicular power.

Following on

1. If you are anticipating an interview for a job, set up a role-play. Give the 'interviewer' some clues as to what to ask.
2. Talk to your partner about a financial concern.

3. Think of three problematic situations at work you would like to address. Ask yourself your three key questions and write down answers for them. If you want to go further, with someone's help, use role play to practise one or more of them.

4. Imagine yourself in any of the following scenarios and practise negotiating a price which leaves you feeling neither guilty nor cheated:

   a) For the past two months, you have been giving someone a lift to work. You do not have to go out of your way and you enjoy the company but you want to ask for a contribution to the petrol.

   b) Your friends know you cook well. You are asked to cater for a large party. Even though you enjoy cooking you are aware of all the work involved and would like to ask for some payment, over and above the cost of the food.

   c) You are a professional illustrator and a friend asks you, as a favour, to design a special birthday card. He expects you to do it for nothing as it is such a small job. You want to negotiate some payment.

   If none of these feel close enough to your own life, identify a situation which is more relevant and which will give you an opportunity to practise.

5. Starting with the phrase 'I have to . . .' write down the list of responsibilities you have in your life. When you come to the end, write down 'I choose to . . .' and then copy down the list. See if there is anything you feel personally responsible for that you could delegate to someone else.

6. Make a list of positive qualities you bring to your work. It is easy for women to minimise qualifications and achievement. Practise asserting your strengths and successes out loud to someone who will then reciprocate.

18

Women and Authority

How do we manage to be authoritative without being authoritarian? Remember the difference between perpendicular power and personal power: how do we handle the power or authority that is attached to a position that we hold? How can we carry out the role and responsibilities of our legitimate power over others without oppressing those below us in the hierarchy?

I don't believe that men handle this conflict any more effectively than women but many men feel more at home with the aggressive, competitive model because of conditioning.

It is not uncommon for female executives to themselves feel under enormous pressure to perform in a particular way and that because the *modus operandi* in the workplace culture is already established – by generations of men before them – they simply have to follow the same rules . . . or fail. When we're anxious about what someone else will think of us, it is an easy step to do as others do: be abrupt, arrogant, intimidating, show we mean business, look tough and be as hard as nails. If you choose this option, it is important never to lose sight of the fact that this approach stems from anxiety, not genuine confidence or a sense of personal power.

Some women are content to emulate this model and make it their own, either by being 'one of the men' and overtly tyrannical or by using the adaptation of 'velvet-gloved aggression': what employees experience in response to female bosses who adopt this particular strategy is being ever so sweetly, ever so charmingly and ever so softly *crushed*.

However, many other women feel more ambivalent. They don't feel comfortable 'pulling rank'. They do not want to risk alienating others or to jeopardise the possibility of co-operation:

they move from a sense of concern for the other person and try to balance this with their authority . . . but then hesitate. When we don't want to behave in an overtly aggressive manner, we tend to moderate our behavior to our detriment: we often speak too softly and unsteadily; our communication lacks firmness and clarity. Our words are vague instead of specific; we fail to take ourselves seriously and we are insufficiently direct in our approach. As a consequence the totality of our message is weak and often ineffectual, leaving us (and others) frustrated.

The lack of any obvious middle ground leaves us disadvantaged. So if you're one of those women who would like to know how to be authoritative, effective and even ballsy *without* being a bitch into the bargain, this chapter is very relevant.

The balance is to be found in managing authority assertively. This is part of setting limits. We looked at the importance of boundaries and setting limits first when saying no; we looked again when reviewing the emotion of anger. Personal boundaries are an integral part of personal power and anchored in self-esteem. In the workplace we have to juggle with our personal boundaries but also with the boundaries of our particular role: the authority, requirements and responsibilities that are a necessary aspect of that role.

Before looking at personal skills in this context, again we need to take a step back and look at the wider picture. The core principles underlying assertive behavior and communication need to be seen against a backdrop of the general culture of the workplace which promotes very different values. Identifying the unspoken norms helps you to find alternatives. Uncovering what you perceive as dominant values at work doesn't take long. Consider the following questions:

- What are the accepted norms: what is considered acceptable or unacceptable behaviour?
- What are the goals?
- What kinds of behavior are prized and what earns disapproval?

- What do you have to do to fit in? What must you avoid doing?
- What does it actually mean to 'act male' or to be one of the boys?

We often take the surrounding environment so much for granted that we can't see the detail clearly at first. As a guide, this is a profile of the dominant culture of a typical organisation, assembled from the responses of course participants over the years:

Context

Permanent inequality in a fixed linear direction means that hierarchical power dominates. Those above have more power that those below; they have greater access to various resources and higher remuneration. The higher the position, the more valued the work: directorial/managerial responsibility is given higher kudos than administrative or clerical responsibility.

Aims and means

The sole goal is financial: the higher the profit the better. Ever increasing profit becomes the only yardstick of success and the means to these goals are competition and battle waged by fair means or foul. Aggression is therefore the sanctioned and primary mode of behaviour. Ruthlessness and bullying are acceptable as a means of eliminating competition.

Interpersonal relations

With the ascendance of the audit culture, the human dimension in the workplace has been transformed by encouraging an impersonal environment which discourages relationship. Employees are viewed as 'resources' whose performance is subjected to various systems of monitoring through, for example, input and output indicators and returns, risk assessments and reviews, as a means of quality control with a view to making delivery more competitive. Even in those professions which previously revolved around relationships with pupils, students, patients or vulnerable members of the public, employees have found themselves far more involved in administration of targets and standards than in direct engagement with their charges.

Within this framework, certain norms develop:

✦ Integrity is swallowed up by the sanction of dishonesty. This is inevitable and becomes the norm when an individual is judged by performance. How you appear is what matters: you must be seen to be arriving early and leaving late, to be dedicated, to maintain a confident manner at all times. This leads to the well-known phenomenon of bullshitting: appearing always to know what you are talking about, even (and especially) when you don't.

✦ The blame culture. Following on from the strategy of bullshitting is the necessity to hide, deny or find a fall guy for any error. There is no room for mistakes, for vulnerability, for being human.

✦ The predominance of self-interest. Independent promotion takes precedence over colleagues: you have to watch your back, choose allies, avoid enemies, manipulate people and fiddle the system. Research has shown that within the audit culture, the dominance of individualism has damaged professional relationships and generated an implicit norm: the 'me-first' of egotism. (See Susan Long in Bibliography on Page 20)

These values may come as no surprise but consider your personal reaction to them.

• Do you feel uncomfortable or resigned to acknowledging 'this is the way it's done'?
• Do you ever find yourself in conflict with these values?
• Are you uncertain of alternatives?
• Are there occasions when you blame yourself for not fitting in with them?
• Do you ever feel 'unprofessional' precisely because of your dislike of the prevailing norms?

The answer to these questions for many women is 'yes'. Time after time, women (and some men too) find themselves working in a climate that they find soul-destroying, frustrating and unpleasant. A sense of alienation, though, is not a position of strength especially when there seems to be no other option. This discourages us from considering other approaches or dismissing them as woolly, unrealistic, impractical and naive. The combination of a lack of alternative plus the tendency to deride anything that doesn't fit into the dominant culture often leaves us feeling powerless, individually and collectively.

Experiences that reinforce a feeling of powerlessness include:

- Being discouraged from criticising or challenging the *status quo*
- Confusion and doubt in response to 'double talk', dishonesty and fudging
- Incompatibility of values and being personally undervalued
- Not speaking the same 'language'
- Lack of confidence
- Overwhelming history of tradition if working in an institutional setting
- Backlog of personal emotions related to the above
- Isolation

One step towards regaining some personal power in this context is to identify any underlying values that many women sense are truer to their own beliefs and preferences: alternatives which would promote more satisfaction, a feeling of self-respect and, significantly, would contribute to a better working climate all-round.

There is a world of difference between, on one hand, feeling you are inadequate because you've got it *wrong*, and on the other, realising that your personal values are as relevant, important and as legitimate as the dominant ones. Your values aren't wrong, just not mainstream. They may be minority values. They may be labelled as soft, unrealistic, naïve and belonging to cloud cuckoo land. But nevertheless, if they are your values, don't lose sight of them: they may be shared by more individuals than you realise.

Handling confrontation at work

When you have occasion to criticise inadequate performance or deliver bad news whether this means confronting a colleague, someone higher up than you on the ladder or someone lower down, you are faced with a choice: *how* do I handle the situation?

Do you comply with the norm? The template for handling criticism at work is familiar and already in place. It is worth examining in some detail. Consider the following examples of statements of someone who believes he or she has *no* problem at all with giving criticism to an employee:

'Dave, we'll make this quick. You've been here, how long, three months now? You seem to have a problem with the other guys on the team and they're not happy so I'm not happy. If you don't do something about it, I'm going to have to let you go.' (*Nothing specific but generally threatening*)

'Cheryl, this is unacceptable. Do a better job next time.' (*No specific change requested*)

The disadvantage of vague suggestions is two-fold. First, if you do not *say* exactly what you want, the other person will not *know* exactly what you want. So how can they agree to do what you ask if they are not clear about what it is they are agreeing to? It also makes it difficult for you if, three weeks later, you complain 'I asked you to improve your performance' and the reply, justifiably, is 'I have'. What do you say? *You* know you meant something else but if you don't spell it out, you have little redress.

Apart from being ineffectual, this approach is also aggressive but has become standardised and unfortunately confused with assertiveness. It is what I call 'the hit-and-run' method, because it allows you to put your point across without taking any responsibility for your behaviour. Each aggressive interaction leaves the other person defensive, perhaps hurt or disappointed but the obvious advantage of this strategy is that it enables you to avoid having to deal with the other person's *feelings* in response to what you have said.

Other hit-and-run tactics include informing an employee of their dismissal by email, by text or even putting all their belongings into a black plastic bag for them to discover when they arrive for work on a Monday morning. These tactics are rationalised by subscribing to the view that employees are units of labour, not human beings. For many people, therefore, a personal reluctance to criticise directly is reinforced by a system in which this behaviour is officially sanctioned.

Institutionalised aggression occurs in classrooms, the boardroom, the staffroom, the office, on the shop floor and in hospital wards. Even official feedback or personnel reviews are little more than opportunities to hand down one piece of criticism after another with no specific alternative suggested and zero opportunity for or interest in the other person's response. Because aggression is *de rigeur* in the workplace – integral to the competitive and entrepreneurial ethos – you will find men and women in authority who don't think twice about the fallout from aggressive behaviour: a kind of take it or leave it attitude.

Even if you are not that comfortable with this way of dealing with criticism, you may feel there is no other way. Some individuals, facing the task of criticising members of staff or colleagues, have to 'psyche' themselves up because, as we saw in Chapter 14, criticism is generally perceived as a weapon. We tell ourselves: 'I know this is going to be unpleasant and hurtful, but there are times when you have to sit someone down and be really brutal with them because it's necessary and it's for their own good. Things can't go on as they are.' Mentally preparing ourselves, we build up the tension and take aim.

It is remarkable how common this perception is, as if it is *inconceivable* that criticism could be constructive, without being hurtful, nasty and ultimately an ordeal both for you (the critic) and your 'target'. The art of constructive criticism takes on a particular importance in the workplace. If you apply precisely the same guidelines as we looked at earlier in a personal context, you would find it possible to criticise someone professionally without it being brutal, without it being devastating and without having to build yourself up to do the dreadful deed. The recipient (as opposed to target) could learn something useful and even feel supported by the process. What is usually overlooked is that assertive (and therefore constructive) confrontation actually increases an employee's willingness to improve and to co-operate precisely because of being treated as a human being.

Balancing the two faces of power

If you want to take a chance and try a more enlightened approach; if you're interested in exercising the kind of authority that enables and facilitates motivation and co-operation instead of subscribing to the culture of aggression, you need to balance two faces of power in your own mind. Embarking on a confrontational exchange with someone at work still requires the use of self-disclosure and the answers to your three key questions worked out beforehand.

If you follow the principles of opening and closing the conversation, you'll find that it's perfectly possible to be straight, direct, clear and unequivocal in your message, all without aggression. This is *not* just a psychological strategy: it requires you genuinely to consider the person in front of you not exclusively through the labels of enemy, subordinate, loser or rival: it requires you to look at those labels or categories and then see beyond them to a wider reality. The label – the object – ceases to be all there is: you see in the round, with more breadth. This is when your communication becomes assertive. Make no mistake: the assertive option is *not* a soft option. It can be very powerful but is rooted in another kind of power.

Wendy was head of human resources and had received complaints about one of the directors, Mike, regarding missed meetings and generally substandard performance. She had already passed them over to Simon, the CEO, but nothing had happened. She knew this was because Mike and Simon were buddies which explained the lack of action: the problem was also that she disliked Simon immensely. She hated his arrogance, his cronyism, his sexism: everything about him really.

So far, she had not said anything because she didn't think she could do so without an unpleasant fight. What can she do? First she has to let go the perception of him as enemy: otherwise she will not be able to even begin the dialogue. Secondly, she has to be clear about the answers to those three questions: What is happening? How does she feel? What does she want to be different? The answers in Wendy's mind are:

- Simon is ignoring the complaints about Mike
- I feel furious and powerless
- I'd like Simon to deal appropriately with Mike

(*She enters Simon's office having pre-arranged a time to meet.*)

Wendy: Simon, this is not easy for me. (*Simon looks at her and waits.*) I want to keep this brief. As you know, I've informed you of three complaints about Mike's work performance and it seems you haven't passed them on. I'd like to know why.

Simon: (*bristling*) I have no idea what you're implying, Wendy. I haven't passed anything on precisely because I conducted my own investigation and found the complaints to be completely groundless. I suggest you check your facts before accusing me of anything. (*Stares at her threateningly*)

The tension between them is palpable. Wendy is torn between her loathing for Simon and her nervousness. She'll either have to back off or fight back . . . or she can choose to stay out of the warzone and stay with her request. She takes a very deep breath.

Wendy: OK. Simon, I really don't want to get into a fight with you. It would be pretty pointless as you're my boss. But I want to say this. We've had complaints about Mike from three separate members of staff. They know that I pass them on to you and then nothing happens. What I would like you to do is deal with these complaints appropriately. (*Repetition and reinforcement*)

Simon: But I've already . . .

Wendy: I'd like to finish, Simon. I am not on some personal vendetta. I'm asking for the sake of the whole department because as long as these problems are seen to continue, it is doing us all a lot of harm. (*Stands up*) I'd like you to consider it, Simon. I won't take up any more of your time. (*Moves to the door*)

You can't change the system but you can challenge your own fear of speaking up by speaking truth to power instead of allowing yourself to be intimidated. Wendy will never change her opinion of Simon but she was able to state clearly what she wanted – in the face of antagonism and yet without hooking into it – and make her exit. By putting aside the concept of 'enemy', she was able to stay with her own personal power and be effective. This is the source of real confidence.

Another constituent of personal power is integrity, being true to oneself. There are times when we have the opportunity to assert our own values even if these are at odds with the mainstream. Helen found herself facing this kind of challenge when she heard that a long-term employee faced losing his job because of restructuring in the company. She didn't like the man particularly but objected strongly to the proposed procedure of waiting until the Friday before he was due two weeks' leave to tell him not to come back after his holiday. She believed that it was unfair to treat him in this way.

She had tried, at the time, to say something to her own superior but had been dismissed as being too sentimental and reminded that this was the way things were done. She was left with a sense of guilt and self-reproach: an emotional state often masking feelings of anger and powerlessness. It is the loss of integrity that damages our self-esteem so deeply.

Practice 1

She set the scene by making an appointment to see her superior, giving him due notice of the importance of the matter.

Helen: I'm here because I've been thinking about Peter and the decision to sack him.

Gavin: (*shrugging his shoulders*), 'Yes it's tough but he's got to go.

Helen: I feel that he should be told in another way..it's not a very nice way to do it.

Gavin: There's no *nice* way.

Helen: No, but I feel that he should be treated decently . . . (*faltering*).

Helen learned that self-disclosure is vital. This means avoiding phrases like 'I feel *that*' which tend to preface thoughts not feelings: make an honest declaration because, if a value is important to you, only you can express this.

Practice 2

Helen: This is awkward for me (*self-disclosure*) but why I'm here is because I feel uncomfortable (*self-disclosure*) that Peter should be dismissed in such an insensitive way.

Gavin: We are not here to be sensitive.

Helen: I realise that I am in the minority, but it's important to me. Even if you take no notice, I want to state here how strongly I disagree with the manner of Peter's dismissal. It has a demoralising effect on the whole department when one person is treated in this way.

Gavin: (*looks at Helen and pauses . . . does she have a point perhaps?!*) So what do you suggest, a whip round and a party?

Helen: No, I'm being serious. He isn't popular, you know that. But I would like to see him, with you if necessary, and tell him in advance. I think that's a fairer way to treat one of our employees.

Helen had no idea whether her boss would alter his position on the matter but, by clearly stating her proposed alternative, she was able to live with her integrity more intact.

Sometimes it is inevitable that we have to face up to a harsh reality and be the bearers of bad news but even legitimate rejection can be handled without aggression. As her manager, Lisa was faced with telling Annette, a junior employee, that she had not been given a permanent position in charge of web-site development. The problem was exacerbated by the fact that Annette had been temporarily promoted to this position but, although she had been efficient, the interview panel had found her teambuilding skills were not good enough.

The three answers for Lisa were:

- Annette hasn't got the job
- I feel awkward about telling her
- I have to give her the news

Even when it seems too obvious to ask yourself these questions, the answers will always help to focus on what you are feeling and where you're going in the conversation so you start off from an internally stronger position.

Lisa: Annette, thanks for coming (*pauses . . . looks at her directly*) This is a difficult situation but I have to tell you that you didn't get the job, I'm afraid.

Annette: Why not? I thought I'd done really well!

Lisa: You have in some ways but the panel decided you lacked team-building skills.

Annette: What the hell does that mean?

Lisa: I think they mean you need to be more approachable and to consult others more as well as managing your responsibilities.

Annette: And how are you supposed to learn that?

Lisa: Well, I suppose you could go on a course.

Annette: (*her eyes filling with tears*) I am *so* disappointed. I really thought I'd have a good chance. I thought I'd done the job really well.

Lisa: (*sympathetically*) I'm sure you must be disappointed. I would be too.

Annette: Why didn't anyone say anything before?

Lisa: I guess you didn't have a proper appraisal because you took the post temporarily. (*Needing to close now*) Look, Annette, I think it's best that we end this meeting now but I'd be happy to see you again when you've had time to consider things. If you decide you do want to improve your skills somehow, we can talk about it at a later date. Is that OK? (*Annette nods and get to her feet.*)

Lisa: Thanks for coming in and I'm sorry it wasn't good news.

This kind of interaction doesn't take much more time than the hit-and-run strategy but the difference in effect on employees is remarkable. Handling authority assertively is not about losing face or scoring points. It is less concerned with winning as an outcome than emerging from an interaction with an appropriate balance between yourself (and the demands of your role) and respect for the other person.

19

Your Body – Friend or Foe?

This chapter looks at our relationship with our bodies: not in a sexual context – this is the theme of the following chapter – but the ways in which we listen to or ignore, accept or reject our bodies; whether we are familiar or unfamiliar with what occurs in our bodies; whether we feel truly at home within our bodies or view them more as a project we are lumbered with and constantly need to improve upon. More often than not, a woman doesn't so much cherish her body as the 'temple of her soul' as engage in a virtually life-long struggle with it: the result is a conflict between body and mind, appetite and excess, between feelings and reason, indulgence and punishment, truth and pretence.

Many women see their bodies, if not as an out-and-out enemy, then certainly with the unfamiliarity of a stranger. We are often suspicious and uncertain as to how our bodies might respond. We try to keep them under control: we disguise them, stuff them, starve them, decorate them, mutilate them, hide them, restrict them or deprive them. We use them to attract, seduce, satisfy, console, give birth and serve others. If they slow down with overwork or old age we sometimes show them little respect or compassion: we push them beyond their limits or regard them as useless and unattractive, no longer worthy of care and attention.

Image-consciousness has risen to new heights in our culture in the course of last three decades: the 'image is all' ethos affects every one of us, whether or not we subscribe to it, and it is no longer exclusive to the female gender. Image-consciousness erodes integrity and the consequence is that women of all ages remain deeply ambivalent about their bodies. We are (often intensely) preoccupied with how much our bodies measure or weigh or the calorific count of the foods we put into them; we submit them to fitness regimes, remove evidence of any natural hair, hide them behind veils or flaunt them in provocative and revealing clothes.

One of the prerequisites for satisfying and fulfilling sexual encounters with another person is a familiarity, respect and sense of harmony within our own bodies. Instead of concentrating exclusively on external assessment of our bodies as a measure of our self-esteem, I believe it's important to start with our sense of our *selves*: how do I relate to this body of mine, not only its external image but also my interior existence (emotions, instinct, intuition, spirit)?

Much has been written about how women are perceived and treated as sexual objects in various cultures: my focus in this chapter is less on external structures and more on how women have internalised the concept of 'body-as-object' and the psychological repercussions of doing so.

The most common response to looking at a reflection of one's entire naked body in a mirror (if we ever let ourselves do so) is that, instead of regarding our reflection as an image of wholeness, we gaze with critical evaluation on an assembly of parts. This perception derives from being conditioned to look at the human body in fragments: whether sick or healthy, the human body tends to be viewed in discrete units. One of the effects of fragmentation is that we tend to perceive our bodies as a collection of body parts – breasts, hips, genitals, legs, eyes, lips, hair, waist, thighs, buttocks – each of which can be singled out as an attractive asset to make the most of or an unattractive flaw to conceal: instead of wholeness we see bits or objects to which we attach relative value. In a butcher's display, for example, you don't allow yourself to think of the essential 'cowness' of a cow, the magnificent creature with a strong straight back, its deep bellow, its softness, its extraordinary eyes, its *being*. You don't acknowledge the essential being of the lamb or the pig, each a prime creature in its own right because they are reduced to fragments of the whole: a chop or sausage, mince or steak to be consumed and enjoyed.

We learn to see our bodies in fragments. Although, as very young girls, we experience for a few years a unity and integrity of body, mind and spirit, at the time of realisation of being a potential sexual object, this unity is broken. Our physical identity and self-hood are split: who we are versus how we need to be seen. Living this divide can last a lifetime during which we lose touch with the wonder of our being. It is not hard to understand that when anything is reduced to an assembly of parts, it doesn't function as a whole. When we assess our bodies as fragments, we lose sight of our totality, our humanity and of our intrinsic femaleness: at some deep level we stop seeing the interconnected beauty of all we are – inside and out – and once detached from this connection, we learn to see, assess and treat our bodies with the same objectivity with which they are viewed through outside eyes.

This launches many women on a treadmill of monitoring, compensating, covering up and imitating. After a while, external persuasion isn't necessary because it's internalised. In the end we become inured to being objects, to the demands of being pleasing and attractive in body and behaviour. This explains why women often choose to undergo all sorts of major surgical procedures without any persuasion (sometimes even despite attempts at *dis*suasion) from the men in their lives to whom they want to stay attractive: our bodies have been transformed permanently into objects in our *own* perception.

Current trends to 'sexualise' little girls before puberty, turning them into self-conscious objects at an increasingly younger age, mean that even those few precious years of bodily integrity – when there is no division between mind and body – are ever dwindling. Awareness of being potential sexual objects brings many attendant anxieties about one's image in comparison to others. When the seeds of self-consciousness are sown, we become increasingly vulnerable to the cultural pressure to be attractive and to present ourselves in a certain way: of the significance of an external image. How we look becomes more significant than who we are: projecting an external image overtakes cultivating inner integrity. This initiates a burgeoning and lifelong evaluation of one's own body according to some internalised ideal and from this moment, we start to compare and compete with other females for the right to be considered an object of attraction and desire.

The catch is that being in the female body is not without its disadvantages. Recognition of inequality between the genders means that it takes only a small mental step to connect this inequality to being born in a female body. Depending on which culture we are born into, the disadvantage of being female may be obvious within the family unit or at school; it may become obvious later only through sexual encounters or when a woman enters employment. Whether she's making sandwiches in the local deli or on the board of an insurance company, she'll soon spot the inequities. Some young girls become tomboys; some develop anorexia to try and put off developing physically into womanhood. Whether we put all our efforts into endorsing our feminine role or rebelling against it, this process affects every one of us.

Nature as 'nuisance'

Women's bodies have been traditionally valued as safe havens, sources of comfort, decoration and pleasure. They are vital vehicles and carriers of reproduction. Our bodies offer softness and curves, a refuge from the angular, linear world. Every natural aspect of the female body defines her as non-linear. We bleed. Our bodies are round and soft and fleshy. They are unpredictable, curved, messy, chaotic and susceptible to rhythmic changes. Many of us are subject to emotions that can't be understood logically and seem to function according to a system that isn't rational or straightforward or controllable.

In a world which privileges certain qualities over others, nature (in all its myriad forms and meanings) has become a casualty. Natural aspects of a woman's body are no exception. This antipathy ranges from hiding menstruation, to morbid obsession with eradicating smell – perfumed tampons during our periods, perfumed mini-pads in between, perfumed douches just in case – to removing any natural body evidence of reality: wrinkle, cellulite, body hair, smell, soft tissue or roundness. In the western world, women look at other women's bodies through the same critical eyes of distaste for fat or the effects of ageing – 'Did you see her thighs?' or 'Why doesn't she do something about those breasts?'

Many of us put our efforts from an early age into being as feminine and as attractive as possible. The catch is that those women who are adored for their bodies as they *naturally* occur are in the minority. Most of the time, relentless efforts are made to eradicate nature. All natural hair from legs, arms, underarms and face must disappear; waxing the bikini line or removing every trace of pubic hair are currently synonymous with being sexually desirable. A whole range of medications has been manufactured to help us with our ongoing struggle: HRT is on hand to suppress natural menopausal symptoms; anti-depressants to suppress natural emotions. Laxatives substitute for natural digestive processes; scientific formulae for natural breast milk. And then, of course, an infinite array of 'age-defying' preparations.

Although attempts to hide or delay signs of ageing have been around a long time, now more than ever before, the fear of ageing has intensified: young women are persuaded to buy products in their thirties to have a better chance of staving off the inevitable, hoping that by the time they get to sixty, some drug will have been found to guarantee perpetual youthfulness.

Cosmetic surgery – ranging from Botox to facelifts to 'corrective' surgical intervention – is no longer the prerogative of the rich and famous: celebrities merely lead the way in the trend. In fact some women go so far as to claim that the right to choose cosmetic surgery is a testament to being 'liberated'. This claim reminds me of the paradoxical psychological dynamic (known as the Stockholm syndrome) which occurs when a captive shows a devoted loyalty and grateful willingness to submit to a captor who has absolute control over her life: it is debatable whether cosmetic surgery is a symptom of enslavement or liberation.

It is rare to encounter a woman who truly loves and celebrates her body as it *is*. This means that for the majority, having a woman's body entails a lifelong struggle to suppress the natural in favour of an imposed and artificial ideal. Yet, despite our best efforts, our bodies disappoint us because they will not conform. Our bodies betray us. Even cosmetic surgery does not last forever: skin stretches with time and still more work needs to be done.

So is there any way we can build a more celebratory relationship with our bodies, or at least a less critical and more compassionate one? An assertive attitude to your body means learning to understand it, to trust it and to care for it. It especially means learning to live with your body in *harmony* rather than struggling against it.

Tiredness

We have already touched on the issue of tiredness: how we often fail to heed signs of fatigue in our bodies. These signs will vary with each individual but they are often specific: your skin comes up in a rash, your stomach may tighten giving you indigestion, your back may twinge or your legs ache. You find yourself having less and less energy. If you detect and follow the signs in good time you can prevent yourself overstretching your physical and psychological resources.

Health

Finding out what suits *you* is important. There is no point following tedious or expensive diets and punishing yourself unnecessarily. Monitoring what you put in your body means knowing how to restore the balance: too much of one thing means you need to take in a little more of something else. Young women now are more acutely calorie conscious than any previous generations but try and appreciate your body: not as a thing to be clothed and paraded and judged but as *you*.

Learn about what your body tells you: how your appetite and digestion changes with your emotions; how it varies with the pattern of hormonal changes in your body, such as your menstrual cycle. Try watching without judgement and criticism, allowing yourself to feel a bit more bloated for a few days without giving yourself (your body) a hard time because you can't wear your favourite jeans for a while. Learning what is good for your body and bad for your body need not be expensive or time-consuming. Once you start thinking about having *a relationship* with your body, it is easier to notice how you are treating it and what you can change.

Sometimes women go to the extreme and decide, for all sorts of reasons, to treat their bodies like machines: rigorous exercise regimes and diets are followed with intense discipline to keep the machine 'lean'. If you're one of those women, ask yourself whether your approach is rooted in care or control, in acceptance or a wish to knock your body into submission.

Care includes repairing the wear and tear caused by the stress of our lives. Tension and anxiety are inevitable a lot of the time, more than we realise. We flake out in the evening and seem to be constantly sighing with tiredness and moaning about another day, wondering if we will ever have the stamina to get through. Making time to rest is important and learning how to relax, without always needing the help of alcohol, is vital. Appropriate rest may mean more organisation of the way you spend your time: relaxation can take as little as five minutes but makes a remarkable difference. Find out what suits you: walking, meditating, gardening or yoga for example. Learning to breathe and relax in the middle of a tense and important meeting, discussion or journey helps to reduce the stress and strain on your body. Breathing deeply at any time helps.

Find a way to exercise your body in a way that you can enjoy. Going for a walk, cycling, running, swimming, dancing, T'ai chi or pilates: all these forms of exercise can be part of a daily programme. What are some of the ways in which you could make more time for this in your life? Remember it is no good setting your goals too high because you are likely to find it difficult to reorganise your life. Start small. Taking five minutes a day to do some sort of exercise is a *possible* goal and therefore one you can reach.

Understanding how to care for your body in health will help you care for your body in sickness. If you go part way to finding out and taking responsibility for your health, you can take some responsibility for your body when it is not healthy.

Emotions

Chapter 11 described the importance of listening to your emotional body cues instead of ignoring them: going *against* your body means denying to yourself what you feel; going *with* your body means accepting the need to express those feelings in some way. Attuning to your body means taking the time to see what you really need instead of fighting it or resorting to food or drink as a means of suppression and temporary relief. Listening more carefully to what your body is communicating puts you much more in command of your life.

Saying 'no' and 'yes' for your body means saying 'no' and 'yes' for yourself. Having learned the truth of this, many women benefit from assertiveness training by being able to say 'no' and 'yes' for their bodies, seeing it as an important statement of doing something for themselves: saying 'no' to cigarettes; saying 'no' to sex when you don't want it; saying 'no' to extra work when you are tired; saying 'no' to eating all the children's leftovers; saying 'no' to swallowing back tears; saying 'yes' to cycling; saying 'yes' to an extravagant box of chocolates; saying 'yes' to a long luxurious soak in the bath; saying 'yes' to an extra hour in bed; saying 'yes' to sexual pleasure; saying 'yes' to a weekly swim; saying 'yes' to buying yourself a bunch of flowers; saying 'yes' to the offer of a lift when you are tired or saying 'no' to the offer of a lift when you need the exercise. Look at ways in which you can say 'yes' and 'no' for your body and yourself in your own life.

Information, familiarity, care and pleasure: it sounds like being a friend to your body which is exactly what it is. It is important to respect, cherish and care for your body, for yourself. This is far more than an encouragement to get slimmer or fitter or healthier. It is certainly more than improving the exterior and more a question of healing the split between outside and inside. As we'll see in the next chapter, excessive preoccupation with the external image we project does not lead to consistently high self-esteem. Of course, there is the short-term satisfaction of having our worth and status confirmed by admiring eyes but in the long term, we risk losing touch with the core of who we are and failing to build a resilient self-esteem which we need to achieve a measure of emotional independence.

20

Self-Esteem

A long-term consequence of a preoccupation with how we look to others, remembering that this involves both the need to be attractive in physical appearance *and* behaviour, is a chronic self-consciousness: in many women, this leads to confusion about who we really are, what we want, how we feel and what we think we should keep hidden from others. In short, we risk becoming over-dependent on outside reflections.

A woman looks in real and imagined mirrors to see how she appears to others. She also looks to the mirrors in people's eyes, which reflect back how she appears. In one mirror she sees a particular image. In one person's eyes, she sees another. Maybe in someone else's eyes she sees yet another. The images may conflict or converge. At times, she thinks that the reflections show all of who she is, at other times one single facet.

Reflections give reassurance of our existence, our credibility and our worth. We become accustomed to relying on reflected evaluation. We develop 'winning ways' in parallel with 'winning bodies'; we become expert at responding to other people's cues, testing the ground for approval, making the right impression, matching and adapting our actions, words and movements. Obviously, if we choose to live, work, sleep, talk, travel and generally share our lives with other human beings, it would be pointless to stay in a vacuum and close our eyes and ears to everyone else. Problems arise when we become over-dependent on outside approval and validation to the point of breaking the thread of connection with an internal, grounded sense of self.

A constant preoccupation with concerns about what might happen, what the response will be or what someone else is or might be thinking decreases our ability to focus on our own *inner* responses. This is why we lose touch with what we want and feel and also why, when considering changing our familiar response to a situation and behaving uncharacteristically, the first worry which comes to mind is 'but what will they think of me?'

Over-dependence on how others see us makes for a fragile self-esteem. How does Dulcie see herself? Dulcie escapes into daydreams where she sees herself in fantasy – the model, the boss, the star – to avoid looking at herself realistically because what she sees in reality is hopeless and inadequate. Her self-esteem is low and she depends on others to strengthen it. This works to some extent but it is never enough to compensate fully for her own conviction of her lack of worth.

And Agnes? She punishes the vulnerable and fragile parts of herself that allow her to feel hurt. She keeps them firmly locked away. She is quick to attack first before she is wounded, rejects before she is rejected. Her self-esteem looks high but isn't and she is often quite desperate to be loved and accepted even though she would rather die than admit it.

Ivy appears to think highly of herself. She seems to be quite satisfied and confident although secretly she subjects herself to all sorts of critical pressures and punishes herself pitilessly when she fails to meet her own expectations. In order to avoid rejection, she holds on more and more tightly to the control in her relationships, ever more desperate to avoid any risk of losing approval.

Self-esteem is not conceit or arrogance: it does not depend on being a winner every time. It does not depend on any kind of pretence or denial of vulnerability. In the context of this book, self-esteem is based in a strong, anchored sense of self which survives both failure and success; it survives the buffeting caused by the aftermath of mistakes, disappointments and even occasional disasters.

Selma accepts herself as she *is* which means acknowledging both her strengths and weaknesses. The more she values herself and feels strong in herself, the more she can allow herself to look at those aspects of herself which she doesn't like very much but can acknowledge. The more she accepts herself with limitations, the more she is  open to listening to other people's criticism and learning from it, without sinking into self-reproach. The more open she feels, the more she is free to be herself. She can take the risk of changing without clinging desperately to the known and familiar.

She conveys her certainty of her own value as well. She is open to acceptance and love from others: if she is rejected, she is not demolished. If she is not accepted by others, she can choose to weigh up the importance of their approval against the importance of being true to herself. From an inner base of certainty she can risk the uncertainty of change.

Anchored self-esteem survives the inevitable fluctuations of acceptance and rejection from others. You can recognise when your self-esteem is low: your inbox is empty, a friend forgets you never take milk in your coffee, a stranger scowls at you . . . and your feeling of worth plummets. You are left wondering what you have done wrong. What have you done to deserve this? This contrasts with those good days when everything you do feels right: you can dismiss a frown or a disapproving comment because you feel resilient and secure enough in yourself.

Fluctuations of self-esteem in relation to others are connected to the extent to which we feel accepted and loved.

Self-acceptance It is natural to want to belong, to fit in with those who are important to you. Problems occur only when how acceptable you are depends *solely* on how others see you and rate you. Then it's more difficult to take the risk of trying something new: you won't want to rock the boat. Consider the various roles you have in your life and see if you can identify the spoken and unspoken expectations of those roles. Are you aware of not meeting an important personal need because it would conflict with someone else's view of you? Do you give a reflected image too much significance and let it undermine your self-esteem?

You can make a positive decision for yourself and still be haunted by uncertainty. Davina looks in the mirror. She has started a job to make a life of her own which has meant employing someone else to care for her family some of the time. She discovers how much she has relied on reflected approval since she's now feeling the effects of the disapproval from her particular circle of friends. It makes her question whether being a woman really should mean being a selfless and devoted mother.

Hilary decided to stay at home and look after her children. Everywhere she sees mothers who manage a career as well. She is tired of feeling she has to justify not going out to work. She looks in the mirror and wonders if she should be doing both and worries that a real woman should be achieving everything at once. She looks at herself and experiences the discomfort of not knowing who she really is any more.

Sam is single, in her mid-forties, doesn't have children and has noticed a distinct coldness from her married friends. She has sensed a covert assumption that to have been married and divorced is preferable to remaining unmarried; at least if a man had chosen her *once* this might have upped her credibility in others' estimation. All this takes its toll on her self-esteem.

How much of our behaviour is based on a need for reflected approval and how much is it a choice we make for ourselves. Somewhere there is a balance. What do you see when you look in your mirror?

Whose eyes reflect back your measure of acceptability? What standards do you have to measure up to? Whose standards do you need to reach in order to qualify for acceptance within each category of your life? Do you have to be happily married? A size 10? A perfect mother? A sparkling hostess? A sexually satisfying partner? A socially-conscious citizen? A charitable neighbour? A grateful daughter? A competent housewife? An inspiring leader? An inventive cook? A reliable employee? An uncomplaining saint? A tower of strength for others? Have a successful career? Boast a hundred friends? Conceal your age well?

If you can get some idea of how much you depend on others for a feeling of acceptance, you can explore possibilities for building a sense of *self*-acceptance, not instead of, but alongside acceptance from outside sources. With more balance, you have more emotional room to manoeuvre.

Lovability also matters. Being loved gives us a feeling of confidence which is unparalleled whereas feeling unloved and undesirable makes us feel miserable, wretched and useless. Feeling loved regenerates itself so that if we feel loved, we feel lovable. This makes us attractive and people warm to us, so we continue being lovable . . . but it works in reverse as well. We are all sensitive to rejection but however much we may try and prevent it happening, rejections, both slight and serious, occur throughout our lives. The following examples give an idea of the kinds of experiences which can rock our self-esteem:

1 Someone forgets your birthday or an important anniversary.

2 You are feeling very enthusiastic about something that has happened to you but your partner couldn't care less.

3 You reach out to give someone physical affection and they withdraw.

4 One of your parents continually compares you un-favourably with others.

5 Your partner criticises your appearance.

6 You offer to do someone a favour and you are turned down.

7 You are turned down after a job interview.

8 Someone you find very attractive tells you: 'I want to keep this platonic'.

9 You show something you have written or something you have made to someone important in your life and they are clearly unimpressed.

10 You give someone a present you have chosen carefully but the response is one of indifference.

11 You don't get an invitation to a meeting or party to which everyone else seems to have been invited.

12 You feel like making love but your partner isn't in the mood.

Our sense of rejection will be affected by the importance of the particular person rejecting us, our own individual 'crumple buttons' (see Chapter 13) and our mood at the time. Sometimes it takes a lot to shift our self-esteem but, at other times, a mere glance or a trivial gesture is enough to trigger a whole rush of past unresolved and unexpressed feelings of rejection. Given that we are bound to encounter rejection in some form or other throughout our lives, it is useful to know how to handle it assertively with long-term and short-term strategies.

The long-term strategy is to learn the skill of loving yourself, something which we often find problematic. Learning how to be a friend to yourself day-by-day will stand you in good stead in an emergency. Once you have built up a reserve of self-sustenance on the inside, you can withstand many pressures and assaults from the outside. I see this like strengthening our immune system: building emotional immunity allows us to better survive the effects of various viruses – rejections, knocks, isolation, moments of disappointment or being misunderstood by others – to which we will inevitably be exposed in life. A weak emotional immune system makes the impact of such experiences all the greater.

It can also be important to discover ways to explore and draw comfort from separateness. Do you enjoy your own company? Do you dread periods of solitude or look forward to them as a welcome relief? If you do have some time on your own, do you spend it doing what you enjoy doing – even if that happens to be nothing at all – or do you spend the time fretting and worrying about everyone else? Being on your own is also a good way of finding out what is actually happening on the *inside*, especially important when so much of our lives is taken up with concern for what is happening *outside*. Just a few minutes each day, a few hours each week can be enough to remind yourself that there is a part of you to be noticed, to be attended to, listened to and cherished. This part of you need not live up to *any* expectations: it is fine just as it is. Find out who you are essentially, apart from all the roles and responsibilities you have in your life.

Short-term strategies for coping with rejection involve keeping afloat in the shallows rather than disappearing into the deep end. There is always a danger of allowing the experience of being rejected to become skewed psychologically into a conviction that somehow we deserved to be rejected because of being inherently *rejectable*. This makes it imperative to hold on to the knowledge that we are worth being loved, that we are still lovable, even though we may not feel loved at that precise moment.

One way of doing this is to identify more specifically what you *feel* in relation to the particular rejection: in other words, to go beyond the word 'rejected' and find out what lies underneath. Very often, our deeper feelings are associated more with anger than grief: this realisation makes it easier to sidestep the trap of blaming oneself and to move on emotionally instead of clinging to the misery of it all.

Then you can arrange to be good to yourself in some way. Here are some practical examples of tried and tested antidotes:

- A walk by the sea/in the country
- A glass of wine
- Music
- Phoning a good friend who loves you
- Being with people who love you
- Sleep
- Vigorous exercise
- Writing out your feelings uncensored (not for sending!)
- Having a good cry
- A treat of some kind

Following on

1. Use the ideas in the chapter to find three things in your life you could say 'no' or 'yes' to for yourself. Remember to start with small goals.

2. Write down a list of situations when you felt rejected. Then consider what exactly you felt at the time: ignored? unheard? unimportant? hurt? resentful? invisible? not good enough? Next, note down what you actually said at the time. Did you express those feelings or not? If not, why not? Finally, think how you would like to have handled what happened more assertively; how might you handle something similar in the future?

3. Since self-esteem is so much tied up with our need for approval, it is interesting to explore this in more detail. Consider whether there is a person in your life whom you are aware of wanting to please so much that you cannot be yourself and worry constantly about what they might think. Perhaps you feel inhibited and uncomfortable in their company because you believe they don't like you. With this in mind, answer the following questions: perhaps go through it out loud with a friend.

    a) What does this person like or not like about you?

    b) Is this based on impression or evidence? What sort of evidence?

    c) What difference would it make if this person were to like you?

    d) What do you need to do to get this person to like you? Are you honestly prepared to do it?

The answers to these questions will tell you whether your worry is absurd or whether you are genuinely worried about the person's opinion. If this is so, you can practise applying the skills of negative assertion and negative enquiry (see Chapter 13).

4. *Pleasure exercise.* Take a large piece of paper and write down, on the left-hand side, a list of twenty pleasures – these can be very simple. Here are some examples: the taste of chocolate, the sound of the wind, sowing seeds, the delight of an ordinary flower like a daisy or pansy, the smell of coffee, an absorbing book, laughing with a close

friend, sunshine on your back, the smell or sound of the sea, dancing, holding the hand of a small child, a long hot bath, a cat curled up on your lap, the smell of warm bread, strawberries in season, a sunset, an open fire, clean sheets, singing when you are by yourself, the feeling of peace when everyone has gone to bed, holding a baby, a favourite piece of music, a cuddle, looking at the stars, having your hair washed, silence, skinny-dipping, eating in the open air or watching the world go by.

When you have written down at least twenty, the next step is to divide the rest of the page into three columns. In the first column put a T or an A which stand for Together or Alone. This means whether you enjoy the pleasure on your own, or whether you need someone else to enjoy it with. If it is a pleasure which can be enjoyed alone *or* together with someone, put T/A. In the second column put a £ sign – a large £ indicates an expensive pleasure, a small £ sign indicates that the pleasure costs a little money. In the last column, write down how long it is since you enjoyed that particular pleasure. This does not need to be precise – just an idea of whether it is hours, days, weeks or months. Then take the time to see what your list says about your approach to pleasure. Are there opportunities all around you in your everyday life? Are there some things you have not enjoyed for a long time with no good reason? Do you have more pleasure alone or with another person? Do all your pleasures cost money? What do you learn about yourself?

21

Assertiveness and Sexuality

Sex, sex, sex . . . newspapers still titillate our Sundays with it, advertisers exploit it, magazines urge us to be better at it. Though there has been little change in the sensationalism associated with sex, social attitudes to sex have certainly altered since I first wrote this book when I was also running sexuality groups and working as a psycho-sexual counsellor. At that time, this was considered pioneering work. The topic of sexuality had previously been shrouded in more ignorance than information: better left alone, not talked about, hidden, denied, repressed and remaining a dark presence lurking in the cellar somewhere. Researchers in America had then only recently examined sexual behaviour in minute detail in a laboratory environment so that every aspect of the process of sexual arousal could henceforth be identified, measured, catalogued and labelled.

Their results gave an enormous boost to the emphasis on mechanics of sexual performance. In the intervening years, encouraged by the proliferation of access to pornography through internet sites, the preoccupation with performance has gained so much ground that the idea of sex as an expression of love, warmth, celebration and reciprocal pleasure seems now almost quaint and old-fashioned. We are awash with sexual information but little or no contextual reference to relationship, intimacy, care, respect or love.

I still believe that sex is one of the most important ways in which we can communicate with another person through our bodies: a loving embrace can afford us relief from tension (sexual and otherwise), reassurance and a feeling of physical and emotional well-being. But these relational aspects of human sexuality suffer from current cultural pressures which persuade us to see sex – like other activities we engage in with others – as an opportunity for showcasing our abilities and talents. The focus is now more on what we can achieve: when, with whom and how successful we can be.

When I wrote my book on women and sexuality (*The Mirror Within*), I coined the term 'Superlay' to describe how this particular stereotype could pressurise us, as ordinary women, into believing we had to be superb performers in bed. Superlay, as a stereotype, was characterised by being endlessly turned on, always eager for sex, orgasming easily and many times over, hugely desirable and totally in control.

What I explained then was that this image had been moulded perfectly from male fantasies: this was the kind of woman every man wanted, even if she could be a little disconcerting in the flesh. Superlay remained more in realms of fantasy: the women who commanded huge audiences in television series like *Dynasty* and *Dallas* were tough, glamorous, wealthy and powerful: liberated certainly but not overtly sexual.

In the late 1990s, '*Sex in the City*' spawned a whole new confidence in millions of women. These Superlay stereotypes came to life: they inspired and gave heart to many ordinary women who, despite having neither the glamour nor the wealth of the fictional heroines, felt permitted to be as raunchy and sexually independent as men. This was hailed as the apogee of female sexual liberation.

Does it follow that women are now more assertive in sexual relationships? The answer appears to be no: there is certainly more evidence of aggression. A friend of mine, who has been an agony aunt over these decades, tells me that a major change in the vast correspondence she receives every week is now the proportion of boys and young men who write because they're worried about the size of their penis, having been subjected to mockery or scorn by young women. It seems as ordinary now for young women to go out with the intention to score: to target potential males; to fragment them into 'tight butts', 'six packs' or 'dreamy eyes' and to use them for casual sex without any concern for the human being inside the body. This is one of the repercussions of the dominance of aggression in our culture and the belief that this is the *only* way to be seen to be powerful regardless of whether you are male or female.

Has the legacy of Superlay enabled women to be more sexually independent? We may generally feel more permission to take the initiative, to express sexual needs and claim the right to sexual pleasure. However the uncertainty behind the phrase *'I'd be lost without you'* doesn't appear to have lost much of its psychological hold. Many women feel that when they do not have a partner, they automatically lose their sexual viability and are judged to be sexually unattractive. Only when they have a partner, usually a man, does their sexuality kick into life.

In addition, you may find yourself hanging on to a relationship in spite of a lot of hurt and hassle simply because you don't want to be left *alone*: if this happens your personal validity – as a woman – risks disappearing along with your partner. This un-certainty is evident from early on in our sexual lives: many young girls and young women throughout the world have sex for the first time (and many times after that), not through pride or celebration of their sexuality, but out of anxiety about not belonging or fear of disapproval (or worse).

Declarations of sexual independence also sit uncomfortably with the fact that many women today feel pressurised to eradicate every wisp of hair and extra ounce of flesh from their bodies to guarantee a partner's erection; to agree to experimentation with a threesome, for example, or to use pornography as the only way to keep a partner sexually satisfied.

Finally, we can't ignore the changes wrought by the develop-ment of new technologies in this period. These have enhanced the phenomenon of fragmentation, described in Chapter 19, not only by way of the exponential growth of pornography but also because our means of communicating has altered. On-line relationships offer little possibility of real intimacy: sharing your edited thoughts and pictures is not the same as face-to-face relating. There is no real contact, no possibility of person-to-person communication: you select the fragment of information you want to disclose and engage with someone else's edited fragment: alter ago meets alter ego.

Communication in sexual situations

None of these changes has had much impact on the way we actually speak to each other in a face-to-face sexual context. All the aspects of assertive communication described in earlier chapters are as applicable in the bedroom as they are in the supermarket or office: difficulty with making clear and specific requests; saying 'no' clearly and firmly to sexual activity when you do not want it rather than conceding your needs and wants as less important than your partner's; the need to recognise your feelings of anger, hurt and fear and to express them assertively; the need to be familiar with your body and your responses; not allowing your fear of criticism and disapproval to dominate your relationship; facing the difficulty of not knowing how to make a constructive change or initiate a constructive dialogue in a sexual relationship that has become stuck in a rut and unsatisfying.

Sexuality is at one level just another theme and another context in which we have these three options of expressing ourselves aggressively, passively or assertively: what makes it harder though is that we tend to be more vulnerable. Unless you're a professional, you're likely to feel some sensibility when engaging in sexual activity with another person. This is easy to accept when you love the person because the deeper the feelings, the more open you are. Many women still feel anxious about communicating with people who are most important to them and with whom they feel most vulnerable. Let us look at the sort of issues that arise in women's lives which illustrate how assertive skills are relevant within a sexual context:

Betty, thirty-eight, widowed six years ago, is beginning to relate to a new man for the first time. She has two children, aged ten and twelve, and has maintained a low sexual profile since her husband's death. Now faced with her new lover, she lacks confidence. She feels like a novice again: she knows what she wants but feels unable to speak up or to find the actual words to ask him to change the way he touches her. She can respond passively as she has up until now letting the situation continue, with her resentment building up steadily. She can let this go on until she explodes about what a lousy lover he is; or what may happen is that, like Ivy, she will find some indirect means of saying 'no' to him, cutting him off. She will probably avoid sex by saying that the children are unhappy with him staying the night, using that as an excuse. An assertive option would be to use the skills already described to set a time to talk to him directly.

Heather, forty, has enjoyed her marriage for fifteen years, but feels that sex with her husband has become routine, predictable and dull. She wants to find ways of renewing and reviewing their marriage and exploring new possibilities with each other.

Janet's marriage finished four years ago. At fifty, after a series of temporary flings, she decides she wants to remain celibate for a while, to step back and consider what she really wants before getting involved with someone else. When she meets a man who asks her out, she hesitates to make her limits clear: she is afraid of being labelled frigid or weird. Her anxiety pushes her into anticipating every encounter as a potential threat. She overacts and leaves both herself and the other person embarrassed. She has to practise making a clear statement at the beginning of the friendship, setting limits so that everyone knows where they stand.

Marianne is twenty three and has not really wanted sexual activity since the birth of her first child, a year ago. Her partner has been kind and understanding but nevertheless has wanted sex so she has 'given in', even though it has sometimes been painful for her. She is trapped into believing that it is her duty after all: she is his wife and if she does not give him what he wants, he may go and find it elsewhere. An assertive option is to talk about it to her partner and negotiate a compromise around what kind of sexual activity they both want: for instance, oral sex as an alternative to sexual intercourse.

Meg, unmarried, forty-seven, has recently embarked on sexual relationships with several ongoing partners. Her close friends of long-standing appear shocked by her behaviour. She allows their disapproval to feed her own uncertainty about whether or not she is doing the right thing. She can choose to keep her friends from intruding on her own pleasure and enjoyment and assert her right to choose her own sexual lifestyle, making a clear statement to that effect if necessary.

Before attempting to make any changes in your own life, it is worth considering some rights which apply specifically in a sexual context.

1. *I have a right to whatever information I want about sexuality.* Sex education in this country still provokes controversy so young people are even more dependent on the internet, their peers and whatever the media portrays. Some information will get through but it is unlikely to be comprehensive and will be low on the dimension of relationship. If you think back to the manner in which you learned about sexual behaviour, you will probably find that, like many people, it was a haphazard process of misinformation and mistakes and learning through trial and error. Many magazine articles give some facts but overwhelmingly claim to have the secret to making you a better and sexier lover for your partner. No pressure then!

   Even as adults, there may be things you do not know but are afraid to ask because everyone is meant to know everything nowadays. Talking with other women in a spirit of enquiry rather than competition is a good beginning. Many of us talk to our best friends about important and intimate things but not sex. Yet once you overcome this reluctance you may find you can learn a lot and that sharing your own experiences can be very fruitful with the proviso that you talk with friends you trust and who are not trying to impress you.

2. *I have the right to choose my own sexuality.* By this I mean the right to sort out for yourself the person you are and want to be sexually. This may mean not being sexually

245

active but remaining celibate; or relating to one man or to one woman, to several men at once or to several women; to both men and women at the same time; to be married and monogamous or to be single and monogamous. Consider your needs in the light of what you want at any given stage of your life: what suited you at twenty may not suit you at fifty.

3. *I have the right to ask for what I want sexually.* Many women continue to balk at the idea of saying what they want and don't want. If sex is only for the convenience of your partner then you risk doing yourself a great disservice. You also risk accumulating resentment and then finding a way to express your disappointment in a hurtful and aggressive manner. Despite apparent liberation, it is still tempting for heterosexual women to blame a man for not knowing exactly when and how and what they need in terms of sexual pleasure. Taking a more active role, asking and asserting your right to enjoyment is an important way of learning to take an equal and responsible part in bedtime activities.

4. *I have the right to sexual pleasure.* The emphasis here is on the word pleasure. Enjoyment. Fun. Frolics. Laughter. For this, of course, you need to feel friendly and relaxed towards the person you are with. If either of you is nervous, tense, intently concentrating on a goal or putting on a star performance, then fun will usually be in short supply. Instead of making it all a chore you can consciously decide to let go and enjoy yourself. This has a lot to do with your body, understanding how it works, how you respond and essentially trusting yourself enough to let go.

5. *I have a right to choose my form of sexual enjoyment.* Again, the experts, the gurus and the mass media tell us which positions, which type of orgasm and how many are best, how long and where to do it, what to do before and after. Take time to find out about your body, learn about your responses: become familiar with what turns you on a

little, what blows your mind and what definitely turns you off. The 'zipless fuck' (casual sex with a stranger) may be exactly what you want: on the other hand, you may be a woman for whom this remains an exciting fantasy but in reality you need the safe and familiar to turn you on.

Vicky was twenty-eight and, after a couple of serious boyfriends, was feeling isolated and confused. She described how what mattered to her was not only the physical act of sex but also affection and tenderness. Once she voiced her thoughts, she found many others echoed them: she was not alone in seeking something different, more concerned with relationship than only the mechanics. She hadn't liked one boyfriend watching pornography: it made her feel uncomfortable and without being able to articulate just why, she felt it made a difference in his attitude to her somehow. She felt he wasn't the same person he was at other times. She didn't trust him as easily and therefore felt less able to relax herself when it came to sex between them.

6. *I have the right to change my mind.* There is a psychological pressure which makes it almost impossible for us to get started into something sexy and then realise that our hearts (and bodies) are not really in it, that what we would really prefer might be a cup of tea or a good sleep or to sort out the agenda for tomorrow's meeting. If this happens, can you acknowledge your right to change your mind?

It does not help that there is an assumed line of inevitable progression towards the goal of intercourse. You may start with a kiss and enjoy it and maybe you are happy with a cuddle but the last thing you feel like is sex. So what do you say? Can you assertively extricate yourself and say you really do not want to make love? Can you assertively set your limits in this way? Do you even know what your limits are in the first place?

Sometimes it is necessary to find the words, however

awkwardly, to communicate clearly instead allowing feelings of guilt that you are going to let someone down or worries that you will be considered disappointing or be accused of being a prick-tease to keep you silent. There is always an emotional cost in going along with sex when you don't want to.

Saying no

Most women I have met admit that they have participated at times in some kind of sexual activity without really wanting to. They have done so feeling reluctant, half-hearted, sometimes in physical pain, yet have still agreed to have sex rather than make a clear refusal. If you recognise this to be true for you, that you have said 'yes' or said nothing (assumed to be a 'yes') to some kind of sexual activity when in truth you really wanted to say 'no', then see if any of the following reasons are similar to your own:

- Fear of being accused of being frigid or a tease
- Fear of it meaning that you *are* frigid, that there is something wrong with you
- Fear of provoking an argument and then having a grumpy partner who turns over in a huff and fidgets through the night so you don't get any sleep
- Fear of rejection if you do not say 'yes' and then feeling lonely
- Anxiety that your partner will look elsewhere for satisfaction
- The belief that it is your duty because of being a wife or partner or because you have to repay a favour

It is not only women who fall into this sexual compassion trap. Men also fall into the trap sometimes and end up making love with someone when they are not really interested in sex. Mechanical sex of any kind usually hides other feelings. Not wishing to hurt the other person's feelings by rejecting them or appear uncaring or not wanting to lose them to someone else . . . the trap is the same: assuming that the other person's needs are more important than your own.

Sometimes we think we will 'warm up a bit' and 'get in the mood'. This can and does occur and, with luck, your own enjoyment will neutralise any feelings of doing it for the other person. Very often, however, the warm-up does not get quite warm enough, nothing takes off and you don't ever really feel as engaged as you could do.

We can act on false assumptions not only about female sexuality but about male sexuality as well. Two myths in particular are relevant to our subsequent responses.

Man is a sexual beast: in other words, a man has uncontrollable needs. Once he is aroused and has an erection, he has to find some relief, otherwise he will explode or implode: either way it will do him untold harm. Although there is no evidence to support this, men and women continue to believe it and women feel guilty and can be made to feel guilty enough to 'do something' about an erection. Another common belief is that as you have 'caused' the erection, it is your responsibility to do something about it yourself and provide relief. This unquestioned assumption is so prevalent that it feeds into accusations that women are responsible for their own rape.

The question of arousal and erection is not as straightforward as it appears. A man cannot control whether or not he has an erection. The mistaken belief that a man can 'get it up' at will can cause a woman to feel rejected if her partner fails to get an erection when she wants one but distinctly offended if he gets one when she finds it inappropriate!

The man must initiate and orchestrate: despite our claims to be equal, this sexist assumption has not disappeared and continues to contribute to women's difficulties in making clear refusals or taking responsibility for articulating their own needs. The idea that the man should be basically in charge and know what he's doing lingers on. Even if a woman is happier to initiate when she feels like doing so, thinly disguised expectations can still obstruct a genuine sense of shared endeavour: our capacity for disappointment seems not to have diminished at all.

Keeping it equal

Reviewing your sexual attitudes, needs and priorities can take time and certainly requires interest and motivation. How can assertive skills be applied and put into practice in sexual situations? Consider Agnes, Dulcie, Ivy and Selma in action:

You have been out to dinner on your first meeting with a man then gone back to your place for coffee. You come face to face with the classic assumption that coffee is merely a euphemism for sex. It is getting late and he is getting amorous. This leads to a caress which leads to a grope which leads to him getting noticeably aroused. You are tired and want to go to bed . . . alone.

Agnes' tactics: she turns round and yells, 'Get your hands off me! You must be joking': message loud and clear and designed to be humiliating.

Dulcie's tactics: she may attempt to push his hands away and mutter something like 'I really am very tired, it's getting late'. Her confusion and perhaps misplaced guilt keep her locked in passively. So she allows herself to submit to sex right there on the sofa.

Ivy might attempt an indirect repulse like 'I'd love to but it's the wrong time of the month'. Or 'I don't feel very well', (like Dulcie, feeling afraid to be called a prick-tease or frigid and afraid to make him angry). She may go ahead anyway but get her own back later, for example, by spreading defamatory rumours to mutual acquaintances: 'He was lousy, all talk and no action; he couldn't get it up to save his life.' These put-downs can temporarily relieve the feeling of unfairness and bitterness and anger at allowing oneself to be used.

How would Selma deal with it? She could say 'no', for a start, which is a word missing from many women's attempts to refuse. The conversation might go like this:

Selma:	Look, it's late, I would like to go to bed alone.
Man:	But you're really turning me on. *(Manipulative bait)*
Selma:	I don't want sex with you right now, I want to go to bed alone.
Man:	But wouldn't it round off the evening nicely?
Selma:	It would for you, but no, I don't want sex with you and I think it is time for you to leave.
Man:	What's the matter? Are you frigid or into women? *(Argumentative bait)*
Selma:	There's no point in being unpleasant. Please go now. No, I really don't want to have sex with you.

You can acknowledge other lines of reasoning but still maintain your refusal, as in the following examples:

'Yes, it has been a nice evening, but no, *I don't want sex with you tonight.*'

'No, I am not a prick-tease, *I don't want sex with you tonight.*'

I can see that you are aroused but you could always masturbate: *I don't want sex with you tonight.*'

I can see that you are angry, but *I don't want sex with you tonight.*'

No, it is not something you did wrong. It is just that *I don't want sex with you tonight.*'

Of course it's unlikely that you would find a man who persisted *so* strongly but we are often so indirect and ambivalent that the clear message of 'no' has a chance of slipping away unheard.

When matters have escalated in a long-term relationship, the problems are more acute. Let us take the example of a woman in a long-term heterosexual relationship where sex has been generally okay but she no longer feels like having intercourse. She is worried, tense, feeling overburdened and consequently distracted from pleasure.

Agnes's tactics: she might shrug aggressively as soon as her husband touches her and say 'Not *now*, for heaven's sake, stop pawing me' or start a row knowing that sufficient distance would stave off enthusiasm and physical contact.

Dulcie goes along impassively or resorts to indirect means like going to bed early or pretending to be asleep when he comes to bed or leaving in a tampon after her period has finished because she knows that this will put him off so he'll hopefully leave her alone.

Ivy might opt for a 'headache' or a combination of the above mentioned tactics. Perhaps, as he makes the first move, she mentions his mother to deflect his interest or she pointedly gets engrossed in an erotic novel quite enjoying his exclusion and obvious discomfort.

Selma makes a statement of how she is feeling: tired, unenthusiastic, lukewarm or whatever. She might suggest ways of changing the household arrangements so that she could have some help so as not to be so tired; suggest that they make time to sort out together what was happening to their sex life; offer an assertive compromise like wanting to be close and affectionate but not sexual or happy to stimulate orally or manually but not intercourse. Whatever is negotiated is negotiated as equals with respect and care for each other's needs.

Assertive compromise or 'prostitution'? Even without an open financial transaction, many women 'sell' sexual favours for something other than cash. When you reach an assertive compromise with a partner, it is not the same as using sex to bargain for the bathroom to be redecorated at the weekend or distracting him from getting angry with you or keeping him hooked and happy. It is important to be clear whether or not you are involved in some unwritten trading agreement. If you are not clear, then you won't be able to communicate assertively: you will have too much investment in controlling the situation to follow the guidelines of constructive criticism.

Sex is certainly a powerful commodity and because women invest so much in being objects of sexual attraction, they are well aware when they have something that men want: sometimes women feel that this is the only real power they possess. Reclaiming sexual independence is not the same as using (or abusing) the kind of power we wield between our legs.

The dampening effect of unspoken feelings

One of the first steps in looking at sexual relationships across the spectrum is to watch for other feelings. When feelings are not expressed openly they have a habit of colouring our behaviour, including behaviour in a sexual context: when we are intimate and close to someone, we are less guarded.

It can be useful to look at how emotions interfere with spontaneity and sexual enjoyment. Unexpressed anger related to other areas of our lives can easily find expression as a refusal or withdrawal from sex. Performance anxiety about doing the right thing, fears about loss of love or approval, an unmet need for closeness or to share some sadness can also interfere with sexual arousal. When unexpressed feelings linger in the crevices of a relationship, they prevent honest communication and so build up resentment. Sexual activity can end up reduced to an empty, mechanical echo, loveless and dishonouring with both people engaged in some bizarre paradox of intimate physical contact while in their hearts, isolated and alone.

How do we give ourselves the best chance of real intimacy? Do we opt for accommodation or negotiation? What does equality really imply?

Shared responsibility Accommodation is the passive option: you may think you are being equal but check whether or not you are really fitting in with the other person's needs and settling for a quiet life. You may adopt a quasi-maternal role: you feel sorry for your partner and forgive shortcomings like you might those of a child. On the other hand, you may prefer to idealise your partner as perfect and not *want* to acknowledge his shortcomings as being realistic makes you feel too insecure.

Blaming is the aggressive option which is tempting but disastrous in terms of clear communication as we have already discussed. It is easier to allow someone else to bear the brunt of your own non-assertive behaviour and its consequences. Before you launch into blaming, remember it takes two: even if you believe you've suffered someone's bumbling fingers groping over your body for twenty years and feel like exploding with self-righteous fury, a full fifty per cent of the responsibility lies with you for your own lack of communication about what you wanted the other person to change.

Blaming encourages us to use such epithets as 'You're a lousy lover' or 'You're as responsive as a brick', 'There must be something wrong with you, you're abnormal'. Remember to preface your statements with how you feel, and this should be easier now you've practised: for example, 'I feel uncomfortable', 'I would like', 'I find it difficult', 'I'm afraid', 'I don't know when you're aroused' or 'I'm unwilling to let go'.

Assertive negotiation is equal: you are in it together and you want to make it work.

Talking is important We have usually imbibed the myth (from watching too many fictional sexual encounters on screen) that to talk about sex is to lose the magic and break the spell; that it should just be natural and you should not really have to speak about it. This creates three difficulties: first, you feel guilty and foolish and that you're a real killjoy if you mention something: why not just shut up instead of putting an unnecessary dampener on the proceedings? Secondly, we are hampered by believing that 'The Perfect Lover' actually exists: that if your lover were sensitive and really loved you and was utterly attuned to you, then they would know what to do, how to send you into ecstasy, would touch exactly the right places for exactly the right amount of time with exactly the right amount of pressure . . . so saying there is something wrong feels like a put-down, that it is *their* fault. They may well feel offended, inadequate and in the wrong perhaps because, deep down, you think they *are* in the wrong! Thirdly, the habit of not speaking leads to loss of vocabulary: we do not know what words to use. Words feel awkward and clumsy or clinical and distant. With practice you can overcome this problem. Two helpful guidelines are: choose your moment and request a change.

The moment is not in bed! If you want to criticise your lover in bed, no matter how assertively you are inclined, you risk provoking a defensive response. A male lover may well lose his erection and blame it on you. But, even so, the atmosphere is so highly charged that you are better advised to talk at a completely separate time of day, neither just before or during or after sex.

Keep it brief and clear. You do not need to have a seminar but, on the other hand, resorting to non-verbal communication is sometimes misleading: some groans and grunts sound the same whether they are communicating 'more, more' or 'enough, enough'.

Remember the existence of those psychological archives (Chapter 14) especially if you are confronting a difficulty within an established relationship: keep out of any history between you. Deal with one thing at a time and remember it's a joint venture. Be direct and specific about what you do want: help your lover to know how to be more loving and to give you more attention.

The purpose of assertive criticism is to be constructive. It means looking at the strengths of your relationship as well as the weaknesses. It entails being open to criticism and being prepared to accept some of the responsibility for change. It also requires compromise and a commitment to care for the real human being you see before you – not simply an object of your fantasies. It is very, very easy to have sex without emotional intimacy: assertive skills bring the possibility of intimacy a step nearer.

Following on

1. Talk to someone close about your feelings about sex. Honest sharing can be another important way of learning.
2. If you have difficulty finding the words to use when you want to communicate, take ten minutes to write down on a piece of paper *all* the words you know for genitals and sexual activities – slang words, clinical words – just to help yourself feel more comfortable.
3. Learn what turns you on, what you do actually find erotic and pleasurable.
4. Identify three things which you could change and three things which your partner(s) could change to make sex more pleasurable. The next step is to communicate these assertively using the guidelines described in this chapter.

22

A Middle-Aged Woman in Your Own Right

Inevitably the passing of thirty years means I am now middle-aged and, although this additional chapter overlaps with some of my own personal experience, it is written also with an acute awareness of changes in attitudes towards ageing during the intervening years.

I know I am not alone in feeling taken aback by my reflection in the mirror where I can scarcely recognise the image in front of me. Inside I feel very much the same person I have always been but, suddenly, I am faced with what I have become in the eyes of *others*. Clearly this refers back to the idea of psychological reflections in Chapter 19: getting older adds yet another dimension to our preoccupation with managing the impressions of others, especially when those impressions are overwhelmingly biased against anything associated with the natural process of ageing.

Coming to terms with getting older today is compounded by the dictates of a popular culture which defines social validity by chronology: this means our subjective awareness of an ageing body and our subsequent emotional and personal adjustments are inescapably moulded by a deeply comparative, competitive and hierarchical world that relentlessly promotes the primacy of youth. However comfortable we are on the inside with getting older, it won't be possible to remain impervious to all the negativity on the outside. What chance then do we have of retaining and maintaining any kind of self-esteem in the middle and end years of life in the face of this generalised fear and repudiation?

Even if we put aside the gender bias, there is a lot of evidence to indicate how underlying attitudes become manifest in personal and institutional behaviour. In the last year alone in the UK, for example, there have been over a dozen separate reports of research itemising details of appalling neglect or outright abuse associated with treatment of the elderly. This includes being relegated to a low priority by GPs or consultants in deciding whether treatment or facilities should be made available to them; neglect and indifference towards those in hospital wards, neglect and even cruelty towards those in their own homes as well as those residing in what are ironically called 'care' homes. It is brutally clear that the elderly population is not valued. There is now pressure to sell homes and downsize in favour of the young and headlines in the media intimate that continuing financial burdens of old people's care will mean correspondingly fewer resources for students in the future and fewer community facilities (such as libraries, youth centres) in the present: all this fans an incipient intergenerational resentment.

So what do we do? Give up? Hide? Take our place among the ranks of the invisible to remain un-named, uncounted and unheard but grateful for a tiny little place to exist. Allow others to take over and do what they think best for us? Hope that assisted suicide becomes legal by the time we find ourselves too frail to protest at our own mistreatment?

I don't have clear solutions to offer to these dilemmas as I am still working them out for myself but as I listen to people, work with people and witness attitudes to ageing, one aspect stands out. The most pernicious influence is the received opinion that ageing is universally and unequivocally a *bad* thing, implying a total loss of credibility and worth: our ambivalence and anxiety in the face of this negativity incline us towards denial.

On several occasions in these pages, I have emphasised the corrosive effect of denial on our self-esteem: denial of problems in a relationship; denial of tiredness; denial of the existence of sexism or denial of the truth of what we are feeling. Collusion with denial of age has the same effect, at an individual and collective level. As with the emperor's imaginary suit of clothes, we play along by pretending that youth is all. When we are constantly bombarded with female celebrities and stars who relentlessly insist they will *never* go grey or have wrinkles (because they are 'worth it'), our self-esteem can become dependent on the denial of age.

Our cultural obsession with hiding, fighting, cheating or even conquering age and eventual death leave us vulnerable and gullible, which is, of course, what the advertisers (through their expert psychological research) exploit: we spend a fortune on things that will help us stay in denial. Fortunately there are some well-known women in their 60s and 70s and even beyond who are strong enough to maintain a glamorous image without cosmetic surgery and I thank them for doing so even though, without their financial resources, few of us can manage in the same way. But we can stop pretending. We can stop hiding. We can stop criticising other women for looking their age.

Have a personal conversation with yourself. Hiding grey hair sits at one end of the continuum: extensive cosmetic surgery at the other. Where, along this continuum, do you feel comfortable? Compromise is not the same as denial: try and make a decision – which is ultimately very personal – that genuinely celebrates who you are rather than traps you on a treadmill in a never-ending effort not to be found out.

Treading the line between compromise and denial is one challenge. Another is to confront some of the myths and stereotypes instead of silently colluding with them. For example, if and when the opportunity arises, it can help not to collude with the 'us versus them' mythology. Challenge this kind of segregation by engaging with those who are younger and whose values are very different. This doesn't necessarily mean having to walk around with the latest smart phone attached to your ear but there are times when conversations can be struck up and an exchange facilitated. Children are more amenable but teenagers and those in their twenties and thirties often have little or no idea how to approach the elderly, regarding them as a bit alien. Many will, if encouraged, be able to break through their own awkwardness and anxiety and make some connection. I remember the astonishment in the voices of some young Occupy movement protesters at drawing people of 'all ages' to support their cause: they had obviously imagined that protest was the sole prerogative of the young. Having a common cause is a perfect means of breaking down superimposed barriers.

Another area to avoid collusion is to refrain from using phrases like 'I'm having a senior moment' when you forget something or find the papers you spent ten minutes looking for in the place where you left them. The vast majority of people are absent-minded from time to time – at any age – so, even if you're only trying to be humorous, constantly blaming silly mistakes or oversights on senility unhelpfully compounds the stereotype.

Similarly, I hear many women prefacing their views with 'I know I'm just a grumpy old woman but . . . ' If you dismiss yourself constantly, others will unconsciously dismiss you too. This is an aspect of the passive and apologetic option already described which can occur at every stage of life. Keep apologising for existing and soon others will stop regarding you as an equal and, in the absence of a clear statement, are likely to make presumptions on your behalf. Although we can all be grumpy at times, this kind of phrase risks becoming an unhelpful way to lower expectations and invite others to discount your views, opinions and concerns.

This had a lot of resonance for Yvonne who wanted to know how she could possibly tackle the issue of looking after her grandchildren. Her daughter, Rebecca, had been determined to go back to work as soon as possible after her children were born: Yvonne didn't really approve even though she knew it was the modern thing to do. Little by little, Yvonne had agreed to more and more care – from two days a week to three days a week – and she was worried that soon she might be asked to extend it again.

What were the obstacles getting in the way of communicating with her daughter? First, she adored her grandchildren and enjoyed the time she spent with them; second, she didn't actually have any specific commitment during the day; third, she knew her daughter was working very hard at her job. On the other hand, Yvonne knew that sometimes she simply wanted to have some time to herself. Her husband, Jim, Rebecca's step-father, had retired from full-time work but still did some consultancy work and sometimes she just wanted to have the opportunity to go off spontaneously for a day or two with him when he was free. She also found a day of looking after two young children extremely tiring.

Was she being selfish and unreasonable? When questioned about what she wanted, she decided that she wanted to avoid having to say 'no' to her daughter. So how could she start this difficult conversation instead of waiting (and dreading) the request.

Practice 1

She decided to bring up the subject when Rebecca came to collect the children, who were at that moment watching television.

Yvonne: Rebecca, love, there's something I want to ask about.
Rebecca: Yes?
Yvonne: I wondered if we could talk about me having the children here. Do you think we could sometimes make a different arrangement?
Rebecca: What do you mean 'a different arrangement'? It's hard enough as it is now, having to pay the child minder two days a week. In fact, I was going to ask you if . . .
Yvonne: I'm not sure I can do any more.
Rebecca: Look, Mum, I'm sorry but you know I only ask because I have to. Toby will be at school in a year's time so it will only mean picking them up.
Yvonne: I'll think about it. I do get quite tired by the end of the day, you know.
Rebecca: Look, it's not forever" . . . *her mobile rings. She looks at it.* Mum, I'm sorry, I must take this. (*Shouts*) Will you two get ready to go home?

One of the common mistakes we make when we attempt to bring up an awkward subject of conversation is that we don't prepare ourselves by asking those three key questions. Yvonne didn't take the time to think through what she actually *wanted* to request from her daughter and she also failed to convey how strongly she felt. This, remember, is *our* responsibility: not the other person's. Putting our feelings into words is possible to do without attributing blame. What are Yvonne's feelings? Frustration? Confusion? A sense of not being heard or regarded as an equal? Being taken for granted and unappreciated? It is important to acknowledge our feelings, *whatever* they are. Remember that it is nonsense to blame ourselves for what we feel although we *are* responsible for how we act on those feelings.

Although she feels guilty at feeling resentful towards her own daughter, Yvonne has to acknowledge that she is human and that, rather than get into the rights or wrongs of the matter, she has the right to express her needs. So what does she want? This took a while to clarify but, in the end, what felt important to her wasn't the specific number of times she had the grandchildren, but the fact that she wanted to be consulted and be able to *negotiate* her contribution rather than Rebecca simply taking it for granted. That was what Yvonne decided was more important than anything else: she wanted to be treated as an equal.

The next time Yvonne decided to initiate the conversation, she gave Rebecca some notice. She phoned and said she wanted to talk about something and suggested Rebecca meet her in town for a coffee while her husband looked after the children.

(*In the café.*)

Yvonne: I don't know how to start this but I want to talk to you about something important and I feel very awkward about it.

Rebecca: What on earth's the matter?

Yvonne: No, it's not serious. Well, it *is* actually but not awful. I want to talk about looking after the kids.

Rebecca: We talked about that last week.

Yvonne: No, we didn't. We didn't really talk about it. We didn't have time and that's why I wanted to have the time now. (*Rebecca listens.*) I haven't really taken responsibility for what we have arranged and I've been beginning to feel that you take me for granted. I find it difficult to say what I feel because I want to support you and obviously I love having them but I want to be able to negotiate, you know, like equals. Sometimes I think because I haven't anything else important to do, you assume that I'll always say yes.

Rebecca: That's not true. Not really.

Yvonne: I feel caught, Rebecca. I want to say 'yes' to you. And sometimes I want to be able to go off for the day with Jim. Or just read, I don't know, go for a walk, do nothing! I know that's selfish but that's how I feel.

Rebecca: That's not selfish, Mum. I can understand that. I'd love to do that as well sometimes.

Yvonne: I know you would but you have made your choices. You want to work and you wanted children. And I'm happy to help only not all the time.

Rebecca: (*reflects*) I know, Mum. It's not easy but you're right. I did make my choices. So are you saying that you're not going to do the extra day?

Yvonne: I'd rather not. Obviously in an emergency I will but I'd like you to consider some other options.

Rebecca: OK. You know, Mum, I quite respect you for saying that.

Yvonne: Well, I've spent a long time not respecting my own needs so it's about time that I did. I can't expect anyone else to do so if I don't do it myself. (*She smiles at her daughter.*) I can't tell you how relieved I am that we've been able to talk. I thought you'd be really upset.

Rebecca: No, a bit surprised but I'm OK.

Yvonne: Well, if you've finished your coffee, shall we go and have a quick look at the shoe sale?

Standing up for yourself will continue to be a part of assertiveness throughout life. This chapter is not exclusively for those of middle age and older. Obviously when you're still young, you don't ever consider getting old but, if attitudes continue the way they are, everyone will inherit the legacy of hostility and fear towards old age that those of us in our middle years today can anticipate in our future. The writing is already on the wall. Our current elderly population is already suffering from being unconsciously affiliated to the psychological projection of all that contemporary consumer society wants to rid itself of: vulnerability, defencelessness, lack of productivity, slowness, frailty, dependency, illness, the inevitability of death, confusion and senility. If we don't do something about this trend and challenge it effectively, it will be a lot worse in another twenty years.

All characteristics associated with old age listed above can be bracketed together under the general umbrella of powerlessness (in the perpendicular sense). It is important therefore to build and express our personal power to help us approach this stage of life. Old age is not for the faint-hearted. It requires courage and determination to accommodate the effects of natural wear and tear on the body; it takes courage to face up to the end of our lives, including all our disappointments and regrets and a slowly diminishing menu of options to choose from. This is a personal transition and ultimately of course a lone one. If there are indeed any compensations for this stage of life, it's time to find them!

Staying in touch with who we are applies throughout life but is of particular significance when the negativity of ageism saps our strength and makes us doubt our worth. However old you are, you can always give yourself permission to:

- Use your mind
- Face the facts
- Speak directly
- Render a service
- Find a way of being engaged
- Give of yourself
- Savour the present
- Share what you have
- Rediscover joy
- Decide to make a difference
- Release feelings of guilt or sorrow
- Create your own style
- Forgive yourself and others
- Take a stand
- Make an honest appraisal
- Act on impulse
- Use your critical faculties
- Stand up for your values
- Take a chance and be crazy!

23

The Power at the Centre

The concept of personal power was introduced in Chapter 3 and I have referred to it on several occasions throughout the book. In this final chapter, it is time to draw the various threads together. Personal power is, without doubt, the key to assertive communication and behaviour in every context: its full meaning and implications need to be understood at both a rational and emotional level.

Remember that the most recognisable hallmarks of personal power are balance, honesty, emotional awareness, integrity and equality. These can now be reviewed in relation to all the information and illustrations in the previous pages.

Balance

This describes the ability to give equal weight and consideration to your own needs and those of others. It helps us reach out with care and also set limits when necessary. Once we are emotionally inclined towards finding a balance, we enter any situation prepared to negotiate from a position of equality rather than insisting on a struggle for dominance. The quality of balance also applies to the internal experience of the pushes and pulls of outside assessment, both realistic and imaginary. We can learn from others' slights and criticism at times as well as enjoy praise and approval at others yet still, inside, keep in touch with an emotional core that helps us avoid becoming too attached to other people's responses and thereby retain a measure of independence.

Honesty

In this context, honesty applies both to the basis of our communication but, more importantly, means being truthful to ourselves because denial is the very worst enemy of personal power: whenever we are in denial about what is happening to us, we have no access to personal power. This applies to turning a blind eye to persistent sexual harassment; a deaf ear to an offensive racist innuendo; pretending your partner hasn't really got a gambling problem; or refusing to believe your friend is going to die. Only when we stop denying what we know, what we see, what we hear and what actually *is* the nature of our reality, can we take the first step to address it. Maybe we cannot change it but even the act of emerging from denial is to assume a stance of personal power. Then we can identify what we feel and what we can or cannot change: we are able to move from a position of honesty and real choice.

Emotional Awareness

In Chapter 19, I described how habitual self-consciousness has damaged the sense of deep connection with our bodies. Emotional awareness and familiarity offer one possibility of repair. This means taking your feelings seriously and not blaming others for causing them. It entails acknowledging what you feel and being truthful with yourself before possibly taking the next step of putting these feelings into words (*self-disclosure*).

Instead of allowing anxiety to prevent us speaking up, assertive skills show us how to look anxiety in the eye, learn from it, breathe with it, speak through it and emerge on the other side, allowing us to achieve something we didn't ever think we would be capable of. Through repeated practice and survival, we become less afraid of being afraid: we can feel the shift of feeling from uncertainty, hesitation and doubt to conviction, deter-mination and strength of purpose.

Recognition of personal power involves an inner shift of balance. When women first assess their habitual behaviour and consider new responses, there is an automatic assumption that the failure or success of the interaction will depend on who the other person is and how he or she might respond: whether they are old or young, male or female, hostile or friendly, 'higher up' or 'lower down' and so on. We imagine the outcome is pre-determined, that the key to effective change lies within someone else's hands. With practice, the centre of balance moves so we recognise that the key to change actually resides within each one of us.

Integrity

When your mind, heart and body work in unison, you experience being personally powerful: you are being true to yourself. Losing or winning become irrelevant. Integrity is developed by, for example, not pretending to be confident when you're not; not denying hurt feelings when they arise; being proud to have found the courage to stand up for your convictions; being able to leave a conversation when you're uncomfortable and knowing that sometimes a compromise is simply too much for you and you have to say 'no'.

Equality

Personal power is rooted in a commitment to equality. For most people, this is like opening both eyes, instead of looking only through one of them. Imagine looking through the right eye alone, allowing monocular vision. What we see are familiar hierarchical structures of perpendicular power, forever measured in terms of higher and lower, over and under. Once you open both eyes, your vision becomes 'binocular': you can begin to see that *alongside* the differences between you and the other person on the various ladders, there is another point of reference. There is a common point of equality as human beings. The two visions of power merge so that you become able to see perpendicular power from an alternative perspective. Although ladders will continue to define us in societal terms, there is simultaneously a point of equality in any interaction or dialogue. This is when assertive communication becomes possible. Aggression is no longer necessary when you don't have to stay on top: when there is nowhere to climb or to fall.

Seeing yourself as an equal is as relevant whether the person you want to address is 'above' or 'below'. One of the many disadvantages of looking through only one eye is that we hold back from making constructive suggestions because we don't like to challenge someone we see as 'higher up'. This of course includes creative suggestions as well as critical ones.

Priti was in her twenties and found it impossible to speak up and contradict her manager at work. She could not get the senior/junior aspect out of her head. It was only when she focused on the potential of her suggestion to be *helpful* and constructive (as an equal human being) that she was able to speak through her nervousness: she realised she could come across, not as someone speaking out of turn, but as an employee who could contribute an idea that might be of use.

These five principles are the keystones of assertiveness. How do we make them relevant in practice?

Taking the initiative

Our behaviour is often characterised by a pattern of waiting: waiting to grow up, to be asked on a date, to leave school or leave home; for a proposal of marriage, waiting for a child to be born then to grow up; waiting for someone else to notice us, to apologise first, to acknowledge we were right; waiting to achieve the right weight, find the perfect shoes, for someone to stop talking, waiting until we're feel supremely confident, until he's in the right mood or for the perfect opportunity to occur.

Instead of waiting for something to happen, you can take that first step. Maybe there are all sorts of things you have in mind to do: places you would like to visit, people you would like to get to know, a room you would like to paint, a subject you would like to know more about, something you would like to buy. If there is, ask yourself what you are waiting for. Have you ever found yourself waiting for any of the following to happen first?

- For someone to say they're sorry
- For the children to leave home
- For someone to hold your hand

- For someone to show you the way
- For someone to say they're wrong
- For the sun to shine
- For your lottery number to come up
- For someone to do it for you
- For someone else to make the first move
- For someone to give you a good kick
- For someone to make it safe for you to jump
- For someone to come back to you
- For someone to die
- For someone to forgive you
- For someone to mend the stepladder
- For someone to offer to help
- For someone to invite you to speak
- For someone to sweep you off your feet
- For someone to change her/his mind
- For someone to give you the go-ahead
- For someone to guess what you really want without having to ask them

Initiating a change can sometimes involve a major move. Having worked at a PR firm for five years since leaving university, Jodie had to come to terms with a growing realisation that she felt uncomfortable with the values of the company. She found the ethos superficial and demeaning and despite having tried to enter into the competitive spirit, she knew her heart wasn't in it so, instead of continuing to waiting for things to improve, she decided to find something more meaningful. She did some research and eventually was accepted to re-train as a psychologist which meant a big financial adjustment and demanding times of study ahead: but she knew this step would help her feel more congruent in her life, doing a job which matched her personal values.

Taking the initiative applies also to changing the way we behave when we dread dealing with a difficult conversation or meeting. Making the first move helps to feel more in charge of life than sitting around and waiting for the inevitable. Instead of sitting and fretting, anticipating the phone call, the summons to be made, the axe to drop or the pain to go away of its own accord, decide to get up and put an end to the waiting!

Grace was worried about a situation at work. She had had a lot of trouble working with a particular colleague two years previously and had heard on the office grapevine that he was to be transferred back to her department. This meant that they would have to work together again and she knew she couldn't face this. When she practised the conversation, she tried rehearsing her reaction to being called in by her boss to be given the news officially. She handled it reasonably well but not as well as she would have liked. She then decided to take the initiative: instead of waiting to be called in, she asked to see her boss in advance. In this way she could express her concern, state her feelings and suggest an alternative solution *before* the event. She felt much more powerful and was able to handle the interaction far more effectively, first in role-play and subsequently in real life.

Your three key questions

We looked at these questions specifically in relation to confrontation in Chapter 14 but I would go so far as to say that these three questions hold the key to being able to re-connect with your personal power whenever you find yourself in circumstances which trouble you. All too often we dither uncertainly, barely conscious of what is happening yet vaguely aware of feelings of embarrassment, discomfort, fear or irritation.

When you feel disturbed by what is happening around you and sense something is wrong, even if you are confused, try and take a minute at that precise point to ask yourself those three questions: your answers will reveal what your options are.

Clary was in the bar one evening with a group of her friends. Suddenly the topic of conversation turned to Amy who was absent from the group. Amy had been through a difficult time, put on a lot of weight and hadn't been seen for a while. Various unpleasant 'jokey' comments ensued and Clary began to feel very uncomfortable. She felt trapped and didn't know what to do. She considered her three questions and found her answers:

- They are slagging off Amy
- I don't like it
- I'd like it to stop

She decided to speak up:

Clary: Hey, look, listen to me a minute. (*The others stop and look at her.*) I really don't like you slagging off Amy. We don't know what's going on and it doesn't feel right to be talking like this.

Someone says: We're only having a laugh.

Clary: I know, but I feel uncomfortable. I want to talk about something else. Can we change the subject? Dan, how was Barcelona?

Standing up in the minority takes courage but it helps you stay true to yourself without provoking antagonism: nobody has to be right or wrong, nobody has to win or lose. You are simply stating your own limits.

Asserting your values or ideas, even if you're in the minority, helps reaffirm your integrity in a perpendicular world. Christine, 59, had grown up with different social values and did not like a lot of what she saw going on around her. One instance of this discomfort would often emerge whenever she sat and watched TV together with her husband and youngest son who was living at home after his recent divorce. They were watching a popular programme which encouraged participants to be ruthlessly aggressive with each other as they fought for a considerable financial prize and Christine found herself once again feeling uncomfortable. This time she thought about the three questions and her answers:

- I'm watching something I don't want to watch.
- I really hate this kind of behaviour
- I could ask them to turn it off but I'll remove myself instead.

(*Christine gets up from the sofa.*)

Husband: Where you going?

Christine: I don't know . . . the kitchen.

Husband: Why?

Christine: I really hate watching this. People are just being nasty to each other and I don't like it.

Husband: Come on, it's all a bit of fun.

Christine: No, it's not. It's nasty.

Son: Don't be so sensitive, Mum. They chose to take part in this.

Christine: I know. But I really don't enjoy watching it. See you both later (*leaves the room*).

Even though neither her husband nor son were likely to understand her objections, this mattered less to Christine than her choice to stop passively sitting in front of the screen yet again and saying nothing. She didn't win the argument about who was right and who was wrong. Sometimes we find ourselves in conflict with overwhelming odds and reach the limits of our other kinds of power, personal power is still available to us. Being true to your own values and feelings is a private 'win' for yourself regardless of the outcome.

What seeds will you sow for the future?

As we have seen again and again in this book, assertive skills show us how to negotiate with others and honour them as fellow human beings, regardless of the unequal trappings of status and power in which we are all enmeshed. They help us to maintain respect and care for others without losing sight of our own individual concerns, giving us the means to find a balance between self and others, a balance that easily gets forgotten in the general endorsement and insistence that aggression is the *only* way to achieve anything.

The exclusive emphasis on individual self-empowerment – getting what you want when you want it – has eclipsed the reciprocity of an assertive exchange and the dimension of relationship. It's as if we have claimed our rights but forgotten about the responsibilities that accompany those rights.

The illustrations and examples throughout have necessarily focused more on what happens internally as we address the anxieties that arise in conversation. What is less evident in these accounts is something which is intrinsic to actual role-play practice: the importance of the impact on the other person. Even if the speaker is unsure, the difference between an aggressive and an assertive interaction is never in doubt for the person on the receiving end. If you have communicated assertively, the other person will know exactly what the problem is, be in no doubt about what is wanted, when and why. The recipient might feel supported or, at the very least, treated with respect. In addition, he or she may feel surprised, perhaps confounded, disappointed or even annoyed but *never* defensive, hurt, crushed, humiliated or abused: these are only felt in response to aggression.

Being assertive springs from a fulcrum of equality and I believe the true values of assertiveness are now more urgently needed in our relationships on a *macro* and *micro* level than ever before. This touches on far more than individual change and far more than achieving individual empowerment. In this deeply unequal and violent world, it has never been so vital to find an alternative to aggression. When individuality and competition are in ascendance, fear is rife: aggression is predicated in this fear.

When we opt for aggression in any form, it is worth remembering that aggression always generates aggression. Every time we act aggressively in word or deed, we feed the relentless cycle. The recipient of our aggression will, when the time is right and when they too find themselves in a position of power over someone, seize the opportunity to repeat the dynamic of aggression, to pass it on in the hope that it will expunge their own unpleasant and traumatic feelings of powerlessness. Unfortunately the relief is only short-lived so the cycle, once established, becomes self-sustaining.

All forms of aggression – from the mildest to the most lethal, between individuals or between nations – are evident wherever we look in the world as are deep inequalities at every level of human existence. Often I find myself responding to the bigger picture with helplessness and horror, tempted to dissociate myself and close my eyes and ears to it all.

But somewhere I recognise that we are all part of the cycle of aggression. And this recognition indicates some choices. They may seem insignificant in relation to the large scale forms of aggression we witness around us but nevertheless, we exercise a personal choice about every single interaction we are faced with. Assertiveness shows us there is another way: not a weak, wimpish, ineffectual way but a way which demonstrates a different magnitude of power based in compassion. Compassion is the best antidote to the poison of aggression because it immediately transforms an exclusively perpendicular viewpoint.

Each of us has a choice about how we communicate with every single person in our lives: do we treat them as equals or objects? Do we insist on seeking revenge or find the possibility of forgiveness? Do we take responsibility for our feelings or do we blame others? Do we allow resentments to linger and fester until a showdown is inevitable or do we engage honestly with a commitment to finding a resolution? Is it imperative to establish ourselves as the winner in every situation or can we let it go? Do we treat employees as dispensable units of labour or as human beings? Is it possible to resist taking that surreptitious pot-shot at someone we'd like to see suffer? These dilemmas apply to family, friends, strangers, colleagues: any other human being whom we encounter. We will inevitably fall short of our ideals but the commitment in itself, as in all relationships, is what matters: we have the option of refraining from aggression in our own individual lives and in small ways to sow different seeds for an uncertain future.

Index